get the
interview
every
time

revised and expanded edition

Proven Strategies from Fortune 500 Hiring Professionals

Brenda Greene

 **KAPLAN** PUBLISHING

New York

This publication is designed to provide accurate and authoritative information in regard to the subject matter covered. It is sold with the understanding that the publisher is not engaged in rendering legal, accounting, or other professional service. If legal advice or other expert assistance is required, the services of a competent professional should be sought.

Vice President and Publisher: Maureen McMahon
Editorial Director: Jennifer Farthing
Acquisitions Editor: Shannon Berning
Development Editor: Joshua Martino
Production Editor: Karina Cueto
Production Designer: Pamela Beaulieu
Typesetter: PBS & Associates
Cover Designer: Rod Hernandez

Published by Kaplan Publishing, a division of Kaplan, Inc.
1 Liberty Plaza, 24th Floor
New York, NY 10006

Printed in the United States of America

April 2008
10 9 8 7 6 5 4 3 2 1

ISBN-13: 978-1-4277-9714-8

Contents

Introduction

Whether you are a newcomer to the workforce or a seasoned professional, finding a new job is a challenge. On its most basic level, job seeking is a calculated move into the unknown.

The job search usually starts with a few questions: Who can help? What kind of job is out there for me? What can I expect to earn? Where do I want to work? How will a new job further my career? When do I want to make the change? Then it's a matter of handling the in-between details: the research; the networking; the résumé; the cover letter; the phone screen; the first, second, and maybe third and fourth interviews. Finally, you hope the process ends with a fulfilling and lucrative job offer.

It should come as no surprise that the process tends to push those buttons deep in the gut that either energize you or fill you with dread. To paraphrase Dickens, finding a new job can be the best of times and the worst of times.

The first edition of *Get the Interview Every Time* helped thousands to create résumés and cover letters to get their foot in the door. Updated and expanded, this new edition now covers the process of interviewing, as well as how to advance in your new job once you land it.

As in the earlier books, the new edition of *Get the Interview Every Time* gives readers an inside look at the hiring process at Fortune 500 companies. These massive corporations employ millions of workers, so the expertise of their hiring professionals, who see thousands of résumés a month and hire hundreds of applicants each year, is invaluable. More than 71 Fortune 500 hiring professionals—specialists, managers, directors, vice presidents—weighed in on the hiring process at their companies. They either participated in one of the two surveys that were conducted in 2003 and 2004, answering detailed questionnaires on what Fortune 500 companies want to see in applicants' resumes and cover letters as well as how they recruit the best talent, or they provided specific information on topics such as panel interviews, electronic submissions, what Fortune 500 employers value, and even the questions they are most likely to ask during an interview. And the new material in the book's final chapter, based on interviews with three Fortune 500 senior executives, focuses on how to get ahead—without too many serious missteps—once you land the job. Some of the data gathered in this book will surprise job seekers—and even career consultants.

It's always a good idea to break down a major undertaking—like finding a new job—into small pieces and work through the process step-by-step. The new format of this book will allow readers to tackle the various stages of the job search in this manner.

Naturally, the economy plays a part in how many people are hired each year. When the two earlier books were written, David Leonhardt of the *New York Times* called the 2003 economic climate a "Goldilocks economy," one that "seems like a lukewarm bowl of mush."[1] And the average time frame for finding a job back then was 4.2 months. Fortunately, the economic cycle has taken a turn for the better. Jeremy W. Peters of the *New York Times* said in 2007, "The job market looked much like the economy as a whole last month: subdued but strong enough."[2] Add to that the current statistics on the time frame of finding a job, now 3 months (instead of 4.2), and the prospects of securing a good position are even better. Of course, anything can happen, but regardless of the economic climate, don't be passive. There are always new jobs out there for those who actively seek them. *Get the Interview Every Time* will help you to seize the job that is the right fit for you. No matter what kind of job you are seeking.

What's important to understand is that you have to be a good fit for the employer—and the new job has to be a good fit for you.

Once in a while, a new, exciting opportunity more or less drops in your lap—like a gift from above. And occasionally finding a new job is an urgent matter of survival. However, the process of finding a new job usually unfolds with a slow-cooking resolution that eventually gels and then spurs you to make a move. No matter what propels you toward a new job, you always want to look like a professional—like someone who knows how things work. The new, expanded edition of *Get the Interview Every Time* will help you polish that inner gem of yours so that you land the job that allows you to showcase your talent, provide a valuable service, and earn a salary that meets your personal needs.

ACKNOWLEDGMENTS

Detailed surveys—the first in 2002/2003 and the second in 2004—were sent to human resource professionals at 65 Fortune 500 companies. The responses from the Fortune 500 hiring managers, directors, and vice presidents were the crux of my earlier books—*Get the Interview Every Time* and *You've Got the Interview . . . Now What?*—and remain the primary source of information for this revised book as well. The updated and expanded edition of *Get the Interview Every Time* quotes extensively from the information these insiders provided for the first two books.

Since the two surveys were conducted, some companies have merged or no longer rank among the Fortune 500. Some individuals, meanwhile, have moved to other companies or have been promoted. The participants for the first survey were selected from companies on the 2002 Fortune 500 list, and the participants from the second survey were from companies on the 2004 Fortune 500 list. The list, for the most part, reflects the status of the companies and individuals at the time I received responses to the two surveys.*

Corporations change, personnel changes, and everyone gets busier and busier. I am grateful that within this changing landscape, executives at these massive corporations stepped up to share their expertise. I would like to extend my appreciation to the following professionals for their time and thoughtful contribution:

- **Albertson's, Inc.:** Stacy Harshman, employment administrator. Survey 1
- **Allied Waste Industries, Inc.:** Kathy O'Leary, manager, employment services. Survey 1 and Survey 2
- **Alltel Corporation:** Julie Ruesewald, human resources project manager. Survey 1
- **Alltel Corporation:** Lara Crane, manager of staffing. Survey 2
- **Aquila, Inc.:** Carol Eubank, human resources manager. Survey 1
- **Avon Products, Inc.:** Robin Fischer, director of talent acquisition. Survey 1
- **Bank One Corporation:** Jeremy Farmer, senior vice president, human resources. Survey 1

- **Baxter International, Inc.:** Barbara Morris, vice president of human resources. Survey 2
- **BB&T Corporation:** Michael Tyree, human resources specialist. Survey 1
- **BellSouth:** Suzanne Snypp, director, human resources/staffing. Survey 2
- **BJ's Wholesale Club, Inc.:** Paula Axelrod, manager of staffing. Survey 1
- **CarMax, Inc.:** Pam Hill, director of staffing and planning. Survey 2
- **Continental Airlines, Inc.:** Mary Matatall, senior director, global recruiting and staffing administration. Survey 1 and Survey 2
- **Darden Restaurants, Inc.:** Susan Lock, human resources manager. Survey 1
- **Deere & Company:** Sherri Martin, director of human resources. Survey 1 and Survey 2
- **Dollar General Corporation:** Gary Moore, recruiting director. Survey 1
- **Energy East Management Corporation:** Sheri A. Lamoureux, director, human resources planning. Survey 1 and Survey 2
- **Engelhard Corporation:** Rocco Mangiarano, director of human resources. Survey 1 and Survey 2
- **Enterprise Leasing Company:** John Tomerlin, vice president, human resources. Survey 1
- **Fannie Mae:** Trang Gulian, manager of human resources. Survey 1 and Survey 2
- **Federal-Mogul Corporation:** Jackie Coburn, manager of staffing. Survey 1
- **FMC Corporation:** Kenneth R. Garrett, vice president, human resources. Survey 1
- **Gannett Co., Inc.:** Stacey Webb, human resources representative. Survey 1
- **Georgia-Pacific Corporation:** Chris C. Collier, group manager of corporate recruiting. Survey 1
- **H.J. Heinz Company:** Tom DiDonato, human resources vice president for Heinz NorthAmerica. Survey 1
- **Harley-Davidson Motor Company:** Steve Duea, manager of staffing. Survey 2
- **Health Net, Inc.:** Cherri Davies, manager of staffing. Survey 1
- **Health Net, Inc.:** Diane Berk, staffing manager. Survey 2
- **Host Hotels & Resorts, Inc.:** Lisa A. Whittington, vice president of human resources. Survey 1 and Survey 2
- **HSBC North America Holdings, Inc.:** Brian Little, group director of human resources. Survey 1 and Survey 2
- **Idaho Power Company (subsidiary of IDACORP, Inc.):** Dawn Thompson, formerly a human resources specialist now a specialist in sub stations. Survey 1

- **International Truck & Engine Corporation (Parent: Navistar International Corporation):** Bill G. Vlcek, manager of strategic staffing. Survey 1 and Survey 2
- **JC Penney Corporation, Inc.:** E. Humpal, manager of employment services. Survey 1
- **Jabil Circuit, Inc.:** Heather McBride, senior human resources generalist/recruiting manager. Survey 1
- **Jabil Circuit, Inc.:** Heather Otto, employment manager. Survey 2
- **JDS Uniphase Corporation:** Stephen Heckert, human resources senior manager. Survey 1
- **Jones Apparel Group, Inc.:** A. Tejero DeColli, human resources senior vice president. Survey 1
- **Kellogg Company:** Cydney Kilduff, director of staffing and diversity. Survey 1
- **Kindred Healthcare, Inc.:** Donna Campbell, manager of recruiting services. Survey 1
- **Liz Claiborne, Inc.:** Andrea Fenster, director of strategic staffing. Survey 2
- **Lucent Technologies, Inc.:** Sherry Rest, manager, process and technology, recruiting and staffing solutions. Survey 1
- **Marathon Oil Corporation:** R. T. Beal, manager of talent acquisition. Survey 1
- **Medco Health Solutions, Inc.:** Audrey Goodman, vice president of organization development. Survey 2
- **Merck & Co., Inc.:** Tracy L. S. Grajewski, senior director, corporate staffing. Survey 1
- **Office Depot, Inc.:** Anne Foote Collins, director of corporate recruiting and services. Survey 2
- **Pepsi Bottling Group:** Cecilia McKenney, human resources vice president. Survey 1
- **Phelps Dodge Corporation:** Art Calderon, director of human resources and strategic programs. Survey 2
- **Phelps Dodge Corporation:** David Pulatie, human resources senior vice president. Survey 1
- **PSEG Services Corporation:** John Garofalo, enterprise staffing and outreach manager. Survey 2
- **Saks Incorporated:** Roland Hearns, vice president of recruitment placement. Survey 1
- **Southern California Edison Company:** Susan Johnson, human resources manager. Survey 1

- **State Farm Insurance Companies:** Leslie Humphries, human resources specialist. Survey 1
- **SYSCO Corporation:** Amy Moers, senior staffing manager. Survey 1
- **SYSCO Corporation:** Amy Reeves, director of corporate staffing. Survey 2
- **Teachers Insurance and Annuity Association—College Retirement Equities Fund (TIAA-CREF):** Carol F. Nelson, second vice president, staffing and relocation services. Survey 1
- **Teachers Insurance and Annuity Association—College Retirement Equities Fund (TIAA-CREF):** Robert Moll, senior human resources generalist. Survey 2
- **Tesoro Petroleum Corporation:** Janie Lopez, human resources consultant. Survey 1
- **The Bank of New York Company, Inc.:** Ken Dean, assistant vice president, human resources. Survey 1
- **The Chubb Corporation:** Mary Powers, assistant vice president, human resources. Survey 1
- **The McGraw-Hill Companies:** David Murphy, executive vice president of human resources. Survey 1
- **The Mutual of Omaha Companies:** Dan Bankey, manager of strategic staffing. Survey 1
- **The Timken Company:** Barry Martin, director of staffing and development. Survey 2
- **Thrivent Financial for Lutherans:** Debra Palmer, staffing manager. Survey 1 and Survey 2
- **Unisys Corporation:** Patrick Dunn, director of workforce planning. Survey 1
- **United Parcel Service, Inc.:** Stacy R. Wilson, human resources administrator. Survey 1

In addition to the Fortune 500 individuals listed above, others contributed to the book as well. I would like to thank Sissy Cunningham, my lifelong friend and coauthor of *The Business Style Handbook: An A-to-Z Guide for Writing on the Job with Tips from Communications Experts at the Fortune 500,* who consistently offers her time, encouragement, and expertise.

Beyond the surveys, many of the Fortune 500 HR professionals were available to answer questions throughout the writing of this book. In fact, I sought their feedback on many topics. I would like to highlight my special thanks for the following individuals' continued availability: Lisa Whittington of **Host Hotels & Resorts,**

Barry Martin of **The Timken Company,** Bill Vlcek of **International Truck & Engine Corporation,** and Rocco Mangiarano of **Engelhard.**

I also spoke with individuals at two other Fortune 500 companies regarding the departmental and/or panel interview. These conversations were thoroughly illuminating and provided the information that forms the basis of Chapter 15. Thank you to Neil Bussell, group manager, **PepsiCo Business Solutions Group,** whose input is based on his career experience, and Peter Thonis, senior vice president of external communications at **Verizon.**

I also received valuable direction and input from the following individuals: Helen Cunningham, director of communications at the **Depository Trust & Clearing Corporation (DTCC);** Dom Gallo, senior director of customer relationship management at **Securities Industry Automation Corporation (SIAC);** Anita Bruzzese, author and syndicated career columnist for Gannett; Kevin Marasco, marketing director at **Recruitmax;** Ted Horton, managing partner at **BCI Partners;** Jeanne Achille, president of the **Devon Group;** Chrystal McArthur, associate dean of Career Services at **Rutgers University;** Ruth Shlossman, a director at **Watershed Associates;** and Trina Lee, public relations manager at **CarMax.**

In addition, thanks goes to Dan Bankey, a manager of strategic staffing at **Mutual of Omaha,** for his thoughtful and extensive comments as well as his insight on what the future holds for job seekers in Chapter 8. Nick Murphy, operations manager at **WorkBlast.com,** contributed excellent direction on the video résumé in the same chapter on hiring trends, as did Phillip Thune, chief executive officer of **HireMeNow.com.** I would also like to thank Heather McBride, formerly of **Jabil Circuit** and now an HR manager at **Fiserv,** Lisa Whittington of **Host Hotels & Resorts, Inc.,** and Donna Campbell of **Kindred Healthcare** for adding great value and insight to Chapter 9 in their critique of a sample resume.

For the revised edition, Meghan Gonyo, a New York account manager of recruiting and sales at **The Creative Group,** Robert Half International, provided invaluable information on the current job market. And Heather McBride, a human resources manager now at **Fiserv,** once again, provided input, this time giving suggestions on how best to navigate those tentative first six months at the new job.

Also new to this edition is the final chapter, which focuses on getting ahead in your new job. The information in this chapter was based on interviews with Charlotte Frank, senior vice president of research and development at **McGraw-Hill Education, The McGraw-Hill Companies;** Shelley Bird, executive vice president of global communications at **Cardinal Health;** and Lisa Whittington, vice president of human resources at **Host Hotels & Resorts.** Thank you for your time and contribution.

In addition, I would like to thank the following individuals for either providing sample résumés or helping me secure other résumés so that many diverse industries were represented: Mary Lou Adelante, Sharon Ambis, Tom Anderson, Mary Beth Barlow, Robert Edward Barlow, Jr., Michael Barry, Amy Bennett, William Berde, Esther Brandwayn, Debra A. Brodsky, Coleen Byrne, Megan Byrne, Marissa Caputo, Nicholas Caputo, Jaclyn Cashman, Min Chen, Cathy Chiavetta, Phil Chiavetta, Helen Cunningham, Steven Felsenfeld, Peggy Gaines, Angelo Guadagno, Kim Horton, Sabina Horton, Luke Kallis, Izabela Karlicki, Suzanne M. Lanza, Michelle N. McKenna, Suzann McKiernan-Anderson, Mark McLaughlin, Kathy Murphy, Doreen Murray, Sasha Oblak, Cheryl S. Peress, Rhonda Price, Andrea G. Preziotti, Alma Rodriguez, Michael J. Rosch, Andrea Caryn Sholler, Nicholas Seminara, Isabel Cunningham Uibel, Martin Ward, and Mary Ward.

Everyone needs an editor, and I was very fortunate to work with Shannon Berning for the new edition. Jon Malysiak was also instrumental in acquiring the earlier books for Kaplan. My development editor, Joshua Martino, did an excellent job of helping me pull these two books together. My copy editor, Paula L. Fleming, provided an invaluable service as did Karina Cueto, my production editor. And my gratitude also goes to Joëlle Delbourgo, my agent for each of my published books, for her support.

Finally I would like to thank my friends and family for their encouragement and support. Myles, Rose Anna, and Marie make all the hard work worthwhile. Rob Scala, the best lead guitarist in Jersey City, keeps the creative sparks flying. Mary Scala for her kind and encouraging words; Rose Greene for her example; Kathy Murphy and Suzann McKiernan for constant friendship and laughter; Sabina Horton, JoElyn Heuer, and Sheila Nadata for keeping me grounded; Martha Lambert for her spirit and generosity; and the Byrne, D'Annibale, Murray, Leonard, Good, Caputo, Chiavetta, and Greene families for their love and support.

---

* The respondents' participation in the survey does not necessarily indicate an endorsement of this book.

PART I

Résumés and Cover Letters

"Résumés that garner interviews exhibit these three qualities: there are no spelling or grammatical errors, they are neat and professional in appearance, and they show relevant experience."

Lisa A. Whittington
Vice President of Human Resources, Host Hotels & Resorts, Inc.

CHAPTER 1

What the First Survey Tells You About Your Résumé and Cover Letter

At the turn of the millennium, Corporate America's hiring process was undergoing a massive overhaul thanks, in large part, to the digital revolution. Suddenly it seemed there was a new hiring game in town. For job seekers, electronic know-how was taking precedence to pounding the pavement.

Job seekers were somewhat flummoxed by the new standards because there was so much contradictory information about the hiring process. All of a sudden, hiring professionals at large companies were overlooking the standard, hard-copy, one-size-fits-all résumé that arrived at their doors via snail-mail and began instead to seek candidates who targeted their electronic résumés and cover letters to specific open positions featured on the company website. Even job seekers with sterling credentials were wondering why they were floundering in the pool of availability while candidates with less experience were securing plum positions. Many job seekers didn't realize that HR professionals were recruiting people who wanted to work at their particular company, not just people who had the skills and qualifications to fit the open position. The game had changed almost overnight.

In 2002 and 2003, I surveyed 50 Fortune 500 HR professionals to help job seekers determine the ins and outs of the recruitment process at America's largest companies. The results of that survey formed the basis of the first edition of this book in 2004. While it still takes a good résumé and cover letter to win an interview at most companies, it also helps to know how America's biggest companies recruit the best talent. Part I of this expanded edition of *Get the Interview Every Time* is based on the first survey and focuses primarily on résumés and cover letters. These HR professionals—specialists, managers, directors, vice presidents—answered a detailed questionnaire on what Fortune 500 companies want to see from applicants. I've updated these results for this edition, but luckily the digital hiring process has begun to take root and the hiring standards are not quite as capricious as they were in 2002.

WHAT IT TAKES

If you're like most job seekers, you want to know what catches an employer's attention. Is it talent? Work history? Education? Relevant experience? And what are the best practices for targeting desirable positions at big companies? How do you even go about it in the digital age, when everyone is scanning, attaching, and emailing as they've never done before?

Remember when all you had to do to find a good job was sit down and write a standard résumé? Depending on your temperament, you either sweated through this exercise or you relished every minute. The process was relatively straightforward: you followed the format that the career counselor gave you, or you reviewed a résumé book in your local library that contained samples you could use as a model. Then you printed your new résumé on quality stationery, mailed it to 50 or 100 of your favorite companies, and waited impatiently for the telephone to ring to set up the sought-after interview.

Today, it rarely works that way. Think *electronic, target, connection, speed,* and *accuracy.* Those are the operative words in hiring. And even though some people diminish the importance of creating a good résumé, you still need to have one—even if your cousin sits on the board of directors at your target company.

Your résumé is your calling card. A prospective employer expects to review a candidate's résumé, no matter who you are or who you know. It's your ticket—actually, a front-row seat—to an interview. Knowing the expectations of America's biggest, most profitable companies gives you a competitive edge. The results of the first survey provide insight directly from those who make thousands of hiring decisions every year—and who also review thousands of résumés each month (sometimes every week). More than 2 million people work for the 50 companies represented in the first survey. That's an extensive amount of hiring experience.

Although plenty of information is available for newcomers to the job market, this edition sorts through the conflicting information regarding a successful job search. The collective wisdom contained in the two Fortune 500 surveys represents a new body of knowledge on the subject of a successful job search because these companies are the standard-bearers and leaders on the business front.

According to the majority of the participants on the first survey, these HR professionals initially take two minutes to review your résumé. That's not a lot of time to make an impression. Because most résumés today are delivered to human resources departments via email, if you're not familiar with all the variables of the electronic résumé, your two-minute opportunity could evaporate on the spot.

All 50 respondents in the first survey said that most recruiting takes place via the company website. A representative from JPMorgan Chase & Co. noted in a *Wall Street Journal* article that 77 percent of its hires in 2003 started on the corporate website, including those in entry-level jobs up to some in vice president positions. So it's essential to have a résumé that is cyber-ready. The new edition of *Get the Interview Every Time* provides simple, step-by-step guidance for posting electronic résumés.

STRATEGY BASED ON FIRSTHAND ADVICE

Finding the right job is a priority, especially because the average American spends between 56 and 61 hours per week at work. Add an average of 1.5 hours per day commuting and the math is easy: working takes up a significant amount of time. Because almost everyone who works needs a résumé, cover letter, and an inside look at the interview process, it makes sense to have a sound strategy based on firsthand advice from the experts inside the human resources departments of America's biggest companies.

That's one reason I've included many sample résumés from diverse industries to compare and contrast (see Appendix). Most of these samples are actual résumés that have passed the two-minute acid test. They have opened the doors to rewarding positions at excellent companies. The samples can guide you in the preparation of your own targeted résumé, but try not to skip right to the sample résumés because reading Part I will help you do the following:

- Research and target your next job.
- Write dynamic cover letters.
- Launch an Internet-ready cover letter and résumé.
- Customize your résumé for a targeted job.

Fortunately, since the first edition of this book, the economy has been on the upswing. Without a doubt, a healthy economy makes finding a job much easier. Still, many job seekers perceive the job market as unfriendly and approach it tentatively. These job seekers have a tendency to jump at any available position—sometimes even unsuitable positions—rather than patiently comb the marketplace for the right fit. The new edition of this book will encourage you to be patient and optimistic. Your ideal job is waiting for you to fill it—and this book will help you find it—but you must actively seek the right position.

In an article posted at CNNMoney.com, Nina Easton, the Washington bureau chief of *Fortune* magazine, tackled the topic of why Americans generally are "bearish" when the Dow is soaring and the economy is growing. Her answer sheds light on the job market of the new century. She says: "In the new economy, we all have to be entrepreneurs with our own lives—with all the rewards and risks and, yes, anxieties that entails."[1]

When I recently contacted the Fortune 500 survey participants, I was surprised to find that many of them—even senior level executives—had moved on to other companies. Holding a job at one company for 30 years is becoming the exception instead of the rule. There's a good chance that you, too, will work for seven or eight different companies—or maybe even change careers and find yourself in two or three different industries. For that reason alone, you need to know the new standards in human resources and how the current hiring environment works. You need the skills and information to be an entrepreneur of your own life.

THE RESULTS OF THE FIRST FORTUNE 500 SURVEY

Recruiting practices at large corporations have changed dramatically during the last ten years. Nowadays, job seekers are expected to maneuver their way around the new hiring landscape electronically. They must target individually tailored résumés and cover letters to specific open positions that are, more often than not, posted on company websites. According to the survey, even though it is still essential to network and prepare a professional-looking résumé and cover letter, it's also necessary to know that most companies recruit new employees via the Internet. Moreover, 70 percent of the Fortune 500 hiring professionals surveyed for this book said that they prefer résumés sent electronically.

Experts who participated in the survey were virtually unanimous in stating that résumés need to be not only individually tailored for targeted jobs but skill-specific and results-oriented as well. And it must be immediately obvious to a prospective employer that the job seeker is a good fit for the company and its culture.

In a two-page, 24-question survey, Fortune 500 hiring professionals answered questions regarding their respective hiring practices. Their responses provide an inside view of what they look for when acquiring new talent. Here are just a few of the questions:

- How are most résumés delivered to the HR department?
- Is a cover letter attached to every résumé?
- Does a computer program screen résumés?
- What is the ideal length of the standard résumé?
- What's the single most important piece of information on a résumé?
- How much time is spent reviewing a résumé for the first time?
- What are the grounds for sending a résumé to the unwanted pile?
- Where should applicants begin their job search?
- What does the company do with blind (unsolicited) résumés?

Some of the responses confirm what you already know, but most answers will surprise you. Did you know, for instance, that most résumés at Fortune 500 companies are delivered via email? As shown in Figure 1.1, 70 percent of the respondents prefer this method (11 respondents prefer snail-mail and 4 prefer fax; all percentages were based on the number of respondents who answered the particular question). One thing is certain: nowadays a job search requires access not only to a computer but also to the Internet.

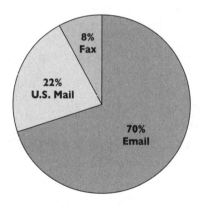

FIGURE 1.1: RÉSUMÉ DELIVERY PREFERENCES PIE CHART

WHAT THE EXPERTS SAY ABOUT COVER LETTERS

That electronic cover letter you agonized over for hours may not be read. It's your résumé that must catch the attention of the recruitment officer—only then will your cover letter get a look. In fact, most emailed résumés are submitted without cover letters: 74 percent of the respondents claimed that no cover letters were attached at the time of submission. When a cover letter was attached, only 40 percent of the respondents read it before the résumé. The remaining respondents read the cover letter only if interested in the candidate. Trang Gulian, a manager of staffing at Fannie Mae, said she "only reviews a cover letter if more information on the candidate is needed."

But just because hiring professionals don't read all the cover letters submitted doesn't mean they don't expect to see one. On the contrary, data suggest that although the hiring professionals look at résumés first, the next thing they read (if they are interested) is the cover letter. Cutting corners and blasting a solo-flying résumé out into cyberspace may not produce good results.

Taking a casual approach toward writing the electronic cover letter may be counterproductive as well. In fact, 84 percent of the survey respondents expected the e-cover letter to conform to high writing standards, the same standards traditionally applied to a standard cover letter; only two respondents indicated that it's not a strike against the candidate if the electronic cover letter is informal.

What about the standard cover letters sent by snail-mail? Are they considered dinosaurs? Not yet. If well written and insightful, such cover letters could help you stand out above the rest. Tracy Grajewski, a senior director of corporate staffing at Merck, said she wants the cover letter to "tell how focused the person is on his or her job search and give an idea where to refer the résumé."

So what do Fortune 500 professionals expect from standard and electronic cover letters?

- They accompany every résumé you send.
- They are brief but error-free and accurate.
- All pertinent contact information is included (name, address, telephone number, email address).
- Accomplishments are highlighted in a short paragraph.
- The position being applied for is specified.

The Fortune 500 participants had a great deal more to say about what they expected in cover letters. See Chapter 5 for more details.

If you're wondering whether your résumé and cover letter get the human touch, you can rest assured that only 36 percent of the companies use computer programs to screen applicants initially. If the company does screen, however, those résumés and cover letters should include key words that computer programs can pick up. Even though the majority of respondents (64 percent) don't yet have the capability to screen, it's just a matter of time before they jump on board. Why? Because manually screening the thousands of résumés that Fortune 500 companies receive is labor-intensive.

Eighteen of these companies receive between 50 and 100 résumés a day, 12 receive more than 100 résumés a day, and 4 of the 50 companies claimed to receive more than 500 résumés per day (Alltel, Chubb, Continental Airlines, Unisys), as depicted in Figure 1.2. Only 22 percent of the Fortune 500 companies receive fewer than 20 per day.

The survey results clearly indicate that the momentum in recruiting is shifting swiftly toward the Internet. It's safe to assume that what Fortune 500 companies do today, smaller businesses will do tomorrow. It makes good fiscal sense. According to Cambria Consulting's Bernie Cullen, a partner at the Boston-based human resource consulting firm, companies can "cut their costs [finding] new employees by nearly 90 percent compared with traditional recruiting techniques"[2] via the Internet.

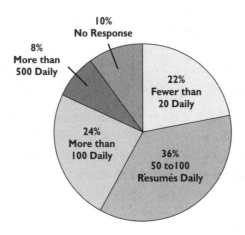

FIGURE 1.2 RÉSUMÉS RECEIVED PER DAY

WHAT'S AT THE CORE OF A GOOD RÉSUMÉ?

When asked what they look at first when reviewing a résumé, 80 percent of the respondents said "related experience." Dan Bankey, a manager of strategic staffing at Mutual of Omaha, recommends, "Focus your energies on the specific jobs that match the talents and interests you have—and individually tailor your efforts toward convincing the candidate companies that you can provide measurable ROI when hired."

Human resource professionals are primarily concerned with filling open positions. When an applicant can match the experience of the person leaving the company, the transition is smoother and less costly. (Replacement typically costs around $14,000; the Society of Human Resource Management [SHRM] claims the cost is usually a third of an employee's salary).[3]

Surprisingly, neither an applicant's educational background nor previous place of employment was a top criterion. In fact, only one respondent said educational background was the first thing he examined, and only one respondent said where the applicant worked before was first. Four of the respondents stated they first look at the format and style of the résumé. If that meets their expectations, then they proceed to examine the applicant's qualifications. One respondent said that he checks grammar and spelling before proceeding, and two said they look at a combination of the four factors mentioned.

Another surprise is that the "accomplishments" category was not checked off by a single survey participant. Although a candidate's prior accomplishments may be a deciding factor in whether the candidate will be asked to interview, this category seems to come into play only once other criteria are met. As many respondents made clear, accomplishments must be backed up with verifiable numbers, results, or promotions. Hiring professionals are wary of overblown accomplishments and "hype."

If you're wondering how long is spent reviewing your résumé for the first time, you should note that you don't have all day to capture a recruiter's attention. Thirty-six percent said they spend 2 minutes, 34 percent said they spend 1 minute, 22 percent said they spend 30 seconds, and 6 percent said 5 minutes. One respondent said it depended on the résumé.

This information should actually encourage you because it differs from conventional thinking on the subject. For example, according to the résumé design page in OWL, the online writing lab of Purdue University, which is geared toward recent college graduates, "Employers will usually take, at most, only 35 seconds to look at this one-page representation of yourself before deciding whether to keep or discard it." According to the *Wall Street Journal,* "Employers overlook significant experiences because they typically scan a résumé for just 15 seconds."[4]

Whether you have 15 seconds, 35 seconds, or 2 minutes, you still must grab the recruiter's attention quickly. That's why it's important that your related experience is immediately evident on the résumé. The best way to capitalize on this experience is to make sure your résumé contains relevant key words and a focus statement.

As for the length of your résumé, the survey indicates a general consensus. When applying for a management position, the standard is two pages, according to 74 percent of the respondents. Only 18 percent of the respondents thought one page was standard, and only 8 percent thought three. Two respondents said it "depends."

The preference for brevity makes sense when you consider that recruiters at large corporations look at hundreds of résumés each week. They need to zero in on the pertinent information quickly. Creating a ten-page résumé is almost certain to diminish your chances of getting a thorough examination by a recruiter.

START YOUR SEARCH ON THE COMPANY WEBSITE

It's best to begin your job search by narrowing down the companies you're interested in and then going to their websites. But before you go to the career page and start filling out a profile or searching for a specific job, spend some time getting a feel for what the company is about. Research is crucial to gaining an edge, according to the Fortune 500 respondents.

When asked where applicants should begin, 74 percent said to start at the company website. Surprisingly, only 18 percent said networking should be the first option, a finding that flies in the face of the commonly held belief that networking is the most important key to a successful job search. One respondent advised reading the classifieds, another said to go to job fairs, and two advised all of the above.

When asked where their companies advertise jobs, 60 percent said these jobs can be found on the company's website, 12 percent said they use newspaper classifieds, 6 percent said they use online job boards, and 20 percent said they used all of these. One respondent said that an agency was his company's primary source.

Although the survey results reinforce that time spent on a company website is highly advantageous, you need a strategy. Surfing haphazardly through innumerable company websites and job boards could be counterproductive if you neglect other strategies. Try to aim for balance: add some job fairs, networking, and even cold calling to the mix.

Developing a strategy before sitting down at the computer is crucial. Pinpoint the companies that interest you and target specific jobs. And pick up the language of the workplace as you go along—the lingo is continually evolving, and you want to be able to communicate effectively at all phases of the process. Once you've narrowed your target, you'll be able to make the best use of your time on the Internet.

DON'T NEGLECT THE BASICS

It is essential that before posting your résumé on a company website or online job board that you make sure your information is accurate and error-free. Run everything through the spell checker—twice. For extra insurance, you should have another person read your material for grammar and spelling errors or inaccurate gaps in your employment history. It's easier to make mistakes than you think.

When asked what the percentage of errors was for submitted résumés (see Figure 1.3), 36 percent of the respondents said that 10 percent have errors, 44 percent said 25 percent have errors, 16 percent said 50 percent have errors, and two respondents said 75 percent of the résumés they see contain errors!

Errors are one reason your résumé flounders; in fact, 14 percent of the respondents said spelling and grammar errors disqualify even the most accomplished candidates. But there's another important reason you may not get a response.

When asked about the grounds for rejecting résumés outright (see Figure 1.4), 54 percent of the respondents reported a lack of computer skills, 18 percent said applying for a position that isn't open, and 12 percent said stipulating a specific salary. Only one respondent considered a gap in work history a serious issue—and jumping from one job to the next can set off alarm bells.

Most recruiters in human resources departments at Fortune 500 companies are practiced at detecting incongruities in the information you provide. Even if the information seems straightforward and direct, many verify the facts, especially when a candidate gets past the first stage of the process. In fact, exactly 50 percent said they "always" verify information on résumés, 28 percent "usually" check, and only 22 percent "sometimes" check at this stage of the game.

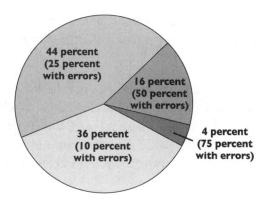

FIGURE 1.3: RÉSUMÉS RECEIVED WITH ERRORS

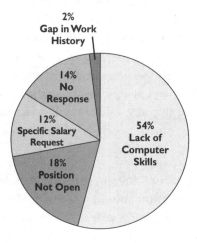

FIGURE 1.4: REASONS FOR DISQUALIFYING RÉSUMÉS

And what about the ubiquitous "personal information and interests" sections on many résumés? According to the Fortune 500 respondents, if the information isn't relevant, don't include it. Forty-two percent of respondents said they prefer not to read about applicants' outside interests, 28 percent said such information was "acceptable," and 14 percent advised including it only if those interests are applicable to the job. Mentioning your love of poker and mountain climbing could work against you, so remember to keep all the information on your résumé relevant.

Once you send the résumé, there's a good chance it will be acknowledged; at least the majority of respondents (54 percent) always acknowledge receipt of your résumé. Of the rest, 30 percent acknowledge receipt only if they are interested in you as a candidate, and 10 percent said that acknowledgment depends on the method of submission (which generally means that if you email a résumé, an automatic response is generated). Only 6 percent of the respondents said they never acknowledge receipt of résumés.

Whether or not you receive an acknowledgment, once the résumé is sent, you have no control over the outcome. Make sure your initial effort is thorough, accurate, and well-researched. Don't sit back just because you sent one résumé to a prospective employer and you're dead set on getting that particular job. Continue your efforts. That way, if the job doesn't materialize, you have other options (and less disappointment).

WHAT ABOUT MANAGERIAL POSITIONS?

The job-hunting landscape is changing as much for management candidates as it is for newcomers to the job market. When asked how they recruit for managerial positions, 40 percent of respondents to the first survey said that résumés are still used, 26 percent said they rely on a recruitment agency, 18 percent said management positions are filled by a referral from someone in the company, 12 percent said they use the company website, and 4 percent rely on the classifieds. Based on the cost savings and the trend toward using more information technology, you can expect the percentage recruited via the company website to grow steadily during the next few years.

What is particularly interesting about the survey results is that your dream job may present itself up to a year after you submit a résumé. Most of the Fortune 500 respondents keep your résumé on file for a year or more; in fact, exactly half of the respondents said they do this. And 24 percent said they keep them for up to six months, whereas 6 percent said three months and one respondent said one month.

Sometimes you may have the urge to send a résumé blindly to a company that you would like to work for in the hope that eventually a suitable position will open up. The good news is that only 12 respondents said they would not consider such résumés at all. Half said they file them for future openings and six route them to the appropriate departments. Four hold on to them indefinitely, especially if the candidate is recommended by either a personal friend or someone within the company.

When asked if they ever filled a position by using a résumé from their files, 76 percent said they do (even though this does conflict with how they view less recent résumés on online job boards). Only 12 percent said they prefer new résumés.

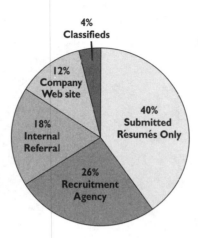

FIGURE 1.5: RECRUITING FOR MANAGERIAL POSITIONS

Generally, when you are most eager to move on to a new job, you get one shot at a company. Meghan Gonyo, an account manager at The Creative Group, a division of Robert Half International, says it's better to find out how an individual company's recruitment system works *before* you send the company your résumé.[5] You want to avoid having your "name keep popping up in their system," which suggests that you might not be as focused as you need to be. That's why the next chapter about researching the company is crucial. At every stage of the job search, you need to come across as a professional—someone who is focused, direct, and clear about your goals and objectives.

CHAPTER 2

Getting to Know the Job Market

The planning stage—your *preliminary* research—may be the most essential step in the job-seeking process according to the Fortune 500 survey participants.

All major corporations expect applicants to be familiar with the company's website. They want to see that you've done your research and they want to see that you are interested in working for that particular company. Nowadays job seekers have easy access to a company's business, culture, and employment opportunities, so there are no excuses for not knowing about the company you hope to work for.

Companies have spent millions and dedicated significant resources to ensure that their websites have valuable content and are user-friendly, and for good reason: when it comes to hiring, company websites are incredibly cost-effective. According to a *Wall Street Journal* article by Kris Maher, Merck, for instance, has saved "several million dollars over the past year by relying more on its corporate website to find candidates."[1] Websites enable companies to hire from a broad range of candidates without using expensive search firms and advertisements.

Once you've decided to pursue a certain company, it's also helpful to examine its literature from previous years, as it will give you a good idea of how the company has evolved. Annual reports, press kits, brochures, price lists, and other publications are readily available online. If you already submitted your résumé and are waiting for the telephone to ring, put this in-between time to good use by reading all the literature you can find on the prospective employer.

GETTING ORGANIZED

Start a job file. Then file the literature in a folder—after you read it. That way, you have all the information you need if you are asked to come in for an interview—a week, a month, or three months later—or if you have to make your way through an unexpected phone screen. This kind of preparation tells the company you are interested in becoming a part of the team. Review the information periodically and definitely check out the company website before an interview. You don't want to go to an interview and ask questions that could have been answered easily just by reading some basic information on the company website.

Brian Little, a group director in human resources at HSBC, reaffirms this advice: "Research before you send a résumé. Nothing wastes more time than looking at résumés that should have never been sent in the first place."

Even as you use cyberspace, a hard copy folder will aid in your research. Create a folder for your job search and start jotting down relevant information on each company. Put news clippings or annual reports in the file, so they are easily accessible. The calendar feature in some email systems allows you to keep a record. Set up an email account dedicated solely to your job search. It will keep your job search focused, and all relevant information will be in one account (and you won't have to sift through hundreds of emails to find the last one you got from a prospective employer). Make sure you have a professional email address, such as JeanXSmith@ yahoo.com (rather than chickflex@hotmail.com). In addition, the calendar feature is an excellent tool to help you keep track of your progress. Write down the names of contacts, the companies you want to research, and the action you took. Having this information readily available saves you the trouble of backtracking in case you are suddenly called in for an interview. During the job search, you will be navigating unfamiliar territory and gathering new information. Getting companies mixed up happens, but you can reduce the risk of making a blunder by creating a system for staying organized.

It's tempting to get off track when searching for a job. If you're like most people, you'll find it challenging to research potential employers and create a targeted résumé that whittles your work history down to two pages of relevant, but dynamic, material. You may look for any excuse—the lawn needs mowing, the cat needs to be fed—to put off your search. Stay on track. The average time frame for finding a job—three months—can easily be bumped up to six months or a year if you lose your momentum and spend your search time on extracurricular activities.

Even if a bout of procrastination overcomes you, be sure to devote a few hours to more general research. A look at the following career sites can get your brain in gear: check out Flipdog.com, CareerJournal.com, Monster.com, Salaryexpert.com, and Wetfeet.com. Not only will you pick up useful key words for your résumé, but the sites may also stimulate enthusiasm for the task at hand. These sites provide guidance to job seekers on such topics as interview techniques, salary scales, and résumé writing tips.

Keep in mind when you post your résumé on a job board that many recruiters look only at recent entries. If your résumé lingers too long on a job board, you cut your chances of being seen, so don't rush to put a résumé out there. Instead do some prep work. Another caveat: Your personal information on the large job boards is not as secure as it should be. In August 2007, Monster.com's "system had been hacked, in a security breach that resulted in the theft of confidential information for more than a million users."[2]

And another thing, matching skills between employer and employee on mainstream job boards is more difficult. That's why many recruiters are switching to job boards operated by professional groups. According to one health care technology recruiter: "About 15 percent of people who respond to a job posting [on the professional group job board] have the right skills, compared with the 2 percent results . . . at mainstream job boards."[3]

In addition, relying solely on the big job boards may suggest to an employer that your search is unfocused and your approach is passive. At all times during the job search, you want to give the impression that you are proactive. Posting your résumé on a mainstream job board at this stage may not create the best impression.

One advantage to browsing the job boards is that companies often use them to pull in candidates to their own company websites. For instance, say you find a position that interests you on HotJobs.com. You click on the position, and your browser leaves the HotJobs site and brings you to the prospective employer's website, where you then have to follow the company's application process. According to Creative Group's Gonyo,

> It's all about reaching the job seekers, maybe even those who are passive job seekers. Companies want to find out where these job seekers are literally hanging out in cyberspace, so even though they maintain that their company network or website is the proper way to pull somebody into their system, these companies can direct traffic in different ways.

An excellent source for company profiles and research is www.hoovers.com.[4] The information on the site is reliable, the contact information is current, and you can get a quick overview of a company if you don't have time to do more extensive research. (Everyone can access the profiles, but you have to be a paid subscriber for more in-depth information.) Also, you'll get more information than you can handle by putting a company name through a Google search.

MORE THAN THE CAREER PAGE

When you go to a company's website, take a look at the company's mission statement or its profile of the "archetypal employee." Not only will you find useful key words, but you'll also get a good idea of whether the company is a suitable fit for you.

The mood of employers has shifted significantly. Compared to the ego-driven mentality of the 1990s, the emphasis has shifted to service—to the customer, the client, or the user. In Jim Collins's book *Good to Great,* the author contends that the values embraced by the companies he profiled and the words they use to describe their corporate culture include: "disciplined, rigorous, dogged, determined, diligent, precise, fastidious, systematic, methodical, workmanlike, demanding, consistent, focused, accountable, and responsible."[5] Steer clear of hype and self-promotion and use these words as a guideline for the tone of your résumé.

Most of the recruiters at Fortune 500 companies have examined thousands of résumés, so you can be fairly certain they are adept at detecting sensational claims. Rocco Mangiarano, a director of human resources at Engelhard, sees between 50 and 100 résumés per day. He said in the survey that applicants "should be honest about who [they] are and what [they've] done." And David Murphy, an executive vice president at The McGraw-Hill Companies, said, "Hype does not pay." He added that "exaggerated claims about skills and/or achievement" are his personal grounds for sending a résumé to the unwanted pile.

So, resist bombast. Go instead to the company website and look up its mission statement; most Fortune 500 companies have one (even if they call it by another name). Many of them are simple statements about a company's goals and values; others are more elaborate texts. But all of them will give you direction on the tone you should use in your cover letter or résumé.

For example, the Procter & Gamble corporate website has a section called "Purpose, Values and Principles" that has clues about its culture. P&G's mission:

We will provide branded products and services of superior quality and value that improve the lives of the world's consumers. As a result, consumers will reward us with leadership sales, profit and value creation, allowing our people, our shareholders and the communities in which we live and work to prosper.[6]

If the culture of the company—one "with a mission"—seems antithetical to your maverick sensibility, then you may not fit in well there. You can save yourself and the employer a lot of money and time by finding this out before you accept a new position.

If you were to write a cover letter to this company, you might want to refer to its website material and show how these values are exhibited in your own work history—think "branded," "value creation," "improving the lives of consumers," and "superior quality." Remember, hundreds—and sometimes thousands—of résumés are sent to large corporations on a weekly basis. David Pulatie, a senior vice president in human resources at Phelps Dodge, said in the first survey: "You must create personal uniqueness. When hundreds apply for the same job, you must stand out."

TAKE YOUR TIME

After reviewing the general pages of a company website, proceed to the "career" or "job opportunities" page. There, you will see directions to apply for an open position. Generally, you will be asked to send your résumé directly to the company, or you will be asked to fill out the company's employee profile (which usually utilizes much of the information already on your résumé).

If you are uncertain about how you should proceed, then call the HR department and ask for direction. Creative Group's Gonyo said if you decide to make a call to the HR department, treat this call as a mini telephone screen, even though you are initiating the interaction. Usually, she says, the HR representative will put a note in the company's system that you contacted them. You want that note to be positive.

If you decide to fill out the company profile, do not rush through this process. Have a dictionary on hand and be prepared to double-check the accuracy of your information—from spelling and grammar to dates and company names. Human resources personnel are evaluating your communication skills, so do everything in your power to make sure that any information you provide is accurate and error-free. Take your time. If you are going to be interrupted a few times because you have to pick up your daughter from basketball practice or you're expecting a call from your Aunt Lucy, then it's better to fill out the company profile late at night or early in the morning. It's essential that all your communication with an employer is 100 percent professional.

Most companies expect you to have an email address. If you don't, create one before you go to the company website. On the PepsiCo career profile page, you are given a link and the option of creating an email address with Yahoo! Better yet, get your own email address from Yahoo! or Hotmail. Many times, company websites require you to log on before proceeding to a specific job. Sometimes your email address acts as your username during log-in, so there's no getting around the need for email. Even if you have an address already, it's a good idea to set up a new account to use specifically for the job search. To avoid electronic glitches, get used to your new email before using it.

It is essential you follow directions precisely; several Fortune 500 survey participants stressed this again and again. Dawn Thompson, a specialist in human resources at Idaho Power Company, said, "Pay close attention to the application procedure of the company. [A candidate] who doesn't follow procedures usually isn't considered." So when PepsiCo requests in its career profile that your résumé attachment not exceed 16,384 characters, do not send one that has 18,000 characters. This may sound simple, but many applicants don't follow basic instructions. Don't be one of them.

It is also helpful to be armed with a list of action words (see Chapter 4) to use in the event that you are asked to describe your career objective. Many Fortune 500 respondents said they often reject a résumé because the applicant's objective is fuzzy or too general. Determine what positions are open and available and speak to the employer's need.

If you have to fill out an employee profile rather than send your résumé, you may be asked to write a career objective in your profile. If you don't have one on your résumé, then you'll have to compose one on the spot before submitting your profile. That's when the list of action words comes in handy.

On some company websites, you may only apply for open positions. Others allow you to submit a profile or résumé for future openings. Again, follow the directions.

Make sure you read the job description thoroughly. The description is usually more elaborate than a classified advertisement. Pick up some of the key words from the job description and put them on your résumé (provided you have these skills, of course). If you are sending a "blind" résumé, one that will be held by the company for future positions or jobs not advertised, that's all the more reason to narrow your options. Employers want to see your focus.

Employers want to match candidates whose credentials meet the criteria of the open positions at their company. Job seekers must anticipate those needs and target their résumés accordingly. Revamping your résumé to reflect an employer-directed focus is essential. Employers want to know how you can solve their problems or meet their needs. The more you know about the company, the better you position yourself to customize your résumé to meet the company's needs.

Again, take a look at the Procter & Gamble career site. Besides allowing applicants to apply for open positions via the standard online job forms, the site also offers the opportunity to click on its career advice center and even participate in its "interactive online courses."[7] Another click and an applicant can discover what it takes to succeed at P&G: the "what counts factors." This is valuable information when you are targeting your résumé, as well as when you land the interview.

COMPANIES AS OPEN BOOKS

Match your qualifications to current job opportunities at a company. Many of the Fortune 500 participants said that if your qualifications don't match, your résumé remains active in the company database from six months to a year. But that doesn't always happen. When A. Tejero DeColli, senior vice president at Jones Apparel Group, was asked what the company does with unsolicited résumés, she replied that they just don't accept them. You must apply for open positions—and only open positions. A few other participants also said their companies don't consider unsolicited résumés.

This means you should do some sleuthing to find out what a company's policy is toward unsolicited résumés. If the information is not readily available on the career page, then send the HR department an email or call to ask about its policy regarding unsolicited résumés.

If a company explicitly states that you should not call, then honor that policy. If, however, you are unsure of the company's policy, then investigate further. Stacey Webb, a human resources representative at Gannett, stated that job seekers need to be "persistent. Contact the HR department to express your interest in opportunities with the company."

In addition, this phone call could save you from getting lost in the system. Creative Group's Gonyo says, "Having a personal connection is key." A telephone call will give you the opportunity to find the name of the person to whom you should send your résumé. It's also a good idea to have a list of questions ready before calling the HR department, questions specifically dealing with the application process. Following are some examples:

- What is the standard procedure for applying to the company?
- Are there any openings now?
- Will there be any positions opening up in the near future?
- If a résumé is sent to the department via email, should it be sent as an attachment or as plain text?
- Do you require a career profile (e-form) to be filled out on the company's website beforehand?

Ask good questions because you don't want to sound uninformed or ill-prepared when speaking to an HR representative. As with online applications, your communication skills are being evaluated. You can improve your chances of being hired by being prepared and anticipating an employer's needs.

DON'T GET AHEAD OF YOURSELF

Having the relevant skills that match a job opening is the number one qualification mentioned by the Fortune 500 participants. If your skills are not current or in demand, don't be averse to taking a course to brush up. Finding a new job can take on average three months. In a downward economy, the time frame can extend to a year. If you have to brush up on your computer or accounting skills, do it. Employers appreciate your dedication. Those who succeed in today's challenging environment are those who never stop learning and are willing to seek the information that will make their job search more productive and fruitful. If you don't know about social networking, look into it. If *HTML* is an unfamiliar term, do more homework. According to Dan Bankey, a manager of strategic staffing at Mutual of Omaha, "We're looking for lifetime learners."

As already mentioned, it costs a company approximately $14,000 to replace an employee (and thousands more for senior-level employees). Because a poor hiring decision can be costly to a company, try not to be impatient if the hiring process takes longer than you would like. You can be assured that the bigger the company, the longer it will take to procure a new position. Cydney Kilduff, a director of staffing and diversity at Kellogg Company, said applicants should "be patient—big wheels turn slowly."

And if you really want to work for a particular company, don't give up. David Murphy of McGraw-Hill said, "Do not rely on simply sending a résumé. Work the headhunter. Network your way into contact with the right hiring authority at the target company." Cecilia McKenney, at Pepsi Bottling, added, "Be persistent with the company you want to work for. Pursue jobs with multiple mediums and follow up."

According to the Department of Labor, there are more than 1,200 official job occupations,[8] so opportunities abound if you are willing to pursue what is truly right for you. Do not settle. Instead, do yourself a favor and take the time you need to discover what will fulfill you as well as provide you with a thriving livelihood. That's the purpose of your preliminary research—to help you zero in on the right industry and job. Then, when the job interviews begin, be prepared to research some more.

CHAPTER 3

Résumé Format and Design

Hiring professionals at Fortune 500 companies see hundreds, sometimes thousands, of résumés each week, and generally, they spend no more than two minutes looking at each one. Many survey participants mentioned that an "easy-to-read" résumé was a prerequisite for offering a prospective employee an interview, so choosing the right format and design can make a big difference.

SELECTING THE FORMAT

Creating an easy-to-read résumé starts with the basics and moves toward the finer points. To begin, you must decide what format works best for your skills and experience.

Most résumés follow a reverse chronological format: a time history of your work experience, beginning with your most recent position. Many recruiters prefer this format simply because it is easy to read. A chronological depiction of your work history allows hiring professionals to see how long you worked for each company. It allows them to quickly ascertain your growth as an employee and is a straightforward depiction of your increasing responsibilities.

The functional résumé, on the other hand, is more skills-oriented and avoids a chronological depiction of your work history. It works particularly well when you have limited paid experience, you worked part-time and/or as an independent contractor, you have large gaps in employment, or you are changing careers. For instance, if you want to emphasize the skills for a sales management position that you acquired working as a volunteer soccer coach and fundraiser, rather than highlight your last short-term job as a programmer, the functional layout may be a better choice.

But functional résumés have their downside. Practiced human resources professionals can easily detect any attempt to camouflage weak points in your experience. Even if a recent work gap was legitimate, a functional résumé can send the wrong signal to some employers, who may wonder if you are hiding something. The good news is that an unconventional employment history can still be transformed into a virtue if the information is presented in a strong, honest, and focused fashion.

Creative Group's Meghan Gonyo said, "You have to know how to present your information so that it doesn't look like you jumped around. That's a red flag. The way you present the material in your résumé is key."

Not every work history falls neatly into either a chronological or a functional format. On the contrary, quite a few format variations—the linear, creative, accomplishment, international, key word, targeted, and curriculum vitae, as well as a combination of these formats—may be more suited to your needs. However, they are all derivatives of either the chronological or functional format, so these two formats will be the focus of this chapter.

FIRST THINGS FIRST

Before you choose a format, compile key information—contact information, focus statement, employment history, educational background—so that it can be positioned as needed. This is the backbone of your résumé, and you need to spend a good portion of your time in developing it and, later, revising it. Not only must it be 100 percent accurate and error-free, but it must also be vibrant and focused. If the key information is faulty, even the best design will fail.

At this point, start to transfer all the earlier research you put in your notebook or handheld device into your newly created job data file on your computer. This is also where you will store your key information.

Every résumé should provide the following data: contact information, focus statement, professional experience, and educational background. Avoid listing the following: personal data (height, weight, age, marital status), hobbies, references, and salary requirement or salary history. Your résumé must accentuate the positive. Save sensitive issues (such as a physical disability or criminal record) for later.

Your key information should be arranged as follows:

Contact Information

In the digital age, this information takes up more and more space on a résumé. How much data should you provide? Begin with your name, address, home telephone or cell phone number, and email address. Decide if it's necessary to provide a daytime contact number; if you don't want to include your current work number, a cell number is the best alternative. If you include a URL so employers can view your website, it should be at the top of your résumé under your email address, as in the following example:

> *Martha Hempenstall*
> *111 Avenue A*
> *New York, NY 10000*
> *(212) 674-1000 (cell)*
> *marts@aol.com*
> *www.martsXYZ.com*

Focus Statement

The "focus statement" is known by many names (career objective, expertise, skills summary, professional qualifications, key features, accomplishments, background, highlights, professional profile), but usually it's the brief statement appearing after your contact information. It should pull all of your information together and tell a prospective employer, in a few sentences, about your level of expertise, the type of position you are seeking, or your most significant accomplishments. Information technology (IT) professionals often include a skills summary here that details their proficiency in hardware and software. As mentioned earlier, don't shoot for too wide a target. Try to anticipate what the prospective employer needs and pepper this statement with employer-directed, attention-catching words. (A targeted résumé may change its focus statement from one job to the next, highlighting certain skills for a particular job.) Here's an example of a focus statement (notice that it lists both the position being applied for as well as the candidate's expertise):

> **OBJECTIVE: *Development Associate.*** Strategic writer with eight years' experience fundraising more than $22 million and developing—from start to finish—successful long-term nonprofit, government, and corporate campaigns

Professional Experience

This section is the crux of your résumé. How you list your previous employment experience will depend on whether you use the chronological or functional format. When preparing the chronological résumé, your most recent experience should be listed first followed by earlier professional experience in descending order by date. A functional résumé, on the other hand, emphasizes your skills rather than where you worked and for how long (although it is often recommended that you give dates and where you worked, just in a less prominent position). Sometimes you describe a particular position; sometimes you describe just your skills. The first position in the professional experience section in the functional format is often reserved for the work experience that most closely relates to the position being sought at the new company. Your professional experience section in the functional format will be more skills-oriented and less specific than it would be in the chronological format.

What's most important to remember is that résumés grab recruiters' attention when the experience fits the job. Julie Ruesewald, a senior human resources generalist at Alltel, agrees. She said, "Don't apply for jobs you're not qualified for."

In the chronological format, put the emphasis on the professional experience listed first, as most employers are primarily interested in your current or most recent employment. If it's not obvious what industry you worked for and you are fairly certain the prospective employer won't be familiar with the company, then describe it briefly, either right after the name (technology) or in the description of accomplishments or duties. The first entry usually gets the most space on a résumé. A word of caution to those who feel the need to fudge some information: the Web has made it fairly easy to verify almost anything.

Educational Background

List your degrees and professional certifications in this section. How much space you devote to your educational background depends on what you want to emphasize in your résumé. If you graduated within the last five years or have virtually no work experience, you may want to expand on your college coursework or certifications here. Another common option for recent graduates is to rearrange the order of the key information and highlight the educational section by moving it to the top of the page following your contact information. (One Fortune 500 respondent recommended you list your education first, even if you have a lot of experience.) Whether you place dates next to your completed degrees is a personal decision. Some prefer not to include these dates because they believe it pinpoints their age, even though antidiscrimination laws are supposed to protect applicants.

If you are fluent in languages or have relevant professional affiliations, you may also include these items in this section. If you are in the process of completing a degree, list your anticipated graduation date. Some résumé books and career experts recommend that high school information or unfinished college degrees not be listed, although this issue is not cut-and-dried. As Dan Bankey of Mutual of Omaha said, "Absolutely include any training and continuing education. It can be a differentiator." You need to decide whether mentioning an incomplete degree will further your cause.

Bankey added:

> We sort by years of schooling, so if someone has some college, put it in. High school can be important if it's the highest level one has. We look at the highest level. Falsifying an application can disqualify you; truth and honesty are really important to us. We find that one-third of résumés have something that is not correct, but we'll give a candidate an opportunity to explain it. People really feel the need to have a college degree.

In an interview with the *New York Times,* a Career Couch columnist asked me why people tell lies on their résumés. I answered that people usually lie on résumés because they are eager to get jobs. He seemed surprised at this response. He obviously thought lying on a résumé was a sure indication of some deeply rooted pathology that eventually would develop into a predilection for mass murder. I don't think that's the case. Sometimes people are desperate to work—and make bad decisions.

The recent resignation of Marilee Jones from the Massachusetts Institute of Technology (MIT) comes to mind. Jones, the dean of admissions at MIT until April 2007, had misrepresented herself on her résumé 28 years earlier when she applied for a position as an administrative assistant and stated that she had college degrees from Rensselaer Polytechnic Institute (she was a nonmatriculating part-time student for a year), Union College, and Albany Medical College. (She sounds overqualified for this position, but your guess is as good as mine why the alarm bells didn't go off in 1979.) In defending their decision to hire Jones, MIT Chancellor Phillip Clay said Jones "rose through the ranks and performed spectacularly." And Lawrence S. Bacow, who served on the hiring committee back then and is now president of Tufts, said, "We all make mistakes, and she has acknowledged and paid for hers. That said, she served MIT for 28 years with distinction."[1]

Jones is not a depraved con artist who delights in duping people. She obviously served the MIT community well. But the decision to misrepresent herself early in her career caught up with her. Keep this in mind when you are tempted to lie.

CONTENT IS STILL KING

Your contact information, focus statement, work experience, and educational background form the backbone of your multipurpose résumé. While there's room for variation in the design of a résumé, this information must be correct, readable, and dynamic. Don't spend hours, however, rearranging the information in a hundred different ways. The more accessible and straightforward this information, the better your chances your résumé will hit its intended target.

Content is still king in a résumé, so it's a good idea to determine how best to present your work experience. Think "action verbs" that illuminate accomplishments and skills. Employers want to see results, and they are interested primarily in how you contributed to boosting your former employer's bottom line. Make sure your content reveals this. Even the best design cannot compensate for lackluster career performance. Nonetheless, make an effort at the design of the résumé because a good design makes content more readable.

DESIGN ELEMENTS

What are some of the design elements of an easy-to-read résumé? Balance, symmetry, and white space all contribute to the visual impact of a reader-friendly résumé. No one should have to struggle to review your material. A good design goes a long way toward easing eyestrain, especially when hundreds of résumés must be reviewed.

Adhering to the notion that a résumé should never be more than one page long, some job seekers tend to cram too much information in too little space, making it difficult to find relevant information and perhaps explaining why 74 percent of the survey participants prefer two-page résumés. Unless you are a newcomer to the job market or have limited experience, plan to write two full pages. (Several Fortune 500 respondents said the length depends on how extensive your experience is, but keep the two-page guideline in mind, no matter how accomplished you are.)

You can choose page-width spacing or a column approach to display all your key information in a flattering light. As a starting point, allow one inch for your margins—top and bottom as well as left and right. Sherry Rest, a manager of recruiting and staffing solutions at Lucent Technologies, said, "Although résumés are most often reviewed in electronic format, make sure your printed format has margins that will allow a recruiter or hiring manager to make notes."

Experiment with fully justified or ragged-right margins. Full justification, whereby both margins are aligned, may give you more words per line, but a ragged right margin (the right margin has an uneven edge) is faster to read, according to a study by Microsoft reported in Susan Britton Whitcomb's book *Résumé Magic*.[2] To get a few ideas about indentation, bullets, rules, and columns, take a look at how other résumés are designed. (See the samples in the Appendix.)

If your word processor has résumé templates, experiment with them but don't resort to filling in the blanks. Using templates may encourage you to settle for a run-of-the-mill description of your work history or tempt you to rush through the process of putting the pieces together yourself. The more time spent creating your résumé, the better your objective and design.

Kenneth Garrett, a vice president in human resources at FMC Corporation, said in the survey that you should "know what's on your résumé and be able to articulate it precisely." Your résumé should tell the recruiter that you have thought about who you are as an employee and your career goals because you have spent time presenting this information purposefully.

MAKE IT INVITING TO READ

Your résumé should be a logical arrangement of key information, which is why order and consistency—or the lack of it—play a big role in résumé writing. Chances are your résumé won't even be read if the information is presented haphazardly, so before focusing on the big picture, pay attention to the small details.

Because of the many variables, one of the trickiest parts of writing a résumé is consistency. Typefaces, indents, bullets, wording—all of these elements must be presented in a consistent way. You don't want Montana showing up in three different forms (*Montana, Mont.,* and *MT*) or one job title to be in boldface and the next job title in italics. Because of all these variables, proofread a résumé several times. Make sure verb tense is correct, your punctuation is consistent, and your indents align correctly. Take the extra time to do it right.

Your computer has a wide array of typefaces. Times New Roman, Courier New, Garamond, and Arial are all good choices. They also convert well from one computer system to another, meaning that your carefully formatted résumé has a better chance of looking good when the hiring manager prints it out. Goudy Stout, Raavi, and Gigi will probably send red flags to more conservative recruiters. Mixing up and using several different typefaces in a résumé is hard to pull off, unless you're graphically creative. Err on the side of caution when it comes to typefaces; otherwise, the résumé may look immature, cluttered, or downright unreadable. It's best to use the same typeface throughout the résumé, and as already mentioned, Times Roman, Arial, Garamond, and Courier New are all professional-looking fonts.

You should feel free to use bold, italics, and capitals, so long as they are used in a consistent pattern. For instance, make sure *all* of the names of the companies are capitalized or use bold to highlight *every* position held. The easiest print to read is roman type, so don't overdo the boldface or italics. Practice restraint.

Start with a font size of 12 points for normal text. Some claim you can reduce the size of text to 10, but 10 is hard to read and doesn't print as well. Resist the temptation to squeeze all of your information on one page by going to a smaller font. Instead, it's better to rearrange your résumé—or at least the white space—than to go to 10 point. If it's necessary to fit in one or two extra lines, reduce the text to 11 at the minimum. Smaller fonts may discourage recruiters, especially those who have read innumerable résumés for eight hours straight. Having said all that, for electronic submissions, 10 point is typical.

You may experiment with larger sizes for your headings, but don't get carried away (14 and 16 are more than adequate). By selectively enlarging the typeface, you can highlight something you think is important, hopefully a great job or accomplishment (but not your name).

Positioning your information appropriately is also important. If recruiters have to scour the remote corners of the page for pertinent information, the résumé is missing its mark. Your selling points should be placed up front. Don't hide important information in a lot of detail. Short, direct points and paragraphs are better than long ones, so edit rigorously and try to whittle the résumé down to its essence.

You should invest in quality stationery with matching envelopes if you're mailing your résumé, as well as quality stationery for the copies of your résumé that you will bring to your interviews. Stick to white or neutral colors for a professional appearance. Bright-colored paper (florescent pink or iridescent blue, for instance) sends the wrong message. Use a laser printer or a photocopy machine for extra copies. In the digital age, it doesn't pay to invest in offset printing (and making 100 copies), because according to the Fortune 500 participants, it's better to tweak each résumé for a specific job. In many respects, your résumé will be a constant work in progress.

If you don't have access to a computer (or you know for certain that someone else can do a much better job), then you might want to consider hiring a professional résumé writer. You still have to write your key information, but résumé writers can help you with design, key words, focus, and target. You can find résumé writers in the yellow pages. A certified professional résumé writer (CPRW) has passed competency tests administered by the Professional Association of Résumé Writers & Career Coaches (PARW/CC). These certified résumé writers will assist you in preparing a multipurpose résumé, but you may have to revise it each time you apply for a new position. Therefore, if you do have someone else prepare your résumé, work collaboratively with that person so that in the future, you can tweak your résumé periodically on your own.

For those of you who may need additional help, nonprofit career counseling services are available in every state. Also, every college has a career center that reaches out to students and alumni and, sometimes, the general population. Don't be afraid to seek help. Career counseling firms and job search companies are also alternatives, but be wary. Not all of these firms are legitimate; some charge advance fees and deliver only empty promises. Before you decide to contract the services of a company, review *www.jobscams.com* or visit *www.execcareer.com,* both of which monitor career-marketing companies.

If you go to headhunters, remain proactive. Become as involved in the process as possible, even if they create your entire résumé from scratch and choose each company where your résumé will be submitted. David Murphy of McGraw-Hill recommends that job seekers "work the headhunter." And Ken Dean, an assistant vice president at the Bank of New York, has this caveat: "You cannot rely on [headhunters] to put [your résumé] in front of the correct person." Don't be passive; partner with the headhunter. Stay involved with all aspects of the job search—even though you would like someone else to handle it for you.

Since you are reading this book, chances are you plan to create your own résumé. As long as you have access to the basic tools (a computer and the Internet) and follow a few sound guidelines on language, layout, and design, it's not difficult to create a winning résumé that opens doors.

PULLING THE PIECES TOGETHER

Once you write your key information and choose a format, you are ready to build a résumé. This section provides step-by-step suggestions, showing "before" and "after" versions of both chronological and functional formats. Many suggestions are based on feedback from the Fortune 500 participants.

The two "before" résumés are multipurpose and have wide applications in their respective fields. The "after" résumés are employer-driven and job-specific, which is what most companies expect today. The first résumé in this chapter uses a chronological format; the second is based on a functional format.

According to Stephen Heckert, senior manager of human resources at JDS Uniphase, you should "focus your résumé on a company's current or future job openings. This may mean developing a different résumé for each job opening." If you're worried about writing a new résumé every time you apply for a job, relax. It's not necessary to write 30 different résumés for 30 different jobs. What you ultimately should aim for is a multipurpose but dynamic résumé that can be tweaked every time you apply for a specific job. It's easier than you think.

BUILDING A CHRONOLOGICAL RÉSUMÉ

In a chronological format, you list your work history, beginning with your most recent employer and ending with your least recent employer and describing what you did and how well you did it for each employer. It's a winning format because it's simple and direct. If you have gaps in your work history, this format will reveal every one of them because it is arranged by date. That's why employers prefer the chronological format: it easily discloses whether you have a stable work history with a progression of responsibilities and accomplishments.

The following fictional scenario illustrates why a chronological format can be a good choice.

Mary relocated to northern New Jersey when her husband was transferred. For a few years, she commuted to her job in White Plains, but then the two hours of bumper-to-bumper traffic each day got the better of her. She decided to change jobs but wasn't exactly sure how she wanted to proceed. She hurriedly revised her résumé (Figure 3.1) in response to a classified ad she saw in the paper. She got the job at a local library, and although it was not a permanent solution, the position satisfied her on other levels. She worked in that capacity for two years, enjoying the interaction with the public.

When the position of administrative assistant at a large book distributorship came to her attention, Mary decided to make a move. She had to revamp her résumé to apply for the job. She decided to use a chronological format because of her solid work history.

The résumé that Mary used to apply for the library position indicates she is a competent and loyal employee who worked at a well-known Fortune 500 company for 16 years. She had no trouble securing the position of assistant librarian because she is an enthusiastic and reliable individual with varied interests and talents. Now she wants to set her sights higher—on a position that is more challenging and financially rewarding. She read the description of the administrative assistant position at a Fortune 500 book distributorship[3] on a company website and realized it combines her earlier administrative talents as well as her interest in books:

> The Merchandising Department has an excellent opportunity for an Administrative Assistant. The ideal candidate will be responsible for providing administrative support to the director, managing store inventory, occasionally supporting two vice presidents, managing routine correspondence for the field merchandise department, and coordinating travel schedules and reservations. The candidate will also be responsible for preparing agendas for meetings, acting as liaison with appointments and guests, and assisting the field merchandise department with projects and initiatives. The ideal candidate will be creating reports and schedules using Excel, Word, and other software; performing administrative functions, such as transcribing minutes of meetings; arranging conference calls, and providing backup phone support. Additional responsibilities include coordinating filing systems, ordering and maintaining supplies, and arranging for equipment maintenance. Qualified candidates must have some college and at least four years of administrative experience. They will also have excellent computer skills, including MS Word, Excel, Access, and Adobe Illustrator, and excellent verbal and written communication skills. Additionally, the candidate must have the ability to multitask, be extremely organized, be a team player, and be responsive to deadlines.

FIGURE 3.1 *Mary Smith's "Before" Chronological Résumé*

Mary E. Smith
1 Lincoln Ave., Ridgewood, NJ 07100, (201) 670-1000

Objective

A seasoned professional with excellent administrative and interpersonal skills, I am interested in an executive administrative assistant position.

Experience

1985–2001   IBM Corporation, White Plains, NY

Assistant to the Vice President of Marketing—North America:

- Extensive travel arrangements, both domestic and international
- Executive meeting planning and coordination
- Heavy calendar and email correspondence
- Follow up with staff
- Backup to the Americas Vice President's desk

Executive Secretary to the Director of Marketing—Latin America:

- Liaison to Latin America assignees
- Travel coordination in the Americas
- Heavy calendaring, conference calls, and meeting planning
- Focal point for Latin America secretaries
- Backup to the Vice President of Marketing desk

Marketing Programs Coordinator:

- Coordinate customer and sales force mailings
- Brochure production, inventory, and design
- Alumni and prospect databases
- Email to customer representatives

Education

Little Flower Catholic School for Girls—Philadelphia, PA
(academic as well as business curriculum)

Interests

Reading, exercise, tennis, gardening, needlepoint

References

Available upon request

THE "BEFORE" RÉSUMÉ

If you are wondering whether Mary can just update the "before" résumé and have a chance to interview for the new job, the answer is probably no. Mary's "before" résumé is a chronological, multipurpose document with a broad target. She could find a position with this résumé (as she did at the library), but it will be difficult to get an interview at a top-notch company that can match her skills, her desire to grow, her interests, and her financial needs. She needs to revise her résumé substantially.

Let's take a closer look at the "before" résumé, section by section.

Contact Information

The italicized contact information isn't the problem; the clashing fonts are. The leadoff font is different from the text font. If you are committed to using italics for the contact information, at least use the same type as for the text. She should also remove the comma after the ZIP code (no need to put a comma before a parenthesis). Better yet, though, is to drop the telephone number down to the third line because, in this day and age, providing the prospective employer easy access means including more information. What about a cell phone number instead? Also, an email address should definitely be included.

Focus Statement

Mary's "Objective" is not focused. Instead, it is generic and a bit tired—and it doesn't do justice to her extensive experience at a Fortune 500 company. She will, of course, need to revise it in her new résumé to include her current position as an assistant librarian. But if she resorts to a broad cliché instead of vividly describing what she hopes to attain and what she has to offer the prospective employer, chances are that the eyes of most recruiters will glaze over.

CNNMoney.com's Allen Wastler wrote in "Objection to Objectives" that he finds most objectives or focus statements "silly." He said, "When you think about it, the objective is pretty obvious the moment you hand over the résumé. Writing it out is an exercise in redundancy."[4]

When a focus statement is as vague as Mary's, Wastler may be right. Nevertheless, most HR people appreciate a focus statement. It makes their jobs easier. Even Creative Group's Gonyo concurs:

The best thing is a summary recap—two or three sentences, a summation with their objective—because that lets you know what they are looking for next. People aren't going from one account manager position to another account manager job any more. They are looking to move into new areas, so I need to know why and what they want.

Experience

This is the heart of the "before" résumé. Mary missed an opportunity to show her increasing responsibilities and promotion. Even though assistant to the vice president of marketing was the most current position she held at the Fortune 500 company (that's why she listed it first), she was promoted from executive secretary to marketing programs coordinator. Her promotion isn't obvious in the "before" résumé because Mary decided she preferred working for senior executives to working independently in the marketing department and shifted the information around—a valid personal decision. But for now, she needs to highlight her increasing responsibilities and promotion in the résumé so recruiters pay attention. Simply by providing dates alongside the three positions and moving the marketing programs coordinator position to the second slot, she could highlight the steady progression in her career.

Fortune 500 survey participants made the same point. Sherri Martin, director of human resources at Deere & Company, said she likes a résumé to exhibit "a career history of success demonstrated through advancement." David Murphy, executive vice president at The McGraw-Hill Companies, said that "consistent career development" was one of the three qualities that made a résumé stand out.

The bulleted description of Mary's responsibilities is brief, which is positive, but the sentences should not be fragments. A résumé is more dynamic and action oriented when verbs are used in bulleted sentences (notice punctuation of the bullets in the "after" sample). A résumé is not a memo but rather a formal introduction to a new company. Recruiters expect you to be professional by following the writing style typically found in most professional correspondence. (See Chapter 4 for more information on this topic.)

In addition, the description of Mary's duties is vague when it needs to be specific. Cecilia McKenney, a vice president in human resources at Pepsi Bottling Group, said she expects to see a "clear career progression that shows increasing responsibilities and/or skill organization" in a résumé.

Finally, although Mary sprinkled many excellent key words (nouns or short phrases that describe your qualifications that a computer scan will pick up) throughout the description of her responsibilities, there is room for more. Cherri Davies, a manager of staffing at Health Net, Inc., said her company "screens résumés submitted by email or URL website by key word searches." Make sure your résumé contains enough key words to make it past the first round.

Educational Background

Most résumé books recommend that you do not include your high school or incomplete degrees, even though most job seekers feel they must put something in this section. Because Mary does not have a college degree, she lists high school instead. She could strengthen this section by including continuing education classes that would be relevant in her new position. She should highlight and expand on her computer know-how. Even though working for a large computer company assumes a certain understanding of technology, recruiters (as well as scanners) are looking for specifics. When asked the number one reason for rejecting résumés, 54 percent of the survey participants said a "lack of computer skills."

There is no consensus for the inclusion of "interests" on résumés. Many of the Fortune 500 participants (42 percent) said applicants should not include outside interests on a résumé, 14 percent said to include them only if they were relevant to the job, and 28 percent said it was valid to include them. The safest bet is to include only those interests that may enhance your performance on the job or are applicable to the position. It will not be a strike against you if you forgo including outside interests. Mary can more effectively further her cause if she elaborates on her technical know-how rather than highlight her hobbies.

Finally, it goes without saying that references are "available upon request," so there's no need to include this statement on a résumé.

THE "AFTER" RÉSUMÉ

Now take a look at the "after" résumé shown in Figure 3.2. It's designed and targeted so that it corresponds to the position Mary is seeking at the book distributorship. Compare the wording in the job posting with the phrases Mary now uses to describe her qualifications. As noted in Chapter 1, the Fortune 500 survey participants prefer brief résumés, with 74 percent saying they should be no more than two pages and 18 percent saying they should be no more than one. Mary's résumé does not warrant two pages. Instead, it's a one-page, chronological résumé that highlights what the employer needs.

Mary needed to reposition her information and emphasize the positive. She also had to redesign her résumé so that it exhibited more purpose and logic. Here are the changes that made the difference:

- She sets the heading flush right to counterbalance the document.
- Her focus statement doesn't sound like a cliché and zeros in on what the prospective employer is looking for in an employee.
- She drops the first-person I from the focus statement and follows the style of professional résumés.
- She writes brief but dynamic statements that fit on one page, without squeezing in irrelevant information.
- She lists her most current position using key words (*filing systems, administrative support, conferences*) from the prospective employer's job description.
- She uses dynamic verbs to begin the bulleted information (*provided, guided, maintained, scheduled, generated, managed, acted, transcribed*).
- She uses dates in her description of duties at IBM, showing the progression of increased responsibility.
- She inserts more key words from the prospective employer's job description in her work history at IBM.
- She drops the reference to her high school and instead accentuates her continuing professional educational development. (The job description says the candidate *should have* some college, not *must have*.) The HTML and Web design classes were taken at the library, which is called the Habernickel Technology Training Center.
- She emphasizes her computer skills. Even though her knowledge of Adobe Illustrator (another key word) is not substantial (she never used it on a daily basis at work, nor does she have certification in it), she knows she is adept at learning most computer programs. Mary will enroll in a crash course while she continues her job search.

FIGURE 3.2 *Mary Smith's "After" Chronological Résumé*

Mary Eleanor Smith
100 Lincoln Avenue, Ridgewood, NJ 07100
Cell (201) 670-1000 • E-mail mxsmith@yahoo.com

PROFESSIONAL QUALIFICATIONS: Multitalented, team-oriented, and experienced support person with excellent computer and marketing skills can blend creative, interpersonal, and administrative skills to meet and exceed goals in both a Fortune 500 environment as well as a research organization.

2001–Present **Ridgewood Public Library, Ridgewood, NJ**
Assistant Librarian
- Provide courteous and efficient service to patrons at large public library that is ranked one of the busiest in the county.
- Guide students as well as professionals in research.
- Maintain filing systems and provide backup support to technologist.
- Provide administrative support to library director.
- Schedule classes at Habernickel Technology Training Center.
- Generate publicity for events.

1985–2001 **IBM Corporation, White Plains, NY**
1998–2001 *Assistant to Vice President of Marketing—North America*
- Arranged extensive travel arrangements, domestic and international.
- Coordinated and scheduled executive meetings.
- Managed heavy email correspondence.
- Assumed major responsibility in planning and follow-up with staff.
- Acted as backup to the Americas Vice President's desk.
- Transcribed meeting minutes.
- Met tight deadlines and multitasked adeptly.

1993–1998 *Marketing Programs Coordinator*
- Coordinated customer and sales force mailings.
- Produced brochure, supplying text and design and meeting deadlines.
- Maintained alumni and prospect databases.
- Managed extensive emailings to customer representatives.
- Ordered and maintained supplies.

1985–1993 *Executive Secretary to Director of Marketing—Latin America*
- Acted as liaison to Latin America assignees.
- Coordinated all travel schedules and reservations in the Americas.
- Arranged conference calls and meeting planning with heavy calendaring.
- Teamed with other support personnel to maintain several databases.
- Acted as backup to Vice President of Marketing desk.
- Assisted in preparing agendas and reports for meetings.

PROFESSIONAL DEVELOPMENT AND TRAINING: Selected consistently to attend workshops on time management, marketing, business writing at IBM. Completed HTML and Web Page Design courses at the Habernickel Technology Training Center.

COMPUTER SKILLS: Lotus Notes, Excel, Access, MS Word, WordPerfect. HTML. Familiarity with Adobe Illustrator. Adept at learning new computer skills.

AND REACH A LITTLE HIGHER

Even in a robust economy, competition is stiff and employers are holding out for candidates who match their specific requirements. However, that doesn't mean you shouldn't reach for something better when going for the next job. If your skills are particularly strong, you should at least apply for a position, even if it is not a 100 percent match. Employers understand that job seekers want to advance—in fact, it's probably the most legitimate reason, at least in the eyes of an employer, for moving to another company.

Many Fortune 500 respondents encouraged job applicants to keep plugging away, even after a rejection. In other words, you shouldn't necessarily give up after the first try. Not only does your résumé stay in company databases for an extended period of time, but most Fortune 500 hiring professionals surveyed said they want to see a strong interest from candidates to work for that particular company. Going out of your way to get the necessary training is certainly a good indication of your interest in a particular company. And it shows your persistence and focus as well.

THE FUNCTIONAL RÉSUMÉ

The functional résumé presents an applicant's skills independently from that person's work history. Most experts suggest you include a work history so the recruiter doesn't think you are hiding important information (gaps in employment, limited experience, or short tenures at previous employers). Norma Mushkat cited a survey of 2,500 recruiters done by ResumeDoctor.com in which the functional format was listed as one of the ten top peeves.[5] In addition to these drawbacks, a functional format is more difficult to write.

Then why is an example of the functional format included here? Because it works well for those with unconventional work histories, and a growing percentage of job seekers do not have conventional work histories. The following fictional example presents a good case study of when a functional format works well.

Mikhail is a data processing consultant specializing in information technology. His background is varied and broad: he has worked as an independent consultant at 28 companies in his 30-year work history. Mikhail's résumé is five pages long—and the chronological format of his "before" résumé excessively details every assignment he ever had. Much of the information is repetitive. When he discovered a permanent position for a senior design analyst on a company website, he targeted his résumé for this opening. He decided to use a functional format and cut his résumé to three pages.

Although Mikhail knows it's important to include at least a bare-bones listing of the companies he has worked for, he also knows a bulleted list of his top projects would work better than a detailed description of each job. Mikhail pares his résumé to two pages by listing all the companies in a separate section without the detailed descriptions of what he did at each company. Because the prospective employer is a technology firm, he wants to highlight his technical skills. If the company wants more detailed information about his earlier work history, it can refer to Mikhail's website, where this information is presented in chronological order. Figure 3.3 shows Mikhail's résumé before he revised it.

NOW COMPARE THE TWO

Mikhail's résumé indicates that he is qualified, having consulted for 30 years as a programmer/analyst, but many of his jobs were unrelated. Even though he worked primarily at financial services companies, he needs to point out this common thread in his long history. Consider the posting for the new job:

> Senior Design Analyst with proven ability to analyze system components against project requirements and produce general design and program specifications. Must have strong verbal and written communication skills. Proven ability to lead large development projects through all phases of life cycle with emphasis on testing component.
>
> Extensive experience in IBM mainframe development, including COBOL, MVS, JCL, and mainframe analysis and debugging tools, such as File-AID, Xpediter, etc. Experience with VM operating system a plus but not a requirement. Experience in Order Processing and/or Market Data systems a strong plus but not a requirement.

Mikhail takes note of certain key words, so he can include them in his revised résumé. He has all of the necessary qualifications, but he will have to rearrange his key information to reflect that. Let's take a closer look at the "before" résumé, section by section.

FIGURE 3.3 *Mikhail's "Before" Résumé*

Mikhail Okdamir   *www.okda.com*
1 Condict Avenue
Jersey City, NJ 07300
Business: (201) 866-1000 Cell: (201) 866-0001

SUMMARY

Successful data processing professional with years of experience in various areas of information technology. Skilled technologist and organizer. Excellent writing and communication skills.

SOFTWARE

MQ, CICS, COBOL, COBOL II, LE COBOL, DB2, SPUFI, QMF, VSAM, DOS/VSE, MVS, IDMS, INTERTEST, Viasoft, Xpediter (batch and online), Macro CICS Assembler, Assembler, CEDF, ADS, Easy Test, File-AID, Library Management system, Panvalet, Librarian, Endevor, TSO/SPF, ROSCOE, CMS, SDF, Debug, COMPAREX, MS Word, Visio, HTML, ABC FlowCharter, Windows 98

EXPERIENCE

May 2002–Dec 2002. **HIP NEW YORK. EPO/PPO.** Implementation of new health plan. PHCS Interface project that will expand HIP services beyond tri-state ten-counties area. Provider Incentive Checks system. Coordinated interface process with Fleet Bank Interface system to clear Claims Benefits Checks (FTP). Developed technical specifications for Geriatrix system. Various supporting claim processing projects. Generated entries for general ledger for Provider Incentive checks. Converted user requirements into programming specification. Scheduled new jobs and on-request jobs. Coordinated implementation of jobs involving banks. Prepared technical documentation. Production support. Coding and testing.
VSAM, CICS, COBOL, FTP, XPEDITER, JCL (batch and online)

Nov 2000–May 2002. **MORGAN STANLEY INC.** Mutual funds support. Managed and supervised file expansion project. Developed supporting documentation. Converted user requests into formalized programming specifications. Supported 12B1 process. Interfaced with trust division that supplied input data for 12B1 process. Scheduled new jobs and ran on-request jobs. Prepared and wrote 12B1 Project overview. Generated vouchers for AP system. Balanced AP vouchers before production run. Followed up on daily production. Prepared reports on production problems for management. Conducted meetings with users to resolve various technical questions associated with requirements. Coding and testing of requested JCL and/or program changes.
CICS, DB2, SPUFI, LE COBOL, COBOL II, MQ, VSAM, VIASOFT, INTERTEST, VISIO, TSO/SPF, JCL, MS WORD

Feb 2000–Oct 2000. **BANK OF TOKYO/MITSUBISHI.** Maintained Bank Accounting System (IMMS). Constructed accounting vouchers. Developed technical specifications from user requirements. Advised user on usage of new online systems. Developed guidelines to reorganize VSAM files. Specifications for program and/or JCL changes presented for

FIGURE 3.3 *Mikhail's "Before" Résumé*

approval and walk-through. Developed procedure to add new line printer for printing of checks. Installed supporting software. Coded, tested new programs, program enhancements, and/or supporting JCL. Developed process to update and enhance system documentation.
VSAM, DB2, CICS, INTERTEST, COBOL II, MVS/JCL, VISIO, MS WORD

Apr 1997–Dec 1999. **DEAN WITTER REYNOLDS, INC.** Mutual Funds Processing. Developed systems specification from user requirements. Developed backup procedures. Coded and tested major system components. Developed new programs. Participated in Y2K remediation. Assisted in developing audit trails to prove completeness of Y2K changes. Instructed backup employee on 12B1 changes. Proposed audit trails to prove 12B1 process. Scheduled new jobs for production. Followed up on production moves. Generated proper journal entries for AP system. Balanced and proved voucher file before scheduled implementation. Testing and coding of various proprietary mutual fund programs and/or jobs. Assisted in installation of new developer supporting software (Viasoft).
CICS, DB2, SPUFI, COBOL II, VSAM, VIASOFT, INTERTEST, TSO/SPF, JCL, MS WORD

Sept 1996–Mar 1997. **PAINE WEBBER, INC.** Developed program specification for Taxlot Reconciliation System. Ran ad hoc jobs to support user research. Input files were generated on UNIX platform. Assisted user in developing strategies to process data. All proposed changes presented to management for walk-through. Coded and tested programs and/or supported JCL. Developed required journal entries for AP system. Journals were balanced before added to production. Heavy user interface.
CICS, COBOL II, VSAM, DB2, SPUFI, QMF, TSO/SPF, JCL, MS WORD

Aug 1995–Aug 1996. **PERSHING CO.** Mutual fund support. Client support. Coded and tested major enhancement. Interfaced with users. Developed and prepared service requests for the program and/or JCL changes, which were presented to management for approval. Followed up with user on all implemented changes. Resolved post implementation problems. Prepared required documentation and changes to user manuals. Tested and coded new programs and/or JCL. Scheduled new jobs for production. Verified job dependencies. Generated vouchers for company AP system. Balanced voucher file before production.
CICS (Command), COBOL II, VSAM, DB2, QMF, TSO/SPF, XPEDITER, MS WORD

Feb 1995–Aug 1995. **PETRIE RETAIL CO.** SENIOR CONSULTANT. Major enhancements in Fixed Asset System. Designed new approach to generated audit trails for AP system. Designed enhancements. Presented user with proposed changes. User presentations. Organized/suggested improvements for system documentation.
CICS, VSAM, COBOL, ROSCOE, JCL

Apr 1993–Feb 1995. **MEDCO CONTAINMENT CO.** SENIOR CONSULTANT. Designed online Formulary Rebate system. Prepared specifications for batch process. Prepared presentation for users. Developed screens and written programming specifications. Prepared/suggested improvements for system documentation. Assisted junior-level

FIGURE 3.3 *(continued)*

programmers with Batch CICS debugging approaches. Coded new programs and/or new JCL streams and added the changes to existing processes. Tested and debugged. Interfaced with management in presentations and walk-through.
DB2, QMF, SPUFI, VSAM, CICS, COBOL II, MVS/JCL, TSO/SPF, XPEDITER, MS WORD

Feb 1993–Apr 1993. **BROWN BROTHERS HARRIMAN.** SENIOR CONSULTANT. Developed programming specifications from user requests. Developed program documentation. Developed process to document program and/or JCL changes. Coded and tested all programs and/or JCL changes. Maintained existing; received and delivered system.
CICS, VSAM, COBOL II, MVS/JCL, TSO/SPF

Dec 1991–Jan 1993. **IBJ SCHRODER BANK.** SENIOR CONSULTANT. Designed and tested interface with IECA. Modified various online programs in Auctions System. Designed and implemented new reporting system for federal government. Applied vendor supplied fixes to Custody and Trust programs (Omnitrust). Journal entries.
VSAM, COBOL II, CICS, ADABAS, MVS/JCL

Sept 1991–Dec 1991. **GE INFORMATION SERVICES.** SENIOR CONSULTANT. Vendor. Presented new strategies for functional design approach. Implementation of Batch file transfer and Mailbox system for major investment bank. Coding and testing new programs and JCL.
COBOL II, VSAM, CICS, INTERTEST, MVS/JCL

June 1991–Sept 1991. **LEVER BROTHERS.** SENIOR CONSULTANT. Warehouse replenishment system. Prepared user requested activity reports. Presented report layouts. Developed programs and JCL to generate required reports. Developed and proved input file for AP system.
VSAM, CICS, COBOL II, MVS/JCL, TSO/SPF

Apr 1991–June 1991. **DRESSER PUMP INDUSTRIES.** PROJECT MANAGER. Planned and supervised conversion from DOS/VSE to MVS. Conducted technical interviews and assembled project team. Monitored and resolved business and technical problems. Project manager. Coordinated activities of group of 13. Conducted status meetings.
MVS/JCL, VSAM, COBO I, TSO/SPF

June 1990–Apr 1991. **SHARP ELECTRONICS.** SENIOR CONSULTANT. Manufacturing applications, tracking and reconciling custom broker payments. Maintaining various projects. Testing and debugging.
IDMS, COBOL II, VSAM, CICS, MVS/JCL, TSO/SPF

Feb 1990–June 1990. **IBM PROFESSIONAL SERVICES.** SENIOR CONSULTANT. Worked on client's site. Insurance applications. Interfaced with management. Coding and testing.
COBOL, ASSEMBLER, CICS (Macro), VSAM, MVS/JCL, TSO/SPF

FIGURE 3.3 *(continued)*

Oct 1989–Feb 1990. **DEUTSCHE BANK.** SENIOR CONSULTANT. Trade Entry System. Tax Reporting System. Prepared system outline for trade cancellations. Interfaced with management. Coding and testing.
WANG/COBOL

July 1989–Oct 1989. **MERRILL LYNCH CO.** SENIOR CONSULTANT. Worked defining the requirements for various projects. Trained junior personnel. Tested and debugged. Interfaced with management.
COBOL II, VSAM, CICS, MVS/JCL, TSO/SPF

June 1989–July 1989. **ADP CO.** SENIOR CONSULTANT. Worked on various projects. Maintenance. Tested and debugged. Interfaced with management.
ASSEMBLER, VSAM, CICS (Macro), TSO/SPF

Mar 1989–May 1989. **DREXEL BURNHAM LAMBERT CO.** SENIOR CONSULTANT. Worked on the implementation of enhancements for multicurrency processing. Tested and debugged.
VSAM, CICS, COBOL II, MVS/JCL, TSO/SPF, MVS

Sept 1987–Feb 1989. **BANK OF TOKYO,** SENIOR CONSULTANT. Vista Security Processing system (VSPS). Project manager responsibilities. Resolved production problems in batch and online part of the VSPS system. Planned and supervised conversion of FSPS system from DOS to MVS. Interfaced with software vendor, suggesting many quality and/ or functional improvements. Applied, coded, and tested many vendor-supplied software bulletins.
VSAM, CICS, COBOL II, MVS/JCL, TSO/SPF

Mar 7–Aug 1987. **VISTA CONCEPTS.** SENIOR STAFF CONSULTANT. Worked on securities processing packages for major banks in USA and Canada. Interfaced with clients in USA and Canada. Assisted in defining client's needs and deliverables. Resolved production problems on client site. Interfaced with corporate management. Suggested changes and improvements.
VSAM, COBOL I, MVS/JCL, TSO/SPF

May 1986–Mar 1987. **FIRST BOSTON CO.** SENIOR CONSULTANT. Participated in streamlining and improving the night cycle process. Interfaced with DTC. Coding and testing.
VSAM, COBOL, MVS/JCL, TSO/SPF

Feb 1986–May 1986. **FIRST JERSEY NATIONAL BANK.** SENIOR SYSTEMS CONSULTANT. Participated in the redesigning of stock transfer and accounting systems. Assisted in defining user requirements for CICS-based stock transfer system. Interfaced with DTC. Defined software and hardware requirements for installation of transfer agent software package.
VSAM, COBOL I, ROSCOE

FIGURE 3.3 *(continued)*

May 1985–Feb 1986. **SHEARSON LEHMAN/AMERICAN EXPRESS**. SENIOR SYSTEM ANALYST. Directed and participated in the design, development, and installation of computer-based information systems, Clearance system (Cage Processing). Proposed system improvements and provided various alternatives.
COBOL, VSAM, CICS, TSO/SPF

Nov 1984–May 1985. **SPEAR, LEEDS & KELLOGG.** SENIOR PROGRAMMER/ ANALYST. Participated in the design, development, and installation of computer-based information systems. Assisted in conversion of various applications from DOS to MVS. Assisted in the development and implementation of new Clearance systems. Wrote programming specifications.
CICS, IDMS, COBOL, TSO/SPF, MVS

Aug 1982–Nov 1984. **BRADFORD TRUST.** LEAD PROGRAMMER/ANALYST. System documentation. Wrote programming specifications. Assisted with production problems. Coding and testing.
VSAM, COBOL I, CICS, MVS/JCL

July 1977–June 1982. **MERRILL LYNCH CO.** SENIOR PROGRAMMER/ANALYST. Designed system improvements and provided various alternatives. Prepared programming specifications. Prepared documentation. Project leadership responsibilities.
CICS, VSAM, ASSEMBLER, COBOL I, TSO/SPF

Feb 1974–June 1977. **PERSHING CO.** PROGRAMMER/ANALYST. Prepared programs as necessary. Participated in system analysis.
ASSEMBLER, ISAM, TSO/SPF

HARDWARE
IBM 303x, IBM 308x, IBM 43xx

EDUCATION
IBM: MQSeries Applications Programming (OS/390); MQSeries Introduction (OS/390)

Online Software International: CICS command-level coding: CICS application design; CICS-VS debugging and internals

Merrill Lynch Co.: Management training courses. BDAM assembler interface, CICS macro-level coding (Assembler); MVS JCL; VSAM coding (Assembler)

New York University: Business Programmer Certificate, "C" language course

Chubb Institute: Visual Basic 3.0

University of Economics, Ljubljana, Slovenia: Degree in Business Administration and Management (BS)

Contact Information

Name, address, and telephone and cell numbers are listed; in addition, Mikhail has included the URL of his website. He may want to rearrange the contact information so that it doesn't look lopsided. A flush-left design works well for electronic transmittals of a résumé, but a more balanced distribution of Mikhail's contact information will save space. Also, he will include an email address in the "after" résumé.

Focus Statement

Mikhail's summary doesn't define the type of position he is seeking, nor does it tell the employer what he has to offer. Instead, it is a tired description of just about any garden-variety programmer/analyst. Nothing in this statement stands out to an employer. As with Mary's first focus statement, his target is too wide and it doesn't anticipate the employer's needs. When he revises this focus statement, he will include key words as well as highlight his expertise.

Technical Summary

Because Mikhail is a technology professional, he includes a technical summary so prospective employers don't have to search for this expertise. He lists only those programs and applications that he is prepared to talk about in an interview. In the revised résumé, he will move the hardware reference into the technical summary along with software.

Professional Experience

The chronological listing is too duty-oriented. More emphasis should be placed on measurable outcomes, leadership skills, and problem-solving abilities. Throughout his career, Mikhail has supported, maintained, developed, designed, and implemented systems. However, the progression of responsibility is hard to find in his description of duties. Repositioning this information will make it easier to find, especially by HR professionals who may not have technical backgrounds. The hiring manager with a technical background can always refer to Mikhail's website for a more detailed, chronological description of his background.

Educational Background

Mikhail graduated with a degree from a foreign university but gives the U.S. equivalent so employers are not confused. He needs to state his status as either a resident or citizen. According to Creative Group's Gonyo,

Sometimes it's hard to see from a résumé that a person is not authorized to work in the United States. And you have to make sure that people have verifications and can provide recent references. Including status on a résumé that suggests you may not be a citizen is a helpful addition.

But, if there is some concern that bias may occur because of citizenship status, leave this information off your résumé. Citizenship status will come up at a later point, so be prepared to deal with it then.

He also lists his certifications, which are especially important for technologists, as they reveal that one's knowledge is current. Because he is not a recent graduate (within the last five years), it is not necessary to provide dates in this section.

Mikhail is a seasoned professional who fits nicely into the prospective employer's opening. He has whittled away the superfluous and repetition, cutting his five-page résumé down to three without sacrificing any key information, as shown in Figure 3.4. Here are the changes that made the difference:

- He uses an Arial font throughout at full justification. The "after" résumé easily converts into an electronic version when necessary.
- He uses bullets and rules to separate and add balance.
- His focus statement is no longer run-of-the-mill. Instead, he picks up key words from the prospective employer and inserts them into his own "Qualifications Summary."
- His personal achievements are basically the same as they were in his chronological résumé, but now he opens his bulleted information with dynamic verbs (*defined, redesigned, planned, prepared, designed, participated, tested, developed, constructed, managed,* and *implemented*).
- His work history is included but in a separate section. It doesn't make sense for an independent contractor to make his work history the focus of the résumé.
- His hardware and software expertise are grouped together. Employers, especially technical or scientific firms, want to see that employees' skills are current.
- In his "before" résumé, it was evident that Mikhail had used certain computer languages recently. That's why it was necessary for him to supplement this information in the certification section.
- All relevant information is accessible and accurate. Mikhail checks spelling of technical information by doing a search on hardware and software terminology.

- The functional format is logical and purposeful, exhibiting balance, consistent pattern, and good design.
- Finally, this "after" résumé is much easier to read, because Mikhail has eliminated irrelevant information and cut the five pages down to three while retaining important key words.

You have to decide which format works best for your work history. Even though hiring professionals prefer a chronological format, some work histories just don't fit this mold. Whichever format you choose, though, make sure your résumé conforms to these guidelines:

- Double-check for accuracy. Run it through the spell checker—twice. Ask for objective feedback from outsiders. Your sentences should be direct and brief. Do not exceed three pages in length unless absolutely necessary.
- Make sure you emphasize your accomplishments rather than your responsibilities.
- All of your dates should be accurate and specific.
- Include all contact information, including an email address.
- Make sure you are qualified for the position for which you are applying.

Knowing what an employer wants helps you to design your résumé so that it reflects the employer's needs. To paraphrase a particularly helpful summary of what is typically valued by employers, Susan Britton Whitcomb in *Résumé Magic* says that your résumé should illustrate that you can help a company to make money, save time, make work easier, be more competitive, build relationships, expand business, attract new customers, and/or retain customers. If your résumé exhibits these eight qualities (or at least a few of them), you have a good shot at getting that interview.

FIGURE 3.4 *Mikhail's Revised Functional Résumé*

Mikhail Okdamir
1 Condict Avenue
Jersey City, NJ 07300

Telephone: Cell (201) 866-0001, E-mail: MO111@optonline.net
Website: www.okda.com

QUALIFICATIONS

Self-motivated and experienced senior design analyst with proven track record in design, testing, specifications, development, and enhancement of systems. Adept at solving complex technical problems and communicating to management or team leader status of assignment, including project time lines, issues, and contingencies. Highly skilled technologist with excellent communication and leadership skills can move projects through life cycle in Financial Services sector.

TECHNICAL SUMMARY

Software: MQ, CICS, COBAL, COBAL II, LE COBAL, DB2, SPUFI, QMF, VSAM, DOS/VSE, MVS, IDMS, INTERTEST, Viasoft, Xpediter (batch and online), Macro CICS Assembler, Assembler, CEDF, ADS, Easy Test, File-AID, Library Management system, Panvalet, Librarian, Endevor, TSO/SPF, ROSCOE, CMS, SDF, Debug, COMPAREX, MS Word, Visio, HTML, ABC FlowCharter, Windows 98
Hardware: IBM 303x, IBM 308x, IBM 43xx

PROFESSIONAL ACHIEVEMENTS

• Developed technical specifications and guidelines to reorganize VSAM files. Developed program specifications for Taxlot reconciliation system. Developed and prepared service requests that were presented to management for approval.

FIGURE 3.4 *(continued)*

- Managed and supervised file expansion project while developing supporting documentation. Developed technical specifications.
- Defined software and hardware requirements for installation of transfer agent software. Interfaced with users. Coded and tested all program and/or JCL changes.
- Constructed accounting vouchers and maintained bank accounting system (IMMS). Coded and tested new programs to update and enhance system documentation. Developed supporting documentation.
- Planned and supervised conversion from DOS/VSE to MVS. Conducted technical interviews and assembled project team.
- Participated in Y2K remediation while assisting in developing audit trails to prove completeness of Y2K changes. Instructed backup employee on 12B1 changes. Interfaced with management in presentations and walk-through.
- Designed new approach to generated audit trails for AP system. Designed enhancements and organized user presentations.
- Prepared specifications for batch process while assisting junior-level programmers with Batch CICS debugging approaches. Coded new programs and/or new JCL streams and added changes to existing processes.
- Redesigned stock transfer and accounting systems while defining user requirements for CICS-based stock transfer system.
- Technical know-how needed for last three positions: VSAM, CICS, FTP, XPEDITER, JCL (batch and online) CICS, DB2, SPUFI, LE COBOL, COBOL II, MQ, VSAM, VIASOFT, INTERTEST, VISIO, TSO/SPF, JCL, MS WORD, MVS/JCL, VISIO, FILE-AID

WORK HISTORY
HIP (New York) May 2002 to December 2002; **Morgan Stanley,** November 2000 to May 2002; **Bank of Tokyo/Mitsubishi,** February to October 2000; **Dean Witter Reynolds,** April 1997 to December 1999; **Paine Webber,** September 1996 to March 1997; **Pershing Co.,**

FIGURE 3.4 *(continued)*

August 1995 to August 1996; **Petrie Retail,** February 1995 to August 1995; **Medco Containment Company,** April 1993 to February 1995; **Brown Brothers Harriman,** February 1993 to April 1993; **IBJ Schroder Bank,** December 1991 to January 1993; **GE Information Services,** September 1991 to December 1991; **Lever Brothers,** June 1991 to September 1991; **Dresser Pump Industries,** April 1991 to June 1991; **Sharp Electronics,** June 1990 to April 1991; **IBM Professional Services,** February 1990 to June 1990; **Deutsche Bank,** October 1989 to February 1990; **Merrill Lynch Co.,** July 1989 to October 1989; **ADP Co.,** June 1989 to July 1989; **Drexel Burnham Lambert,** March 1989 to May 1989; **Bank of Tokyo,** September 1987 to February 1989; **Vista Concepts,** March 1987 to August 1987; **First Boston Co.,** May 1986 to March 1987; **First Jersey National Bank,** February 1986 to May 1986; **Shearson Lehman/American Express,** May 1985 to February 1986; **Spear, Leeds & Kellogg,** November 1984 to May 1985; **Bradford Trust,** August 1982 to November 1984; **Merrill Lynch,** July 1977 to June 1982; **Pershing Co.,** February 1974 to June 1977.

EDUCATION AND CERTIFICATIONS
IBM: MQSeries Applications Programming (OS/390); MQSeries Introduction (OS/390)
Online Software International: CICS Command Level coding; CICS application design; CICS-VS debugging and internals
Merrill Lynch: Management training courses; BDAM Assembler Interface, CICS Macro Level coding (Assembler); MVS JCL; VSAM coding (Assembler)
New York University: Business programmer certificate; "C" language course
Chubb Institute: Visual Basic 3.0
University of Economics, Ljublijana, Slovenia: Degree in Business Administration and Management (Bachelor of Science equivalent)
U.S. Citizenship: 1979

CHAPTER 4

Writing That Works

Good communication skills top the list of nearly every employer's criteria for prospective applicants. Don't underestimate the importance of ensuring that all your communication with a potential employer is clear, dynamic, and accurate—whether it's the initial email, a résumé, a job application, a cover letter, or even a thank you note. You don't get many second chances when applying for a job.

In the Fortune 500 surveys, this point was stressed again and again: there is no room for error or inaccuracy in your first introduction to a company—usually your résumé with the attached cover letter. Hundreds of people may be vying for one job, which means that human resources professionals must quickly disqualify candidates. A spelling or grammatical error simplifies this process. In most cases, a résumé with errors goes immediately to the unwanted pile, so make every effort to hone and perfect all your written communication.

For some, writing well is a tall order. But don't be discouraged. Accept that you will have to master this shortcoming. Living in a digital world means that your writing skills are on constant display.

THE MIND-SET

As you research potential companies, think about your career goals, then carefully write your résumé and cover letters. Read about your industry so you acquire the ability to wrap your words around your intention. Job seeking can be stressful under the best of circumstances. Some people just muddle through—trying to get it over with as soon as possible. Many applicants copy a résumé that suits their needs, plug in the pertinent information, dash it off to a prospective employer, and hope for the best. They don't take the time to discover their skills and accomplishments and how best to match them with an employer.

FINDING THE RIGHT WORDS

When conducting your job research, take note of key phrases and words that will be useful in targeting your job. Besides helping you with key words for your résumé, another plus to doing research is that you begin to adopt those phrases and words as your own, in the process discovering the language of your profession. To communicate effectively to prospective employers, you need to know how to reach them in language they understand.

Research helps you communicate on a prospective employer's level. Every profession has its own language, so you should make an effort to learn it.

Learning a profession's idioms is accomplished by reading trade journals, searching the Internet for topics specific to the field, and scouring company websites. In an article in the *Wall Street Journal* directed at people returning to the workforce after an extended absence, it was suggested that "re-entry candidates sprinkle a résumé with the latest buzzwords for a targeted occupation. Doing so shows they know what's hot and helps a company computer scanner catch key phrases."[1] This suggestion is valid for any individual applying for a new job.

A LITTLE EXTRA ASSISTANCE

Don't assume anything when it comes to writing. Even the best writers make mistakes. Before you begin to revise your key information, take the dictionary off the shelf and put it next to your coffee cup, just in case you need it, or use the online edition of *Merriam-Webster's Collegiate Dictionary* at *www.m-w.com*. If you're really serious about writing well, invest in the latest edition of either *Merriam-Webster's Collegiate Dictionary* or *The American Heritage Dictionary of the English Language.*

New words are introduced into the language continually. During the early years of the Internet, hundreds of new words were introduced into the language, and everyone was scrambling to find the right way to use the terminology. No one could figure out if it was *website/Web site, e-mail/email,* or *Internet/internet.* Your dictionary can direct you to the preferred spelling.

Another valuable tool is a stylebook. Although few nonprofessional writers are familiar with this resource, it is invaluable. Stylebooks simplify the writing process by presenting in a straightforward manner the dos and don'ts of both style and grammar. Which stylebooks are the best? It depends on your field; writing styles vary from one profession to the next. For instance, those in the health professions use the *American Medical Association Manual of Style: A Guide for Authors and Editors,* those in science use *Council of Biology Editors Style Manual,* those in writing or academic professions use *The Chicago Manual of Style.* Find out if a particular stylebook is used specifically in your field.

For those who need a more general—and usually simpler—stylebook, examine the following resources: *The Associated Press Stylebook and Libel Manual, The New York Times Manual of Style and Usage,* and *The Business Style Handbook.*

When you get hired, there's a good chance you're going to have to write emails, memos, letters, or reports, so having good resources (a current dictionary and stylebook) are essential not only for your job search but beyond.

THE STYLE AND VOCABULARY

Résumé writing is primarily about verbs, the actions you performed while working. That's one of the reasons why almost every résumé book has a list of verbs to use in your résumé. To get into the writing mode, examine the verbs shown in the following box to see how they apply to what you did in your former positions and what you want to do in your new job. Your particular profession probably has a few verbs of its own, so make sure you jot them down during your research. It's essential for prospective employers to think of you as a doer—and an insider who knows the lingo.

> **Verbs: It's all about what you can DO for the employer**
> achieved, acquired, administered, allotted, analyzed, assisted, authored, automated, balanced, bought, branded, budgeted, calculated, completed, conducted, controlled, converted, coordinated, created, decided, delivered, designed, developed, devised, discovered, divested, doubled, earned, economized, elected, eliminated, eradicated, established, exceeded, executed, expanded, figured, financed, gained, gave, grew, headed, helped, identified, implemented, improved, increased, initiated, installed, instructed, introduced, invented, led, limited, maintained, managed, minimized, motivated, operated, optimized, organized, originated, played, positioned, prepared, prioritized, projected, promoted, purchased, recovered, recruited, redesigned, reduced, relocated, researched, restructured, revamped, reviewed, revised, saved, scored, selected, served, streamlined, supervised, surpassed, tailored, taught, trained, verified, won, wrote

Try to remain consistent in your use of tense. In your professional experience section, use present tense verbs for your current position and past tense verbs for your past experience. Whenever possible, write in the simple present or past tense, unless you are trying to convey a specific time sequence.

Personal pronouns (*I*) and adjectives and articles (*a* or *the*) should be avoided when writing a résumé. Instead of saying "I did this," your sentences should have an implied subject. HR professionals know you managed the development staff, so to conform to résumé style, drop the *I* and write instead, "Managed the development staff." And as Sherri Rest, a manager of staffing and solutions at Lucent Technologies, said, "Don't refer to yourself in the third person," either. Likewise, write "worked in research department" instead of "worked in the research department." Brevity is essential in résumés, even if your writing sounds clipped. Kenneth Garrett of FMC Corporation advised keeping your résumé "crisp, uncluttered, and to the point."

Save the descriptive words—adjectives and adverbs—for your thesis or future novel. The Fortune 500 participants stated, again and again, that they prefer résumés that are concise. Making every word count eliminates the temptation to hype or exaggerate, too. Sherry Rest goes on to say, "Don't try to be clever with your résumé. Just present the facts." And the facts won't be found in your adjectives and adverbs; the facts are in your nouns and verbs.

CAPITAL OR LOWERCASE?

You have probably noticed that the initial letters of job titles are lowercased throughout this book. Follow a different style, however, for your résumés and cover letters. Job titles are uppercased: Assistant Vice President, Customer Service Representative, Senior Analyst, Assistant Buyer, Account Executive, Administrative Assistant. Company names are always uppercased, but another deviation in résumés is that company departments—marketing, finance, sales, communications, accounting, human resources, editorial, and so on—are often uppercased as well. However you handle department names, the most important point is to be consistent.

KNOW YOUR AUDIENCE

Effective writers know their audience. In the case of résumés, your audience will be human resources professionals and, ultimately, the head of the department where you want to work. Understand what your audience knows about the subject and the level of detail they will need to make an informed decision. You may have 20 years of experience in systems, but your readers may have only a cursory knowledge. Cut through the inessential and write so that everyone who comes in contact with your résumé can understand what you're saying. Time and again, the Fortune 500 participants emphasized that you need to be clear. Complex technical detail may be absolutely clear to you, but will your audience understand it? That's your challenge: make them understand what position you want and what you can do for them. John Tomerlin, a vice president in human resources at Enterprise, recommended in the survey that you should "be concise in your wording of your résumé."

One of the best tests for clarity is to show your résumé to another individual, whether a friend, spouse, or family member, and ask for feedback: are your descriptions of your skills and experience clear? In fact, ask several people for their opinions and try not to be defensive when you get their feedback. Everyone needs an editor.

EMPHASIZING THE POSITIVE

Cecilia McKenney of Pepsi said you should be able to "sell yourself," but you won't be able to sell yourself if you're stuck on all your shortcomings. Stop worrying about the gap in your work history or your lack of a graduate degree or your lackluster performance at your last job. Think instead of how you can turn a negative into a positive. Were you an active member of your library expansion board while you looked for work after a downsizing? Did you learn a valuable lesson after your company went bankrupt? This is what employers want to hear about. If there's any one place where you should accentuate the positive, it's on your résumé.

VERIFIABLE HONESTY

Part of a human resources professional's job is to detect exaggerated claims, hype, or downright lies on résumés. No matter what, it is unacceptable to inflate your qualifications on your résumé. When surveyed, 50 percent of the Fortune 500 participants said they "always" verify information on résumés, but that doesn't mean the others don't. They do it at a later stage. Gary Moore, a recruiting director at Dollar General Corporation, verifies all information prior to making an offer.

Will you be able to accentuate the positive and sell yourself while still staying honest? Don't confuse a positive attitude with dishonesty—there is a difference. It's perfectly acceptable not to highlight your lack of a college degree, but don't say you have an M.B.A. when you don't.

WHERE TO BEGIN?

Start with the information you put together earlier for your résumé: contact information, focus statement, professional experience, skills summary, and education. Make sure that the key information is absolutely free of errors.

Now take a closer look at your contact information. Have you included your name, address, telephone number or cell number, email address, URL? Is every letter and digit correct? This may sound mundane, but HR professionals can attest that errors actually crop up in the contact section of the résumé. Sherri Martin, a director of human resources at Deere & Company, said that the information on your résumé must be "100 percent error-free." Don't rush.

ADDING FOCUS

An effective focus statement tells an employer what you are seeking and how you can help the company. You will tweak this section of the résumé again and again, depending on the targeted position. You may call it by another name (career objective, expertise, accomplishments, professional qualifications), but its aim is to zero in on a particular job and explain how you are the best match for that position. Writing the focus statement shouldn't be difficult, because you have already thought about what you want to do in your career.

By the time you are ready to revise the focus statement you've already written and placed in your job search data file, your options are narrowed. According to Janie Lopez, a human resources consultant at Tesoro Petroleum Corporation, "You must be specific on what you are looking for." A mere listing of your responsibilities in your current or most recent job won't hit the target in today's market. When writing the focus statement, plan to write a few sentences that anticipate what the prospective employer needs or what you hope to accomplish at your future position.

If you're worried that your focus statement will limit your opportunities, especially if you haven't figured out exactly what you want to do, then you're right. To get a good job in today's economy, you have to examine your qualifications and experience in terms of how they would fit a specific position. An article on Ohio University Career Services said, "A vague [focus statement] will be interpreted by employers as a lack of direction and self-knowledge."[2]

Take, for example, this technology officer's focus statement:

> **Focus Statement:** Senior information technology professional with more than 20 years' experience seeks management position in high-tech firm. Willing to relocate.

This focus statement needs an overhaul because:

- It lacks specificity.
- It undervalues the IT professional's skill and experience.
- It doesn't tell the hiring manager what the IT professional can do for the company.
- It lacks energy.
- It fails to utilize terminology from the IT profession.

So how do you improve upon such a statement? Begin by describing yourself with your current job title but referencing also the position you are seeking. Tell the employer what you know or what your strengths are and how these skills can benefit the employer. Be specific about your background. Make sure your work history, which will be listed in your professional experience section, can back up your claims. Here's the new focus statement:

> **Focus Statement:** Senior information technology professional with extensive experience managing large-scale development projects. Personal strengths focus on understanding business objective, organizing teams, and delivering solutions. Highly developed skills in leadership, specifically in areas of staff and project management, organizational planning, budgeting and staff development, and development of best practices policies.

Are focus statements required on every résumé? No. Sometimes they are impossible to include because of space limitations. In that case, you must show your focus in your cover letter. What if the prospective employer asks you to skip the cover letter and send an email version of your résumé? Writing a focus statement is still a valuable exercise. Somewhere along the way in the hiring process, your future employer will want to know what you know and how that experience will help the company. So take the time to write a focus statement, even if you don't have a chance to use it right away.

You may have to tweak the focus statement continually during your search. Obviously, you have more skills and accomplishments than you can list in the statement, and the skills and accomplishments you highlight will depend on the position you seek. In one focus statement, you might highlight the marketing skills you acquired five years ago. In another, you might emphasize your ability to meet writing deadlines. Again, it depends on the job.

TECHNICAL SUMMARY

If you're writing a functional or technical résumé, it's recommended that you include a technical summary. It's also a good idea to place it below your focus statement so that HR professionals don't have to search for it. (If you're certain a computer is scanning your résumé, however, you can place it wherever it looks best.) Writing a technical summary is easy because it's a straightforward account of your skills. The important thing to remember is to spell everything correctly. Misspelling key terminology from your field looks sloppy and unprofessional. Also, a computer scanner may miss your reference to Xpediter if you spell it *Expediter.*

A Microsoft *Careers* newsletter advised technology professionals to

> break the section into subcategories, so the reader can quickly scan through your knowledge of programs and applications. Possible categories include technical certifications, hardware, operating systems, networking protocols, office productivity, programming languages, Web applications and database applications. Only list programs/applications that you could confidently discuss in an interview.[3]

THE HEART OF THE MATTER

The section describing an applicant's professional experience is the heart of any résumé. Make sure this information is accurate; you should include the name and address of past employers (street address is not necessary) along with your tenure there (month and year are sufficient). According to a Beta Research study featured in the *New York Times,* "Three years with a previous employer is the average length of time considered to indicate loyalty." If you have a short tenure at a few jobs, don't highlight these dates by putting them in first position or in boldface. Placement of this information will depend on the design you use, but the first line should contain the following information:

June 1980–May 1990   Whitney Communications   New York, NY

The next few lines should provide a little more detail. Let the employer know about your results. If you were promoted, say so. If you streamlined the department, here's the place to tout it. If you never missed a deadline, that's remarkable as well. Numbers are always welcome. These accomplishments can be in a bulleted list or in paragraph form.

June 1980–May 1990   Senior Editor   Whitney Communications

- Wrote monthly column that generated more feedback from readers than any other column.
- Established good relationships with writers and acquired news/articles for features.
- Proofread and copyedited (from manuscripts to blues) for 100-page magazine.
- Met tight monthly deadlines in fast-paced environment.
- Promoted from assistant editor (1982) to associate editor (1984) to managing editor (1986) to senior editor (1990).

Just a reminder: Start this information with verbs (in the present tense if describing a current position, the simple past tense if describing past experience), and because the subject is implied (the missing *I*), you end each bulleted item with a period because it is a complete sentence.

THE LEARNING CURVE

Whether or not you're a college graduate, list any information in the section on your education that tells the employer you're a learner. In an ongoing series in *Investor's Business Daily,* number four on the top ten success secrets was "Never Stop Learning."[4] Your certifications and degrees should be positioned in the education section. A grade point average above 3.0 on a 4.0 scale should be listed; if your GPA was 2.2, don't list it. If you are fluent in languages, mention them. Also list advanced classes, especially those relevant to the current position you are seeking. Usually education is put at the end of your résumé, but if you graduated within the last five years and your work history is minimal, your education should get top billing on your résumé.

Don't be afraid to tell an employer what you did at your last job and be specific. Hal Lancaster, in *Promoting Yourself,* says, "It's fine to state you have an excellent record in doing such and such, but everyone else is stating that, too. How is a hiring manager to know who's the real deal and who's blowing smoke?"[5] Verifiable numbers, solid accomplishments, and promotions will distinguish you, so make sure you highlight them.

"The purpose of a cover letter is to summarize the person's relevant experience, to express interest in the position, and to demonstrate writing ability."

Lisa Whittington
Vice President of Human Resources
Host Hotels & Resorts, Inc.

CHAPTER 5

Cover Letters

In the electronic job market, many people think cover letters are unnecessary. Of the 50 Fortune 500 participants, only 11 said cover letters are attached to every résumé. That's too bad. Without a cover letter, applicants miss an opportunity to display their strengths by providing a more detailed account of their accomplishments than the résumé has room for.

If it weren't for a cover letter, Martin Ward, an IT manager at a major brokerage firm in New York, might not have found a job for a long time. After his company downsized and several hundred employees were laid off, Ward found himself without a job and stuck in the middle of, if not a recession, at the very least a flat job market. He networked with friends, business associates, family, and headhunters. He emailed his résumé to a hundred openings and even sought the help of an Internet job search firm, which reminded him—for a $100 fee—that everyone was in pretty much the same leaky boat.

After following one false lead after another, Ward suddenly remembered a comment made in passing by a senior manager at his former brokerage firm. "If you ever need anything, give me a call," the IT manager had said to Ward just before he left the company. Ward, who is part of the growing phenomenon known as "boomerang employees" (those who return to work for a former employer), wrote a cover letter, reminding the senior manager (who had now moved up in the firm) that they had worked on a project together. That project had added value to the firm, and the impact of its success was still felt years later. The senior manager, who now had more than 40,000 people reporting to him, sent Ward's résumé to the right hiring authority's hands, and he returned to the major brokerage firm several weeks later, despite a "formal HR hiring freeze."

Without a cover letter, Ward's résumé would have likely spun aimlessly in cyberspace's black hole. In a way that a casual telephone call or an impromptu breakfast meeting couldn't, Ward's cover letter showed that he was interested in returning to his former company. By committing to paper the value he added to the company while he was there, Ward convinced his old employer that he still had a lot to contribute.

THE FORMAT TO FOLLOW

Even though many Fortune 500 companies don't require them, cover letters are read if the employer considers you a prime candidate. Jackie Coburn, a staffing manager at Federal-Mogul, said, "Only if I have an interest in the candidate do I read the cover letter," but 40 percent of the Fortune 500 participants said they "always" read the cover letter first. So what goes into a cover letter? Carol Eubank, a human resources manager at Aquila, Inc., said a cover letter should be a "quick summary of why you want the job and how your qualifications match the requirements."

Don't think that means you can dash off an email in a heartbeat and be done with it. You have to put some effort and professionalism into an emailed cover letter. In fact, 84 percent of the Fortune 500 participants said they expect applicants to adhere to the same standards as if they were writing a formal letter. Only two participants said emailed cover letters are more informal and should provide just enough detail to help HR route the résumé to the appropriate job opening or department head. One of those participants who maintains that emailed cover letters are more informal, Stacy Harshman of Albertson's, said her expectation of an electronic cover letter is to "introduce the person and give an idea where the applicant received information about the company."

But what are the expectations of the other 84 percent of the Fortune 500 hiring professionals?

If your cover letter will be sent as hard copy, here's the rudimentary arrangement: your address, the date, the employer's name and address, salutation, body, closing should all be flush left.

A reminder about stationery: When searching for a job, invest in quality stationery. Even if the application process takes place entirely online, you still need a résumé in hard copy for interviews, as well as extra copies to carry around in your briefcase in case you run into an old colleague. Make sure you have enough crisp, neutral paper for the résumés, cover letters, and references, and to further polish your professional image, it's a good idea to purchase matching envelopes. (It may sound obvious, but if you have your contact information professionally printed on the stationery, do not put this information elsewhere in your cover letter.)

Examine the format and notice the placement of information: your address, date, the employer's address, the salutation, the body, the closing. Avoid taking short-cuts with this style. Prospective employers want to see, at the very least, that you are familiar with the basics of business correspondence, so include all of this information, and—here's the difficult part—make sure it fits on one page. Time is in short supply these days, so no matter what, strive to be concise (try not to exceed 250 to 350 words).

According to the survey participants, "neatness" also counts. The cover letter is in a block format, which means all information aligns along the left margin (no need to worry about indentation or tabs). It's centered on the page, with an equal amount of spacing on the top as well as the bottom. An extra line is used to separate paragraphs, except after your closing, which should get four lines to accommodate your signature (in black or blue pen).

Let's review some technicalities first. In the address section, use the postal service's two-letter (no periods) state abbreviation; in the body of the text, spell out the state's name. (Some cities do not require a state be specified; check a style reference for stand-alone cities.) In the employer's address, also include a courtesy title or professional title (Mr., Ms., Dr.). Using a department name will ensure that your letter gets to the appropriate hiring authority. Department names are capitalized in an address. Then use the full legal name of the company. After the salutation, use a colon, not a comma. After your complimentary closing, use a comma.

Now let's look at the body of the letter. At its most basic, it should tell the employer what position you are interested in, where you heard about the position, and how to contact you; and it should reinforce the idea that you are qualified for the job. Your cover letter should be written to a specific individual. (Try not to send a cover letter "To Whom It May Concern.")

But a cover letter can accomplish a few more things, provided it's written well. Think of a cover letter as a means of furthering your cause beyond the résumé. How does Carol Nadata's cover letter in Figure 5.1 do just that?

FIGURE 5.1 *Carol Nadata's Cover Letter*

YOUR ADDRESS	100 Grindall Street Baltimore, MD 21100
DATE	May 1, 2008
EMPLOYER'S ADDRESS	Mr. Robert Leonard Sales Department Consolidated Finishing Corporation 100 Pennsylvania Avenue Washington, DC 21100
SALUTATION	Dear Mr. Leonard:
BODY	I recently read the *Baltimore Sun* profile of your company (April 28, 2008) and noticed that you are expanding your business into the Baltimore area. I am sure you will need accomplished account executives to increase your presence in this area, and I believe I am perfectly suited to help you as I am already familiar with your company's innovative and environmentally sound products.

The enclosed résumé outlines my skills and experience. I am adept at cultivating key relationships with decision makers, so I believe I can grow your business significantly in this area. As you can see from my résumé, I have innumerable contacts in the furniture business—and I invest a good deal of my time through my community service and avid golfing in strengthening my already healthy and profitable business relationships. I believe this will carry over into your business at Consolidated Finishing as well.

I am primarily interested in building your business in the Baltimore area, but I am willing to relocate if necessary.

I will contact you next week to request an interview for current or future positions. If you would like to contact me, I can be reached at my home telephone number at 410-539-1000 in the evenings or on my cell phone, anytime, at 410-556-1010.

Thank you for your time and consideration.

CLOSING	Cordially,

Carol Nadata

Enc.: Résumé

Carol's cover letter shows the following:

- She takes the initiative. Not only does she read up on industry news, but she acts on it, too.
- She spotted a job opening before it even appeared.
- She tells the employer where she heard about the company.
- She anticipates the employer's need: "you will need accomplished account executives to increase your presence . . . ."
- She adds information specific to this position, using language her employer understands: "cultivating key relationships with decision makers."
- She includes information about her extracurricular activities that is not listed on her résumé. (Notice that these activities are relevant to her sales career.)
- She tells the employer that she is willing to relocate.
- She tells the employer she will contact him but provides enough information so that she can be contacted immediately.
- She thanks the employer.

Writing a good cover letter ensures that you will stand out. Try to relish this opportunity to distinguish yourself, yet also know that employers are getting an added look at your communication skills, so the cover letter must be letter-perfect, clear, and concise. Because businesspeople are inundated with information in the digital age, they want employees who know how to zero in on the essentials. Your communication with your prospective employer must show you can do this. In addition, Amy Moers, a senior staffing manager at SYSCO Corporation, said the cover letter should "outline the interests and mobility of a candidate if they aren't in the city where the job is located."

Many job seekers—especially younger ones—will balk, believing that snail-mail cover letters that accompany a hard-copy résumé are obsolete and that the only way to reach an employer is electronically. While it's true that companies are moving in this direction, do not underestimate the impact that a hard-copy cover letter and résumé can have, especially when it is sent directly to a department head (a specific individual for whom you want to work). I know many people who took a detour around the HR department and went directly to the individual hiring manager via snail-mail. They got that person's attention—and an interview. By all means, use the company's recruitment preferences (usually electronic), but improve your chances of getting noticed by following up your electronic submission with a hard-copy cover letter and résumé to specific department hiring managers.

ELECTRONIC COVER LETTERS

When Ken Dean, an assistant vice president of Bank of New York, reads a cover letter, he expects that candidate to "add flavor to anything unusual on the résumé." That holds true for the electronic cover letter as well. More and more companies prefer the electronic application process—for its speed, cost savings, and efficiency.

Many companies require more than an email with a résumé attachment. In fact, often a comprehensive employee profile must be completed before you even get the opportunity to write your cover letter. So don't forget: before you begin any online application process, have your job search data file in front of you. You can pull the appropriate information, and once you've tweaked it to the specific job opening, you can include it in the cover letter.

Stacey Webb, a human resources representative at Gannett, stated that the purpose of a cover letter is "to gain a general understanding of what an applicant seeks in a new position and to give information on background and qualifications." Leslie Humphries, an HR specialist at State Farm, contended that candidates should "sell their interest" in the company. Look at the electronic cover letter in Figure 5.2 (placed in the body of an email, not sent as an attachment) to see if it meets these requirements. Notice that the letter uses plain text, so features such as em-dashes, accents, and italics, which can translate as bizarre characters across different email programs, are not present.

As already mentioned, you are seeking a position at a company, so all of your communication with that company must be formal and professional in tone. Helen Cunningham, in *The Business Style Handbook,* says, "If you are using email for formal correspondence, both within and outside your organization, apply the same standards you would to a letter."

As for the layout of an electronic cover letter, plan to follow the same block styles, but obviously there's no need to include your address, the date, or the employer's address. Instead, you need a correct email address, the correct name of the hiring authority (if it's not a general "contact us" submittal), and a topic for the subject line (usually a job number or position title).

In the sample electronic cover letter in Figure 5.2, the job applicant followed these guidelines:

- Use a contact name in the first paragraph.

- Tell the employer where you found out about the job opening (on the company website).
- Highlight a limited number of positions that demonstrate key abilities (two positions that demonstrate leadership abilities in this case) regardless of how much work experience is listed on your résumé.
- Write a concise paragraph for each highlighted position, avoiding technical jargon but using language that suggests you are an insider.
- Limit the letter to 340 words. (Based on his rough draft in Word, Rob knows his letter is about one page before the electronic submittal.)
- Use numbers to substantiate claims.
- Tell the employer you want to work for the company and that you've researched the company. Rob is interested in working at this "highly regarded" organization and backs up this statement with information he picked up when he was browsing the company's website.
- Tell the employer how you can help. Rob emphasizes his progressive leadership responsibilities.
- Provide your cell phone number.
- Thank the employer.
- Sign off with your name (use an electronic signature if you have one).

As long as it hasn't been stipulated otherwise, call the employer after you send a cover letter and résumé electronically. This is another opportunity to bring attention to your submission, so make sure you handle this call professionally. Even if you have to resend your documents again because of a glitch on the other end, make sure you do so with grace. Paula Axelrod, a manager of staffing at BJ's Wholesale Club, said job candidates need to "be courteous to all [they] come in contact with." But keep the conversation brief—unless the HR representative initiates further discussion.

WHAT IF YOU HAVE NO QUALIFICATIONS?

The Fortune 500 participants stressed repeatedly that they want to know in your cover letter why you think you are qualified for the position. For newcomers to the job market or recent graduates, this topic may be difficult, but it's not impossible. Make your experience at school or in your community marketable—emphasize transferable skills.

Chris Collier of Georgia-Pacific said he wants a cover letter to give an "overview of experience and value-added potential to the company. It should also express a high

FIGURE 5.2 *Rob Scala's Cover Letter*

To: bleonard@siac.com
Subject: Systems Director Position

Dear Mr. Leonard:

After reviewing the SIAC website, I noticed several opportunities in the development area (development director, technical director, and development project manager) and contacted Bill Smith, a colleague of yours in human resources, about these opportunities. He suggested I send my résumé to you for your review.

As you can see by my résumé, my experience includes more than 20 years of progressive leadership responsibilities in large technology environments.
At Chase Manhattan Bank, I was actively involved in developing highly integrated, worldwide applications that supported all aspects of the business --from sales and marketing through operations and finance. My role progressed from programmer/analyst to project leader, then project manager, and finally director.

At Winthrop Stimson, I continued to focus on development but took on additional organizational responsibilities. Beyond leading teams developing mainframe, client/server, and Internet-based applications, I led a group of project managers in department planning and finances (budget of $40 million) and for department staffing and staff development (100 programmers). In this capacity, I was promoted to vice president.

Beyond these roles and responsibilities, my abilities to work with teams and get things done led to being selected for senior teams that drove reengineering and best practices. I have had successes with many different types of business units, and I believe I can bring experience and expertise to your highly regarded organization. (I noticed on your website that SIAC was named "one of the 100 Best Places to Work in IT" by *Computerworld* magazine.) I would like to help you strengthen your leadership team at an organization, group, or project level.

Thank you for reviewing my attached résumé. I will contact you next week regarding this opportunity. If in the meantime you would like to contact me, please call my cell phone any time at (973) 296-1000.

Sincerely,
Rob Scala

level of enthusiasm." David Murphy of McGraw-Hill said a cover letter should "grab my attention by the statement of one or two really salient facts that encourage me to read the full résumé."

It's not always easy to anticipate what's going to grab a hiring authority's attention, but telling this person something that distinguishes you from the rest of the applicants is usually a good start. Maybe you trained as an accountant but also got published in the college poetry review. Maybe you spent the summer in a community outreach program in a culture different than the one in which you were brought up. Maybe you created a fundraising vehicle that is still being used by the parents' association at your daughter's high school. Maybe you coached a Little League team for several years. Maybe you broadened your knowledge of the financial industry during your summer internship. Maybe you created a Dashboard widget while you were at college. Maybe your part-time job in a vet's office allowed you to develop excellent customer service skills. If it helps you to differentiate yourself from the crowd, include it in your cover letter.

CHAPTER 6

Electronic Submissions

The number of positions secured through company websites is growing daily. All of the 50 Fortune 500 companies surveyed for this book prefer electronic résumés, so job seekers must know the ins and outs of posting them.

Of the companies surveyed in the first survey, 70 percent said most résumés at their companies are delivered via email. Either your résumé is sent as a text-only document and is part of the body of the email or it is sent as an attachment (usually a Word document) to the email. The second option is to fill out the company's e-forms on its website, where the information is saved directly to the employer's database. Of the Fortune 500 participants surveyed, 22 percent reported they use this method. All of the 50 Fortune 500 companies surveyed use at least one of these electronic methods to receive submissions—and you can be fairly certain that most companies will eventually follow suit.

An e-form basically amounts to cutting and pasting your résumé into the text boxes provided, but it is often necessary to provide additional information related to the job you are seeking. Completing e-forms is a little more work than sending a résumé and cover letter, so many job seekers avoid them. According to Creative Group's Meghan Gonyo, there is another reason why the e-form is not as popular:

> People are reluctant to fill out, for security reasons, huge applications. And they don't know who is looking at their résumé. There's that whole stigma of the black hole. And, sometimes, when you don't complete the résumé—with your address, your former employer, your references—it doesn't process correctly. A lot of job seekers don't want that information out there. That can be really troubling. And that goes back to if you want

to target a particular company, find out if you can make a connection elsewhere within the company, so that when you do fill out online, that someone is going to look at it. Networking is key.

GETTING PAST THE RESISTANCE

Remember when those electronic tags came along at toll booths? In the New York area, they're called E-ZPass. At first, a lot of griping and grumbling ensued, but the tags didn't take long to catch on. After watching drivers zip past long lines in the exact-change lanes, people started to get the picture. E-ZPass and similar systems became the way to go simply because of their efficiency.

It's the same with the new hiring environment. Submitting electronic résumés is more efficient than processing hard copies. The key, however, is figuring out how to proceed. Based on the Fortune 500 survey, there are various methods for submitting a résumé. Your job is to determine a particular company's preference and then follow those directions to the letter. If the directions seem unclear, it is perfectly reasonable to ask for direction.

Because the 50 Fortune 500 hiring professionals surveyed prefer submissions either via email or online e-forms, those two submission methods are the focus of this chapter. To get all the information you'll need, retrieve the data file you created for your job hunt. In addition to your résumé, it should now contain your company research, several multipurpose cover letters, references, any names you picked up along the way, and various key words relevant to the position you are seeking.

If you don't have access to the Internet, go to the local library or use a friend's Internet connection. If you use the library, it will become your base for job searching, so go in the off-hours in case the library has a time limit for Internet use. Explain that you are filling out an e-form and you may need additional time. (Many company e-forms allow you to save as you go along so you can complete it in stages.) Usually, for a worthy cause, the librarian will grant you extra time, especially if the library is not busy.

For obvious reasons, you don't want to conduct your job search while you're at your current job. Most companies monitor email usage, and your boss may interpret seeking another job from your office as a conflict of interest. If, however, you are asked to send a résumé immediately to a prospective employer—and there's no waiting until you get to your own computer—then use your own email account, which you've already created specifically for your job search, instead of your current company's account.

If you don't have an email address, now is the time to create one. Cory Kleinschmidt, the webmaster of Traffick.com, says the best email portals are Hotmail and Yahoo!.[1] Create an email address devoted solely to your job search. Make a notation of your password and address in your data file. To simplify matters at a later point, use the same password when you go to company websites to fill out their e-forms and create a profile.

Don't forget that your email address will be viewed (and possibly used) by your future employer, so choose a conservative address. You will get a better response from an employer if your address is *TXSmith@yahoo.com* rather than *honeybuns22@ yahoo.com*. If you already have an email address on your home PC and it falls into the "honeybuns" category, create a new email address for the job search. Don't let a silly email address ruin that critical first impression. (This is another reason to have an email account devoted solely to your job search.)

A FEW INITIAL QUESTIONS

Before sending your résumé to a prospective employer, make sure you know the employer's preference for receiving it. If the preference isn't clear in a job posting or company website, then send an email or call and ask. If you're unsure what to ask, consider these questions:

- Should I mail my résumé? Fax it? Email it? (If the employer tells you to mail it or fax it, you can skip this chapter, at least for now.)
- Should I attach my résumé to an email?
- What file formats do you prefer in attachments? MS Word (.doc) or Rich Text Format (.rtf)?
- Should my résumé be in the body of the email (converted to plain text or ASCII, pronounced *askee*)?
- Should I go to the company website and fill out an e-form? And whom should I follow up with? (Try to get a name.)

THE ATTACHED RÉSUMÉ

Many job seekers prefer to send their résumés and cover letters as attachments to their emails because this method retains their formatting (bold, italics, underscore, bullets, etc.). If you are asked to send your résumé as an email attachment, the process is fairly straightforward. Assuming you have Windows and Microsoft Word, here are the basics:

- Put the address (either an individual or department address) in the "To" line.
- Put the job number (if you have one) in the "Subject" line (or the name of the specific job, e.g., Account Executive, Facilities Manager) as well as your name (e.g., Equity Sales Trader-John Smith).
- Write a cover letter in the body of your email.
- Attach the Word version of your résumé by clicking on the "Attach" icon in the email menu.
- Scroll down and hit "File," then select your résumé file. Once your résumé file is highlighted, hit "Open." The file automatically attaches to the email. (The attachment may cover the "To" line, but the address is still underneath.)
- Before you hit "Send," double-check that the email cover letter and attachment are in order. Do not send the email to an employer until you have tested the functioning of your email account and software by sending the attachment to your own and/or a friend's address.

PLAIN AND SIMPLE

You cannot always assume that your MS Word résumé will arrive at an employer's computer in the format in which you sent it. No matter what software your résumé and cover letter are written in, compatibility problems can occur. Some companies do not even open attachments for fear of viruses, and sometimes a spam-protection program will think your email is spam (unsolicited mass email, usually trying to sell something) and filter it into a "Trash" file.

Don't be surprised if an employer requests an ASCII version for email submissions. If the acronym *ASCII* is unfamiliar, don't worry; it's just another term for "plain text." Officially, *ASCII* means "American Standard Code of Information Interchange." It is the universal language of the Internet that can be read by any personal computer. It uses only characters that exist on the standard keyboard (no bullets, foreign currency symbols, or em-dashes).

If you plan to send your résumé in the body of an email, you may cut and paste the original Word version with all its elaborate formatting, but it may not end up on the employer's desktop looking the way you sent it. (Those bullets and em-dashes may convert into question marks.) The best way to send your résumé in an email is as a plain text (or ASCII) document, which requires converting your original résumé as above. Your formatting disappears, and the design of your résumé is no longer distinguishable from the next person's. This can be a blow to those who have spent days designing a unique résumé, but it's better to be universally recognized with your plain-text résumé than to send a document that arrives on the employer's PC as unreadable.

Fortunately, it's not necessary to learn a whole new computer language to make a conversion. Your word processor does it automatically, but you will have to clean up the formatting in your text version afterward. Once you convert, the only design elements you can insert in your new plain text résumé are from the standard keyboard (for example, bullets must be replaced by asterisks and em-dashes by two hyphens.) Follow these steps to convert your résumé to plain text (ASCII):

- Once in your email, retrieve your original résumé from Word. (Drop in all relevant key words for the particular job.)
- Go to "File" and hit "Save As."
- In the "Save As" window, rename your original résumé document "P-text (your last name)." HR will appreciate that your document includes your name. (In the text résumé example in Figure 6.2, the document has been renamed "P-text-Bailey.")
- Underneath the "File Name" bar, go to "Save As Type." Click on the arrow and then scroll down and highlight "Text Only." Then hit "Save."
- When the warning pops up that your formatting will be lost, hit "Yes." (Another option is to use the "Text Only with Line Breaks" when you hit "Save As." It's the same as "Text Only," but it puts in hard returns so the lines break where intended.)
- Complete the conversion by closing the document and then reopening it so you can readjust the margins and clean up the formatting. You may need to add elements that will help organize the material (asterisks, capital letters, readjusted spacing between lines). Fix the alignment, making sure it is flush left. For hard-copy résumés, it was recommended that the font size not be reduced to less than 11 point. A text-only version, however, converts to 10-point Courier that allows for about 65 characters per line, which most email screens can accommodate.
- After cleaning up the formatting in the text version (keep it as simple as possible to ensure compatibility on the other end), save the document again.

With these steps, you have created a universally recognizable résumé. Don't worry about that beautifully designed original. Because you renamed your résumé when converting, your original résumé is still fully intact in the original file, formatting and all. You will need the formatted résumé when you land the interview, so make sure you make a few copies on good stationery to bring with you.

"BEFORE" AND "AFTER" TEXT RÉSUMÉ

Examine the résumés shown in Figures 6.1 and 6.2. Figure 6.1 is an MS Word document whose content is identical to that of Figure 6.2, except that the new text version doesn't have a continued line on the second page with the person's name. That's because the new text résumé will run in the body of your email (no second page). To separate a cover letter in an email from the text résumé, use a

- hyphen line   ---
- asterisks   **

When sending the text résumé in an email, set it up like this:

- Put the employer's email address in the "To" line.
- Put the name of the position being applied for or the job number (along with your complete name) in the subject line. Be as specific as possible.
- The cover letter should be written in the body of your email. It's best to have a name of the person you are sending it to, but if you don't, write, "Dear Hiring Manager."
- Separate the cover letter from the text résumé with either a line of asterisks or a line of hyphens.
- Cut and paste the text version of the résumé into the body of the email below the line of asterisks or hyphens.
- Double-check that everything aligns correctly and that all the formatting is stripped out of the text version. (Sometimes stray elements remain.)
- Be sure your cover letter and résumé are in the same email message. Do not send a cover letter in one email and your résumé in another.
- Do a test by sending it to your email address or a friend's. Check once more that everything is correct.

Examine the original and the plain-text version of the same résumé in Figures 6.1 and 6.2. Experiment before you transmit your résumé electronically to a prospective employer. The two versions of the same résumé should resemble the examples here.

FIGURE 6.1 *William Bailey's Original ("Before") Résumé in MS Word*

William Bailey
1 Dogwood St., Greenbrier, TN 37100 (615) 643-1000 (C) Email: Z34@hotmail.com

CAREER OBJECTIVE: Safety Manager in manufacturing, where expertise in ergonomics, OSHA compliance, workers' compensation, and safety can significantly reduce injuries and decrease costs through preventive measures, employee accountability, and educational programs

SUMMARY OF QUALIFICATIONS: More than 15 years of experience establishing safety programs and developing safety cultures in manufacturing environments. Adept at training and communicating with employees, supervisors, and upper management. Extensive experience complemented by effective communication skills.

AREAS OF EFFECTIVENESS:

Safety Programs
Develop written safety programs that provide overall facility safety.
Develop behavior-based safety programs for employee accountability.
Develop training programs to ensure compliance with OSHA standards.
Conduct air and noise testing to ensure exposure levels do not exceed recommended levels.
Perform ergonomic evaluations.
Conduct workplace audits to identify injury sources; identify corrective action.
Establish facility safety committees.
Involve employees, supervisors, and management to develop safety culture.
Investigate accidents to determine root cause and develop corrective actions.
Educate supervisors and managers on maintaining injury-summary logs.
Analyze injuries to identify trends and develop corrective actions to reverse them.
Quantify safety purchases by showing injury-prevention savings.
Communicate plans and objectives with management to ensure support.
Identify morale issues that can lead to workplace injuries and develop solutions to improve.
Maintain loss records and cost-impact to report to management.
Oversee internal budgeting for loss-prevention staff.

Workers' Compensation
Develop transitional return-to-work programs.
Communicate with claims adjusters to ensure that physicians release injured employees.
Develop drug-free workplace programs.
Educate employees, supervisors, and management on workers' compensation laws.

continued

FIGURE 6.1 *(continued)*

TRAINING:	Provide training of regulatory and nonregulatory topics to employees. Provide train-the-trainer classes for supervisors. Evaluate training to improve presentation and information covered.

WORK HISTORY:

Staff Leasing, Brentwood, Tennessee, 1998 to present
EBI Companies (Insurance), Nashville, Tennessee, 1995 to 1998
Travelers Insurance, Nashville, Tennessee, 1990 to 1995

Accomplishments
Selected as team coach.
Reduced injury-frequency rate by 52 percent, exceeding company goal.
Reduced injury-cost rate by 41 percent, exceeding company goal.

**MILITARY
EXPERIENCE:**

Kentucky Army National Guard, Fort Knox, Kentucky, 1982 to present
First Sergeant/E-8, HHC First Sergeant

Plan and coordinate training and supplies.
Assign soldiers to provide support for five different companies.
Provide retention guidance for soldiers ready to extend.
Maintain Unit Duty Roster, ensuring soldiers perform share of extra duty.
Counsel soldiers on ways to improve performance.
Provide annual performance evaluations of senior enlisted soldiers.
Provide development training for noncommissioned officers.
Effectively delegate responsibility to grow leadership of subordinate
soldiers.
Emphasize safety in every aspect of training.

Accomplishments
Developed and implemented an absenteeism policy that resulted in 19
percent increase in soldiers present in first month.
Retention actions resulted in a 92 percent retention rate of soldiers.
Provide body-strengthening instruction for leaders and soldiers,
resulting in 10 percent increase in strength in past three months.
Consistently receive ratings of "Superior" at leadership development
courses.
Consistently receive ratings of "Excellence" on annual performance
evaluations.
Recognized for excellent platoon safety record while a Sergeant.
Awarded Army Achievement Medal for training that resulted in 100
percent, first-round, platoon gunnery qualification.
Awarded Kentucky Commendation for training, resulting in 100
percent, first-time passing scores from external evaluators on platoon
tactical tasks.
Selected as Outstanding Noncommissioned Officer.

EDUCATION:

Murray State University, Murray, Kentucky, 1990 Bachelor of Science in
Occupational Safety and Health

FIGURE 6.2 *William Bailey's "After" Résumé in Plain Text*

```
William Bailey
1 Dogwood Lane, Greenbrier, TN 37100
(615) 643-1000 (C) Email: Z34@hotmail.com

CAREER
OBJECTIVE:

Safety Manager in manufacturing, where expertise in ergonomics,
OSHA compliance, workers' compensation, and safety can significantly
reduce injuries and decrease costs through preventive measures,
employee accountability, and educational programs

SUMMARY OF
QUALIFICATIONS:

More than 15 years of experience establishing safety programs and devel-
oping safety cultures in manufacturing environments. Adept at training
and communicating with employees, supervisors, and upper management.
Extensive experience complemented by effective communication skills.

AREAS OF
EFFECTIVENESS:

Safety Programs

*Develop written safety programs that provide overall facility safety.
*Develop behavior-based safety programs for employee accountability.
*Develop training programs to ensure compliance with OSHA standards.
*Conduct air and noise testing to ensure exposure levels do not
exceed recommended levels.
*Perform ergonomic evaluations.
*Conduct workplace audits to identify injury sources and identify
corrective action.
*Establish facility safety committees.
*Involve employees, supervisors, and management to develop safety
culture.
*Investigate accidents to determine root cause and develop corrective
actions.
*Educate supervisors and managers on maintaining injury-summary logs.
*Analyze injuries to identify trends and develop corrective actions
to reverse them.
*Quantify safety purchases by showing injury-prevention savings.
*Communicate plans and objectives with management to ensure support.
*Identify morale issues that can lead to workplace injuries and
develop solutions to improve.
*Maintain loss records and cost-impact to report to management.
*Oversee internal budgeting for loss-prevention staff.

Workers' Compensation

*Develop transitional return-to-work programs.
*Communicate with claims adjusters to ensure that physicians release
injured employees.
*Develop drug-free workplace programs.
*Educate employees, supervisors, and management on workers'
compensation laws.
```

continued

FIGURE 6.2 *(continued)*

TRAINING:

*Provide training of regulatory and nonregulatory topics to employees.
*Provide train-the-trainer classes for supervisors.
*Evaluate training to improve presentation and information covered.

WORK HISTORY:

Staff Leasing, Brentwood, Tennessee, 1998 to present
EBI Companies (Insurance) Nashville, Tennessee, 1995 to 1998
Travelers Insurance, Nashville, Tennessee, 1990 to 1995

Accomplishments

*Selected as team coach.
*Reduced injury-frequency rate by 52 percent, exceeding company goal.
*Reduced injury-cost rate by 41 percent, exceeding company goal.

MILITARY EXPERIENCE:

Kentucky Army National Guard, Fort Knox, Kentucky, 1982 to present
First Sergeant/E-8, HHC First Sergeant

*Plan and coordinate training and supplies.
*Assign soldiers to provide support for five different companies.
*Provide retention guidance for soldiers ready to extend.
*Maintain Unit Duty Roster ensuring soldiers perform share of extra duty.
*Counsel soldiers on ways to improve performance.
*Provide annual performance evaluations of senior enlisted soldiers.
*Provide development training for noncommissioned officers.
*Effectively delegate responsibility to promote leadership growth of
subordinate soldiers.
*Emphasize safety in every aspect of training.

Accomplishments

*Developed and implemented an absenteeism policy that resulted in 19
percent increase in soldiers present in first month.
*Retention actions resulted in a 92 percent retention rate of eli-
gible soldiers.
*Provide body-strengthening instruction for leaders and soldiers,
resulting in 10 percent increase in strength in past three months.
*Consistently receive "Superior" ratings at leadership development
courses.
*Consistently receive "Excellence" ratings on annual performance
evaluations.
*Recognized for excellent platoon safety record while a Platoon
Sergeant.
*Awarded Army Achievement Medal for training that resulted in 100
percent first-round, platoon gunnery qualification.
*Awarded Kentucky Commendation for training, resulting in 100 percent first-
time passing scores from external evaluators on platoon tactical tasks.
*Selected as Outstanding Noncommissioned Officer

EDUCATION:

Murray State University, Murray, Kentucky, 1990 Bachelor of Science
in Occupational Safety and Health

SHOOT FOR COMPATIBILITY

In today's digital environment, the primary purpose of design is to make your information more readable. The ASCII version of your résumé may not be pretty, but it is compatible. You don't have a lot of options in plain text, so keep it simple: shoot for readability (and compatibility) rather than visual appeal.

If you are ever in doubt whether the employer wants your résumé as an attachment or as text, then opt for sending it as text. Some career experts suggest sending both an attachment and a plain-text version in the body of the email. A simple preliminary call or email to clarify the employer's requirements will eliminate this guesswork.

Many companies, especially the smaller ones, are still in the process of refining their electronic hiring practices, so there is no such thing as standard procedure. In fact, electronic hiring procedures at some companies can have a lifespan of about six months because they are still developing a process that works. Spend some time on the company website. Read the directions carefully. Then contact the company via email to make sure you understand the process.

ELECTRONIC FORMS

At this point, your data file should contain the following: an original version of your résumé, any pertinent company research, sample cover letters (with a plain-text version of a multipurpose cover letter as well), the names of hiring authorities picked up along the way, a list of key words, and, now, a plain-text (ASCII) résumé. Many companies prefer you use the text version of the résumé to cut and paste into the electronic forms (e-forms) on company websites or job boards. And some sites do the conversion for you.

Think of an e-form as an online version of those paper job application forms you used to fill out in the employer's lobby. The paper forms usually required more than the basic information already included on your résumé (such as a list of references or an essay on your particular strengths). It's the same with e-forms or what some sites refer to as "résumé builders."

Before you log in and submit a résumé or complete an e-form, you will most likely have to create a new account with your email address and password. In addition to requiring the information from your résumé, e-forms often require you to answer specific questions relating to the position you are applying for. You can complete them at your own computer—with the help of a dictionary and stylebook.

Another advantage of e-forms is that they eliminate the guesswork about what to include. With e-forms, the employer tells you exactly what information to provide. (Some sites even specify the character count of the résumé.) Depending on the particular company's website—and there are a lot of variations from one site to the next—be prepared to answer all kinds of questions. Some of the fields in the e-forms are small, so you have to type in the information. Other fields are large, so you can cut and paste from your plain-text résumé. In addition to requesting contact information and that you cut and paste your résumé (some forms refer to the résumé as a CV, short for "curriculum vitae"), an e-form may ask the following:

- Whether you are willing to relocate
- What your GPA was at the highest level of education
- What your salary range is
- Whether you are willing to travel
- Where you heard about the position

Be prepared by having the answers to all of these questions. Already having a figure for a salary range, a list of your technical skills, or a brief description of how your education relates to the position cuts down the chances of error or inaccuracy. Even though most of these e-forms allow you to review and edit the material before submitting it, the more prepared you are, the less likely you will stumble over the details. And there are plenty of details. You may want to experiment with résumé builders on job boards before actually completing a company's e-form.

You'll discover that the e-form process varies from one website to the next. Some allow you to cut and paste your entire plain-text résumé into a data field (which generally ranges between 16,000 and 18,000 characters, or approximately seven or eight pages—plenty of room since you've already honed your résumé to a tidy one or two pages). Other e-forms ask for bits and pieces to be dropped into data fields regarding work history, technical skills, interpersonal skills, and so on. Some e-forms even allow you to paste your Word résumé into the appropriate space. Take a look at the generic e-form in Figure 6.3, which should give you a general idea of what to expect when visiting an employer's site.

FIGURE 6.3 *E-form*

```
* = Required

Name                              *First [        ]  Middle [        ]  *Last [        ]

*e-mail access?                    Yes ○      No ○
*If Yes, Enter e-mail Address      [                        ]
 (Required if you have e-mail access)   (mxsmith@yahoo.com)

*Home Address                      [                        ]
                                   [                        ]
                                   [                        ]
*City                              [                ]
*State or Province                 [    ▼]
*Country                           [United States  ▼]
*Zip/Postal Code                   [    ]
 Country Phone Code                [001]
(*)Home Phone                      Area Code ( [    ] )  [    ] – [    ]
 Work Phone                        Area Code ( [    ] )  [    ] – [    ]  Ext. [    ]
 Mobile Phone                      Area Code ( [    ] )  [    ] – [    ]
 School Phone                      Area Code ( [    ] )  [    ] – [    ]
(*)Non-U.S. Phone                  [                    ]
*How should we contact you?        [                ▼]
 Best days/times to contact you by phone  [                        ]
 What is your salary range?        [                ]
 What position are you applying for?  [                ]

 List your technical skills here (do not exceed 600 characters):
 [                                                              ]
 [                                                              ]
 [                                                              ]

 List your nontechnical skills here (do not exceed 600 characters):
 [                                                              ]
 [                                                              ]
 [                                                              ]

 Attach your resume here (do not exceed 16,000 characters):
 [                                                              ]
 [                                                              ]
 [                                                              ]
```

If you are asked to cut and paste your entire résumé, follow these six steps (for MS Word):

1. Retrieve the plain-text version of the résumé.
2. Highlight the entire résumé.
3. Go to "Edit" and scroll down. Click on "Copy."
4. Go to the e-form and then to the appropriate field or button. Right-click with the mouse and paste the résumé into the appropriate field.
5. Fix the indentation (and anything else that may have gone awry in the transmission) right in the e-form.
6. Take the extra time to proof and edit, then submit the résumé or, if necessary, continue completing the rest of the fields.

If the e-form requires just bits and pieces of the résumé, then follow the preceding steps, but in Step 2, highlight only the pertinent information instead of the entire résumé (for instance, your career objective or your work history).

THE PARTICULARS OF E-FORMS

Some electronic forms are better than others; they range from explicit to vague. On the Alltel site, potential candidates are given a comprehensive overview of the hiring process in four steps. The first step covers online applications:

Go here [a hot link] to search our open positions and submit your résumé. We recommend you first search for a position that interests you. Search often—our postings update daily. Then, build your candidate profile and submit it directly to that position by simply cutting and pasting your résumé and completing our online application. Make a note of your login and password, as you will need these for future access to our system. You will be able to apply for additional jobs using your existing profile.[2]

In another sample, this one from UPS, job candidates are given the choice of whether to use just the e-form or simply submit a résumé:

As the first step in becoming eligible to be considered for employment opportunities at UPS, we ask you to complete the following online résumé/CV. You can either cut and paste your existing résumé/CV here [a hot link], or complete the [e-]form below. When you enter a valid email address, you will receive an automated acknowledgment of receipt of your online résumé/CV. If you do not have an email address, you may sign up for free at http://mail.yahoo.com. The email field is a required field to complete.

Keep your job data file in front of you with all the appropriate information and then follow directions. After completing a few e-forms, you'll get the hang of it. But as already mentioned, not all sites are clear. Some company's websites make it difficult even to find the career link. (Often, if it's not on the home page, then look under "About the Company" or "Contact Us.")

When you first start working with e-forms, there is a margin of error. If any aspect of the e-form procedure is still unclear after contacting an HR representative at a particular company or asking a computer-savvy friend, then you may be better off applying for the dream job you discovered on the Web by more traditional methods—fax or snail-mail—because it's important that you follow the e-form steps precisely to be considered.

SPRINKLE WITH KEY WORDS

When filling out e-forms and submitting electronic résumés, key words take on a whole new meaning because you are applying for a specific job. Read the job description carefully. See what words apply to your qualifications and then use them in your application.

Take a look at the following job description for a network security researcher. The key words are italicized:

> Candidate should have a *Ph.D.* with expertise in *network security*. Candidates must be willing and able to obtain a *Government Security clearance*. Candidates should have a broad knowledge of *IP networking* plus a record of accomplishment (e.g. publications in *peer-reviewed journals*) in some of the following technology areas: *Architecture* and *design of secure data communications networks,* both *conventional* and *wireless, mobile IP, IP multicast, network security,* especially *security* of the *Internet* and *WWW;* security strengths and weaknesses of *protocols* at the *network, transport,* and *application layers; intrusion detection systems; information security systems; firewalls; antivirus systems, honeypots; virtual private networks; footprinting, scanning,* and *hacking techniques;* etc. In particular, we are interested in people who have experience developing *prototype applications* involving such technology and in performing research in the *underlying algorithms* and *computer science*. Candidates should be *creative, innovative* thinkers capable of *identifying* and *proposing new research projects.*

Chances are that your online application won't make it past the first round unless key words are included. Approximately 15 to 20 keywords in the preceding job description should be included on the application—provided, of course, that the candidate has these qualifications. This job description is very specific—make sure you are, too.

In the push to include key words, many applicants randomly include qualifications that don't necessarily reflect their expertise, a problem that is especially rampant in the technology field. Charles Greene, a vice president at Securities Industry Automation Corporation, said,

> Many applicants include all kinds of key words on their résumés, but once they get to the interview, they are incapable of supporting these claims. It's fairly evident after ten minutes who is qualified and who is not. Still, it's a waste of time to include key words that don't apply to your skills and qualifications. Sooner or later, the truth is revealed.

THE JOB BOARDS

If you opt to bypass company websites and use job boards exclusively, the wait to receive a response may be long or indefinite. Two of the biggest job boards, Monster and HotJobs, get millions of hits each month from applicants. In a month, Monster averages about 15 million visitors and Yahoo! and HotJobs normally gets 6 million, so posting an online résumé can be impersonal, to say the least, at these sites. Such sites are helpful, though, as career management tools, because they offer plenty of advice about the hiring process and may be a good place to work out the kinks of your electronic submissions. You may have more success at the specialized job boards (in the writing, engineering, IT fields, etc.); the match rate for the mainstream job boards is about 2 percent, whereas the match rate on the specialized job boards is approximately 15 percent. The only job board mentioned by Fortune 500 participants in the survey was DirectEmployers, a nonprofit association that powers JobCentral National Labor Exchange. Dan Bankey, of Mutual of Omaha, commented, "We love DirectEmployers.com as a leading-edge Internet sourcing tool."

Southern Edison Offers Some Suggestions on Key Words:

- Use enough key words to define your skills, experience, education, professional affiliations, etc.
- Describe your experience with concrete words rather than vague descriptions.
- Be concise and truthful.
- Use more than one page if necessary. The computer can easily handle multiple-page résumés.
- Increase your list of key words by including specifics.
- Use common headings, such as Objectives, Experience, Employment, Work History, Skills, Affiliations, etc.
- If room allows, describe your interpersonal traits and attitude.
- Use jargon and acronyms specific to your industry. (Spell out the acronyms.)[3]

Many employers reportedly use software that scans the most recent entries in a job board's database, so it's important that you "renew" or "refresh" your résumé as often as possible. Another issue in posting your résumé online is privacy: Be careful how much information you release; check each job board's privacy clause, then err on the side of caution. In the article "The New Rules of Web Hiring" in *Time* magazine, Barbara Kiviat wrote that "shotgunning" your résumé indiscriminately out to job boards can be dangerous: "Keep tabs on where your résumé is going. The nonprofit World Privacy Forum last week published a study documenting instances of personal information sold, even identities stolen, from job search sites."[4]

SCANNABLE RÉSUMÉS

Some large companies scan hard-copy résumés into their databases, which takes between 15 to 60 seconds for each résumé. If a prospective employer scans résumés and you are uncertain how to proceed, follow these steps (posted on the Southern Edison Careers page) as a guideline:[5]

1. Use white or light-colored 8½ × 11 inch paper.

2. Provide a laser-quality original if possible.

3. Do not fold or staple your résumé.

4. Use standard fonts, such as Times or Courier.

5. Use a font size of 10 to 14 points.

6. Place your name at the top of the page on its own line.

7. Use standard address format below your name.

8. Use boldface and/or all capital letter for headings.

9. Avoid fancy treatments, such as italics and shadows.

10. Avoid vertical and horizontal lines, graphics, and boxes.

11. Avoid two-column formats.

12. Don't condense spacing between letters.

"Make a contact with someone at the company who is willing to give you background about the company—its culture, the type of jobs available, and business."

Bill G. Vlcek
Manager, Strategic Staffing
International Truck & Engine Corporation

CHAPTER 7

Networking

"Network, network, network" is the advice of Cecilia McKenney of Pepsi Bottling Group. Eleven other Fortune 500 survey participants made it a point to advise job seekers to network as well. Career experts and counselors agree that networking is a vital element in your job search. So how do you do it? And where do you begin? You need to get rid of all the ideas you have about networking first.

Start by considering your focus statement. You need to know—by heart—what type of job you are looking for and what you can do for an employer. Your aim improves tenfold when you are specific and clear, because it's essential you know what you want to do and how you can be of service *before* you start networking. Calling up an acquaintance to say you are looking for a job usually won't hit the mark; in fact, don't even ask for a job. Instead, tell your contact you are looking for a particular type of job in a particular industry and then ask for help—any kind of help that person can provide.

That help may arrive in many different forms. The best kind of help, of course, is to be given the name of a hiring manager, but most networking initiatives begin in a more roundabout way. The majority of people need time to gather their resources. They may have to browse their file of business cards or their electronic address book. Or they may have to take note of the job postings in the cafeteria. Or they may have to spread the word among department heads. Or they may have to make a few phone calls. Or because of budget constraints, they may only be able to provide background information. Call everyone you know to tell them what you need and be receptive to any kind of input you can get.

PROFESSIONAL AFFILIATIONS

Don't limit yourself to professional contacts within a certain company. Sherri Martin, a director of human resources at Deere & Company, recommended that job seekers network through trade and professional organizations. Because industry insiders know what's happening in their fields, let them steer you toward the companies that are hiring or expanding.

Nearly every occupation has a professional affiliation. Simply do an Internet search on your profession and pages of listings appear—whether you're a copy editor (American Copy Editor's Society) or a structural engineer (Structural Engineers Association). If you haven't done so already, you should become a member of the appropriate professional organization. Not only will it help you keep abreast of the latest developments in your field (usually via electronic newsletters), but many organizations also offer low-cost learning opportunities and career guidance as well as insider information on job opportunities. According to Steven Greenhouse in the *New York Times,* the Consortium for Worker Education, a union-affiliated organization that trains 110,000 people per year, actually provides its members, union and nonunion, with free computer and skills-training classes.[1]

Building a professional network takes time. Ideally, you have kept in touch with your direct contacts. When you make contact with them, they will remember your success on a previous project or how easy it was to work with you. If you have lost contact with former colleagues, then start to build another network. Attend job fairs and conferences related to your field. Ask for business cards and share information you have about the industry. Don't wait until you are unemployed to nurture these contacts. Networking is about good relationships, and it works precisely because you have a solid track record—and you have given as much as you take.

If you are employed but concerned you may be swept away in an imminent layoff six months from now, don't hesitate to get the word out as soon as possible. Tell your professional contacts you are considering a move to another company. According to Carlos Tejada in a *Wall Street Journal* article, many companies prefer to "poach" the still-employed from other companies.[2] Companies are skittish about anyone who has floundered too long in the pool of the unemployed.

FROM THE GENERAL TO THE SPECIFIC

Your networking strategies will work best when they begin as general fact-finding missions. Call people—ex-colleagues, former managers, mentors, friends, and acquaintances—and ask them what they know about certain companies. It is highly unusual to get to a hiring source directly or immediately. Count on a few degrees of separation: your friend knows a sales manager at XYZ Company who knows someone in the finance department who is a good friend of the HR director. It takes some time, but follow every lead. If your direct contact puts you in touch with someone who can help you, ask permission to use your contact's name when you initiate communication.

Alumni associations are also excellent resources when job hunting, so look into the alumni association at your college or university. The University of Pittsburgh Alumni Association partnered with its career services department to create AlumNet, "a career-networking program designed to help Pitt students and alumni connect with alumni who can help them advance their careers and explore job opportunities." Rutgers University has a similar network, an online "service that provides a mechanism for alumni to give advice, conduct informational interviews and provide other career assistance," and it even has an Alumni Networking Club. Many of these associations, such as the one at the University of Indiana, ask that you become a member first, but again it's simply a matter of signing up and providing an email address (and sending a donation when you have a few dollars). It's a good idea to make these groups a part of your network. Because networks are reciprocal by nature, you'll be expected to share information and expertise when you are in the position to do so, but it's a small price to pay for having a viable network. In the end, you get what you give.

As with all other research, keep the name of every person you contact in your job data file, especially as you'll want to thank them later for their assistance—whether you get the job they steered you toward or not.

Some people find it difficult to ask for help, but if you're one of them, try to get past this resistance. Even though networking contacts may not be able to secure a job for you, most people welcome the opportunity to be helpful. And remember that once you are gainfully employed, you will have the opportunity to help someone else. Paula Axelrod, a manager of staffing at BJ's Wholesale Club, said, "Don't be afraid to network and use referrals." That's how many positions are filled at major corporations.

THE JOBS NOT ADVERTISED

Networking helps you tap into the hidden job market—the jobs that never make it into the classified advertisements—which is estimated to be between 50 and 75 percent of all jobs. Companies prefer to play it on the safe side when hiring, so many of these jobs are filled internally and many are filled by referrals. You won't know about these jobs unless you make your way into the targeted company. If your tennis partner has a cousin who works at a company you have targeted, ask for the cousin's name. Find out what's going on in terms of hiring at the targeted company. Make an effort to develop personal and business contacts who can help you identify these openings. The networking list you create should be composed of as many individuals as you can think of at various levels in a corporation. What you want is information and advice, not necessarily the offer of a specific job.

Once you have created a networking list, ask certain contacts about arranging an informational interview, which will take no more than 10 or 15 minutes of their time. Nowadays time is a precious commodity. According to Janet Shlaes in "Beyond the Basics: Career Strategies That Work" (the JVS Career Development site), you should narrow the topics you want to cover in these informational interviews.[3] Stick to one topic, such as career advice, industry information, names of key contacts, information concerning planned expansions, the skills necessary to perform a certain job, or how to start out at that company. Make sure the answers to your questions can't be easily found on the company website. One of the worst things you can do in today's overscheduled work environment is waste someone's time. This person is carving out a piece of a busy day to see you, so be sure to say thank you.

Emily Keller, in a *Businessweek* article, said,

> While most informational interviews don't bear fruit right away, recruiters say they are a great way to learn the language of a new profession, ask tough questions about a company's benefits and drawbacks and, if nothing else, gain practice at telling your story and selling yourself.[4]

And it's a good idea to follow up these informational interviews with a note that provides some detail about your progress to date.

Another reason for relying on networking as a primary tool in the job hunt is that your chances of success increase dramatically. In fact, surveys have shown that you have an 86 percent chance of securing a job through networking compared with a 7 percent chance through a classified ad. So why pursue any other method?

The problem with networking is that it takes time, and most people who find themselves suddenly unemployed feel an urgent need to make things happen right away. That's why it's important to build your network before you ever need it; networking should be an ongoing process. If you hear about a company that intrigues you, create a data file before you ever consider applying there. Learn about the company; pay attention to what goes on there. E. Humpal, a manager of employment services at JC Penney, suggests that you network with current employees at the targeted company. Or as Stephen Heckert of JDS Uniphase said, "If you don't have any contacts, try to make some."

When many people hear the word *networking*, the first image that pops into their minds is a dark, cavernous conference hall where everyone is running around with big smiles, introducing themselves, and exchanging business cards with the hope of landing some six-figure job. It all seems a little self-serving, but that's not the whole picture. Networking is about building relationships. This includes touching base with former employers—as Martin Ward, the IT professional mentioned in Chapter 5, did. It means keeping track of the people you enjoyed working with in a former lifetime—easy enough now at the height of social networking, such as at LinkedIn (a professional social network) or even MySpace. It also means building a good reputation in your work life.

Chances are you won't be working for the same company (let alone in the same industry) your entire life—nowadays people hold an average of 12 jobs during their lifetime—so if you haven't done so already, make sure you develop professional contacts along the way. The best way to do that is to show up and work hard, treat people fairly and courteously, be generous, and help others. That way you'll have a professional network without the need of ever having to pass out a single business card.

MAKING THE CONNECTION

An unpredictable economy can waylay your best plans. Perhaps your industry is hit with massive layoffs, and your networking skills, which have gotten rusty while you steadily climbed the corporate ladder, have all but disappeared. Or you may be a recent graduate whose primary goal is to move away from home rather than build working relationships. Or you may have worked at home raising a few children and been preoccupied while everyone else was making those valuable working connections. Or you may have been more of a maverick than a team player during your working life and never felt the need to nurture tried-and-true professional contacts.

According to John P. Kotter, author of *A Force for Change: How Leadership Differs From Management,* you're not unusual. He said, "All too often these networks are either very thin—some people are well connected, but most are not—or they are highly fragmented."[5] So how do you start to build a network when you've either neglected it or have never even begun to build one?

Step-by-step. Talk to people—whether they are friends, members of your church or community organization, professional affiliations, or industry experts—if you're fortunate enough to run into them at a professional conference, job fair, or the dry cleaners. Ask for suggestions or advice. If the conversation goes well, you may get a lead. If the conversation goes extremely well, someone may ask you to send your résumé. Again, though, don't expect immediate results. These things take time. As Trang Gulian, a manager of staffing at Fannie Mae, put it: "Keep trying and keep a positive outlook." And don't burn bridges. You never know when you're going to need help in the future, so keep your list of adversaries down to a bare minimum. Strive, at least, for cordial relations with as many people as possible at your former job.

REAL RESULTS

Networking is about building relationships. Sometimes you can initiate a relationship with a telephone call; sometimes it may take a few letters or inquiries. Whatever you do, make sure you take the time to do some homework about your industry or the company you want to work for. The more you know, the easier your entry into the desired field or position.

Also, remember that many people you speak with as you travel down your career path have been in their profession for years, so be respectful. They know what they're talking about. Listen to them. The art of listening should extend beyond networking. Sherri Martin of Deere & Company said, "If a retain search firm offers you counsel or advice relating to a position it is working on, listen . . . and follow the counsel. [These firms] know what works at the companies they work with."

When you are a newcomer to the workforce, the thought of striking up a conversation with a stranger may seem intimidating. Try to overcome this dread. Take a course on public speaking or perhaps take an interim job and become a telemarketer or a customer service representative to sharpen your people skills. If the ability to talk to people doesn't come naturally, then ask yourself what you need to do to develop it. It's a valuable skill: the ability to articulate what you need and want in a direct and clear manner will bear fruit in other areas of your life as well. If you simply can't bring yourself to strike up a conversation, begin networking online. According to Barbara Kiviat in *Time*, "broader business networking sites, such as LinkedIn.com and Ryze.com,"[6] are becoming increasingly popular. A lot of the initial discomfort of establishing new ties can be overcome online, because you can establish the preliminaries without enduring a face-to-face conversation, and you eventually can make the connections you need in your industry.

In "10 Secrets to Success," a series *Investor's Business Daily* published, the editors found that of the top traits of leaders and other successful people in all walks of life was their predisposition to "Never stop learning." The article suggests you "[g]o back to school or read books. Get training and acquire skills."[7] Whatever you do, do not sit around and bemoan that you can't get a job. If you aren't ready for full immersion in the business world, then do something else useful. Volunteer at a shelter, become a certified yoga teacher, do some pro bono work for a nonprofit, or even read *Time* magazine's "100 Best English-Language Novels from 1923 to the Present."[8]

Many companies are eager to hire employees who know how to turn a negative into a positive. One of the surest ways to do this is to become teachable . . . yet again. Be open toward expanding your arsenal of job skills.

MAKING FORMAL INROADS

If a face-to-face encounter with unfamiliar people is not the best way for you to network and online networking leaves you cold, then consider writing letters of inquiry to the company that has captured your interest. Make sure you do your research and know exactly whom you want to contact at the company to ask for additional information. As Stacy Wilson of UPS said, "Make sure you have [that person's] full, [correct] name." Sending a résumé or cover letter or letter of inquiry to Sir or Madam is too vague—especially for letters of inquiry. Take the time to find the name of the appropriate person to receive your correspondence.

Although a letter of inquiry may resemble a cover letter, its purpose is different. You are still on a fact-finding mission when networking and requesting information or expressing interest. You are not asking for a job yet. You can cover all kinds of topics in a letter of inquiry, especially if you have recently read about a particular company in either the industry news or the general news media. Possible topics include the following:

- Explain your interest in the company and ask where you can send a résumé in the event an opening occurs.
- Request an informational interview with a particular person you read about.
- Ask what skills are required to work at the company.
- Ask if the person knows anyone in particular—in finance, accounting, editorial, IT, engineering, marketing, or sales—who may be interested in seeing your résumé. If the person says yes, ask to use your contact's name when introducing yourself in your inquiry letter to your new contact.

As with cover letters, keep these inquiry letters brief (no more than one page) and concise. In the example in Figure 7.1, a recent graduate expresses his interest in the emerging field of depolymerization, a process that turns waste products into oil, gas, and minerals.

The letter in Figure 7.1 is an expression of interest in a company. In fact, no overt request for a job is ever made; the letter is simply initiating contact. If a response is received, then the writer has another opportunity to build the relationship. Notice that the style of the first inquiry letter is formal. Provided you get a response that is friendly and familiar, then you can adopt a less formal style in your next letter.

The candidate may pursue this relationship through additional inquiry letters or through subsequent telephone calls or even a brief meeting or two. It all depends on the prospective employer. Eventually, you want the opportunity to send your cover letter and résumé to an individual with whom you have a relationship. Make sure all of your communication with a prospective employer is professional and purposeful. Don't waste people's time by being unclear about what you want or what you have to offer.

You may be tempted to spend 90 percent of your time tweaking your almost-perfect résumé. Don't. Your résumé needs to be in excellent shape, but networking is key. Make sure you follow leads (without stalking a job), be patient but also know when to back away gracefully.

FIGURE 7.1 *Example of an Inquiry Letter*

10 Huntington Street
New Brunswick, NJ 08100

August 20, 2008

Mr. William Lange
Director of Engineering
Changing World Technologies, Inc.
100 Hempstead Avenue
West Hempstead, NY 11100

Dear Mr. Lange:

I read Brad Lemley's compelling article "Anything into Oil" in *Discover* magazine. The article suggests your company, Changing World Technologies, Inc., may be on the brink of advancing one of the most inventive technological discoveries of this century.

I am intrigued by the depolymerization process—the possibility of transforming carbon-based waste into environmentally safe oil, gas, and minerals. Turning "600 million tons of turkey guts and other waste" into "4 billion barrels of light Texas crude each year" is an innovation bound to have a major impact on both the environment and global affairs.

Thermal depolymerization is particularly interesting to me because of my background in chemical engineering. I am a recent graduate of Rutgers' engineering program, and I would like to learn more about your company's conversion process. Your website indicates that touring the Philadelphia plant is not feasible. Perhaps you could direct me to an individual at your Naval Business Center in Philadelphia who can speak with me about the skills needed to pursue a career in this field.

I would welcome this opportunity. I will contact you in the coming week to follow up on this request. I can also be contacted via email at *mxwill@hotmail.com* or on my cell phone at 973-296-6000.

Thank you.

Sincerely,

Myles Williams

"In the past, we would work hard to fit a square peg into a round hole, but today, with so many well-qualified candidates in the job market, we no longer have to do this."

Dan Bankey
Manager of Strategic Staffing
Mutual of Omaha

CHAPTER 8

New Trends in Hiring

Just as technology has dramatically changed the applicant's process of looking for a job, so too has it changed the employer's process of making new hires. Today, a growing number of companies are pushing technology in new directions, leveraging their websites with software that gives them more control over the hiring process and a whole new level of efficiency.

In today's recruiting environment, every position posted on a corporate website or Internet job site engenders a flood of résumés. An HR generalist then wades through them all manually to identify candidates. The process usually includes key word searches to hone in on particular skills, knowledge, and credentials. Generally, the first review of résumés is surprisingly quick. In fact, survey results indicate that most of the Fortune 500 participants spend an average of one to two minutes per résumé. Both companies and applicants would no doubt agree that a rapid pass through a pile of résumés is a rather haphazard way to identify the top candidates. Even so, this prescreening part of the hiring cycle is time consuming for companies, especially now that the Internet makes it so easy for job seekers to apply online.

To make the prescreening process more methodical and efficient, a growing number of companies are using recruiting software.

ONE COMPANY'S EXPERIENCE

Technology has literally redefined Mutual of Omaha's recruiting practices, according to Dan Bankey, manager of strategic staffing, who has primary responsibility for hiring. The company uses an "electronic applicant management system" called

Recruitsoft. "It has caused us to really re-examine how we do business," Bankey said. "We believe we stand on the edge of a major shift in how we connect with people interested in job opportunities."

In the past, Mutual of Omaha relied on résumés to prescreen candidates. "The old model for hiring was really driven by the résumé," Bankey continued. While noting that résumés can run the gamut from horrible to outstanding, he added that all of them have one thing in common: "Résumés seek to provide information to the prospective employer as the job candidate wants to present it."

In other words, résumés put the applicant in the driver's seat, with the leeway to decide which information to include, which to emphasize, and which to leave out. Even though this may seem to give the job seeker an advantage, that is not necessarily so, because applicants almost never have a complete understanding of what the company is looking for, what it values in employees, and what resonates with human resources.

Mutual of Omaha has turned the résumé-driven approach upside down via its recruiting software. "Now we obtain information the way we want to see it," said Bankey. "We elicit specific information from applicants that we can easily process and manipulate."

For the company, the advantages of this shift are plentiful. The software does the following:

- Makes data easier to sort and retrieve.
- Filters candidates by matching data against the job requirements.
- Enables the company to ask job-specific questions regarding experience, skills, and interests for each position that is posted.
- Ranks candidates.
- Improves and accelerates communication with applicants.

HOW IT WORKS

Mutual of Omaha advertises job openings online on its corporate website and on other job sites, including DirectEmployers.com. Candidates interested in a specific position apply online, answering the types of personal-information questions that appear on standard paper applications.

The system also asks candidates job-specific questions, which are designed to ensure the company receives both the information and the focus it wants, according to

Bankey. These questions typically explore areas that may not show up in standard applications and résumés, and job seekers are frequently asked to quantify their accomplishments. For example, a sales manager position might include questions on the types of products with which applicants have experience, the size of the geographic areas they covered, the amount of revenue they produced, and their areas of sales management (e.g., recruiting, training, line manager).

To assess skills for a technology position, the questionnaire might ask candidates to list the applications and software they know and to define their level of proficiency. It might also inquire whether they are interested in using those applications or tools again—a query that wouldn't usually come up until the interview.

Mutual of Omaha often takes the opportunity to ask behaviorally based questions as well. For example, the questionnaire for a customer service position might ask how the applicant would handle an irate customer and what the applicant learned from a difficult experience.

If visitors to the Mutual of Omaha site are not interested in specific positions, they have the option to complete Job Finder, a form on which they can list skills, experience, and interests. The company also refers people who send unsolicited résumés or other communications expressing interest in employment to Job Finder. As with the job-specific applications, Job Finder requests information in a format that is easily searchable. The information then resides in the company's database as a source of potential future candidates.

Each time a new job opens, Mutual of Omaha "mines" the database containing job-specific applicants as well as the Job Finder database, explained Bankey. If a close match surfaces from either one, the company invites candidates to consider applying for that specific job.

In screening candidates, Bankey stressed that the company focuses on the information it requested, even though candidates have the option to include résumés and specific comments about themselves. "Getting applicants away from résumés is the biggest challenge," he said, adding that it's only a matter of time. "We're going to take résumés out of the system altogether at some point."

WHAT RECRUITING SOFTWARE MEANS FOR THE CANDIDATE

From the applicant's point of view, a good way to think about recruiting software is that it makes the individual, rather than the résumé, the key driver in the hiring process. Moreover, software that helps companies streamline their process can also make job hunting more efficient for applicants. Indeed, Bankey noted that Mutual of Omaha has actually seen a slight increase in the number of applications it receives.

To utilize these recruiting software systems, applicants will ideally have an Internet connection and enough expertise to use a PC. But for those who don't, some companies offer a work-around. Bankey, for instance, noted that Mutual of Omaha established an 800 number, giving people the option to enter information over the telephone, although he expects eventually to phase out this feature as it is used by only a small percentage of applicants.

Most importantly, applicants need to focus on completing the prescreening questionnaires, investing the time to tailor their responses to the company's requirements. "Job candidates really need to think about how to market themselves," said Bankey. "They need to clearly and concisely relate their background to the opportunities we're trying to fill." (Examples of recruiting software from Mutual of Omaha's Career Pages are displayed in Figures 8.1 and 8.2.)[1]

For applicants who are serious about a particular job, methodology such as Mutual of Omaha's presents an opportunity to put their best foot forward with thorough and thoughtful responses, giving the prospective employer a broader picture of skills and personality than a résumé and cover letter could convey. Although some job seekers may feel shortchanged because they would rather meet someone from human resources in person to discuss their skills and career goals, human resources professionals may take a different view. According to Bankey, "Face-to-face doesn't have to happen this soon."

Another advantage of recruiting software is quicker response times. "We want to recruit the most qualified candidates, and the faster we can get to them, the better chance we have of hiring them," said Bankey. This desire by the company to push the process forward also accelerates the hiring cycle for applicants.

Anyone who makes the first cut at Mutual of Omaha finds out quickly—and has the knowledge that they've cleared a fairly rigorous prescreening process. Likewise, if individuals are not qualified, the company lets them know immediately, thus allowing all parties to avoid wasting time with communications that won't lead to job offers. "The system takes much of the lag time out of the hiring process," noted Bankey.

Yet another plus of recruiting software is that candidates remain in databases. Their information is stored up to three years in the case of Mutual of Omaha; according to Bankey's research, this is well above the average of 6 to 12 months at most large companies. Therefore, even if your application is not suited for a specific job, your information remains on file for other positions or future openings. "Before, it was one job, one look at a résumé," said Bankey. "Now we can re-mine candidates for other jobs." As an example, he explained how Mutual of Omaha receives thousands of letters of interest from interns. "In one day, we used the system to find four interns who were a perfect match."

Recruiting software is just another extension of the technology that can make job hunting both easier and more demanding, and it's probably here to stay. "I believe this is the way of the future—and not the too-far-off future," concluded Bankey.

MORE DETAILS ON E-RECRUITING

Wynn Casino in Las Vegas recruited 10,000 employees in four months, a major feat considering that more than 125,000 people applied for the open positions—from chefs to pit bosses to senior level executives—in an area that has an unemployment rate of 3.5 percent. To handle recruitment, the casino set up an employment center with 40 kiosks, where applicants (some who spoke English as a second language) went through an online screening process. The applicants were asked five questions:

1. Have you done the job you are applying for?

2. What is the level of your experience?

3. How long did you stay in your last three jobs?

4. What types of places have you worked?

5. What is your level of English competency?

FIGURE 8.1

Exit

District Sales Manager (Houston, Texas) – 008492

Job Description

(Apply Online)

Description
Plan, staff and direct a unit of independent contracted agents; develop market and territory strategies to effectively meet the long-term objectives of the division office.

Work with the Recruiting Specialist to build a pool of high potential candidates and ensure selection processes are appropriately administered.

Oversee the formal training programs provided for the agents in all sales, marketing and product areas.

Conduct field training for agents assigned to the unit. Join the agent when making client calls, assisting them as needed to introduce the product, answer client questions and close the sale. Provide constructive feedback to the agent to aid in career development.

Manage the day-to-day performance of agents assigned to Sales Units. Establish performance guidelines including call volumes, product mix, persistency levels, loss ratios, etc. to provide agents with attainable sales targets.

Monitor agent performance, provide feedback for encouragement and evaluate sales results, measuring achievement against planned objectives. Discuss any agent performance issues with the General Manager to seek concurrence for appropriate corrective action.

Manage the environment and activities of the Unit to ensure agents maintain a professional and ethical relationship with each other, Company associates and clients; communicate clear expectations for them as representatives of Mutual of Omaha.

Support the General Manager in the total management of the division office; remain focused on long-term objectives, make sound business decisions in support of Company goals, and comply with all Company policies, Federal regulations and industry guidelines.

Qualifications
Proven sales management skills.

Current licensure or ability to become licensed with Mutual, United and any required Affiliate Company in the state(s) required for the agency.

Successful career as an insurance agent.

Complete understanding and knowledge of insurance products, policies, and coverages, and related guidelines.

Good communication, human relations and motivational skills.

Strong planning and leadership skills; sound judgment and problem-solving skills.

Profile
Job Field   Sales/Marketing
Locations   TX-Houston
Schedule   Full-time
Shift   Day Job

Compensation and Benefits
Pay Basis   Yearly

Flex Time Available? Yes

Send This Job To A Friend

(Apply Online)

FIGURE 8.2

Exit | Help

District Sales Manager (Houston, Texas) – 008492

Hold down the **Ctrl** key to make multiple selections or to deselect items.
Required fields are marked with an asterisk (*).

☐ Accept invitations by email on career opportunities matching this profile.

Personal Information
Please do not include punctuation such as commas or periods in your name and address.
Include name suffix (ex: Jr) following your last name. Please keep your email address current.

First Name*   Last Name*   Initial
[   ]   [   ]   [   ]

Street Address (Line 1)*   Street Address (Line 2)
[   ]   [   ]

City*   Zip/Postal Code*
[   ]   [   ]

Country*   County*
[————Not Specified———— ▾]   [   ]

State/Province*
[————Not Specified——— ▾]

Closest Metropolitan Area*
[————Not Specified——— ▾]

Home Phone   Work Phone
Include area codes in your phone numbers. *
[   ]   [   ]

Email Address*
[   ]

If referred to Mutual of Omaha by an employee, please indicate their name here.
[   ]

Are you at least 18 years of age?*   If not, are you at least 16 years of age?
[————Not Specified———— ▾]   [————Not Specified———— ▾]

Are you related to anyone in our employ?*
[————Not Specified——— ▾]

If yes, who?   Relationship
[   ]   [   ]

Were you ever employed or contracted by Mutual of Omaha?*
[————Not Specified——— ▾]

When? (Month, Year) Where?
[mm ▾] [yyyy ▾]   [   ]

If your name differed from your present name during your education
or while employed for any position noted, please indicate former name:
[   ]

FIGURE 8.2 *(continued)*

Are you currently employed by an affiliate company?* If yes:
—————Not Specified————— ⌄   —————Not Specified————— ⌄

Please list the counties and states you have resided at for the last 7 years:*

Are you one of the following?
U.S. Citizen
Permanent Resident
Asylee or refugee
Temporary resident under on the 1986 amnesty programs*
—————Not Specified————— ⌄

If no, what is your immigration status?

Have you ever been convicted of any felonies (for any reason) or misdemeanors involving dishonesty, moral turpitude, harm to an individual, breach of trust, misappropriation of funds, fraud, or forgery?*
—————Not Specified————— ⌄

If yes, please explain:

May we contact your current employer?*
—————Not Specified————— ⌄

Questionnaire
Please answer the following questions.

1. **Do you have prior insurance sales experience?***
   ○ Yes
   ○ No

2. **What was your personal annualized 1st year commission sales results and what year did this occur? (If not applicable, indicate none.)***

3. **What percentage of these results was from life insurance sales? (If not applicable, indicate none.)***

FIGURE 8.2 *(continued)*

---

4. **Do you have a current life and health insurance license?***

   ○ Yes

   ○ No

5. **If yes, please indicate the states in which you are currently licensed: (If not applicable, indicate none.)**
   *

   ```
   [                                              ⌃ ]
   [                                                ]
   [                                                ]
   [                                                ]
   [                                              ⌄ ]
   ```

6. **Which licenses do you currently hold? (Select all that apply.)***

   ☐ Series 6

   ☐ Series 7

   ☐ Series 24

   ☐ Series 26

   ☐ Series 63

   ☐ I do not have any of these licenses, but I am willing to complete the requirements to obtain these licenses.

   ☐ I do not have any of these licenses and I am not interested in obtaining them.

7. **Have you managed a career agency sales office?***

   ○ Yes

   ○ No

8. **If yes, how many agents were you managing? (If no, indicate none.)***

   ```
   [                                              ⌃ ]
   [                                                ]
   [                                                ]
   [                                                ]
   [                                              ⌄ ]
   ```

9. **If yes, what was the last year you were active as the manager of this operation?***

   ○ 2000-Present

   ○ 1996-1999

   ○ Prior to 1996

   ○ Not applicable

10. **If yes, what were the annualized 1st year commission sales results of your office? (If no, indicate none.)***

    ```
    [                                              ⌃ ]
    [                                                ]
    [                                                ]
    [                                                ]
    [                                              ⌄ ]
    ```

FIGURE 8.2 *(continued)*

11. **How many new career agents were recruited by you in the last year you were there? (If not applicable, indicate none.)***

12. **Are you currently involved in any personal or professional development programs?***
○ Yes
○ No

13. **If yes, describe the programs you are involved in.***

14. **Indicate current professional certifications:***

15. **Indicate the responsibilities in which you have proven experience:***
☐ Recruitment
☐ Interviewing/Selection
☐ Planning Projects
☐ Mentoring/Career Counseling
☐ Coaching and Joint Field Work
☐ Retention Strategies
☐ Affirmative Action Plans
☐ None of the above

16. **Indicate the Financial Service Products in which you have a thorough knowledge:***
☐ Life Insurance
☐ Disability Income
☐ Long-term Care
☐ Annuities
☐ Critical Ilness
☐ Variable Products
☐ None of the above

FIGURE 8.2 *(continued)*

17. **Describe your experience in implementing product knowledge training:***

[text box]

18. **Describe your experience in developing prospecting and/or marketing plans.***

[text box]

19. **Describe your experience in Recruiting and Selection of career sales agents:***

[text box]

Technical Skills ⓘ
Please complete the following Technical Skills evaluation form.
Click on the icon next to **Technical Skills** for Proficiency and Experience definitions.

1. **Mentoring and coaching**

Proficiency	Experience	Last Used	Interest
None	None	Never	None

2. **Coaching new employees**

Proficiency	Experience	Last Used	Interest
None	None	Never	None

3. **Plan, direct, and monitor sales activities**

Proficiency	Experience	Last Used	Interest
None	None	Never	None

4. **Life insurance**

Proficiency	Experience	Last Used	Interest
None	None	Never	None

(Continue)

Then applicants were asked technical as well as multiple-choice questions related to the open position for which they had applied. The results were tabulated and ranked and became part of the overall e-assessment. Kevin Marasco, a marketing director of Recruitmax, noted:

> Actually, over 90 percent of the applications came over the website. [The e-recruiting system Wynn Casino's used] had to make it real intuitive, user-friendly. When the system asked for contact information, the system walked them through the process. It did this for people who are not that computer savvy, so it's real easy and intuitive. Once they get past a certain stage in the process, the system [even] says, "OK, we need to schedule an interview."[2]

Obviously, this situation is unique. Most companies do not need to fill 10,000 open positions in such a short time span, but it's a good idea to become familiar with the basics. If you plan to attend an employment fair or event, bring your résumé, a list of references, even a pocket dictionary. Make sure you are completely prepared to provide all necessary information. According to Marasco, the hiring process can unfold in a speedy fashion when a company utilizes an electronic recruiting system:

> First of all, the technology (we call it an enabler) helps [recruiters] do a better job. . . . You're never going to replace the face-to-face interview. What the technology does is streamline the process and allow recruiters to spend more time building relationships and assessing top candidates, ultimately helping them make a better hire.

Marasco, Bankey, and the other Fortune 500 hiring professionals in this chapter put a lot of emphasis on making the right match and speeding up the recruiting process. The hiring process is labor-intensive and time consuming, so companies are eager to streamline it. Likewise, candidates are eager to speed up the time frame it takes to get hired. That's where a video résumé may come in handy.

VIDEO RÉSUMÉS

Despite all the technological advances in hiring, written résumés are still required to gain entry at both small and large companies. But record growth in social networking—at MySpace, Ryze, and Friendster to name a few—has had a spillover effect on hiring. In fact, LinkedIn, the professional networking site, announced in September 2007 that users can add photographs to their business profiles. And as current thinking goes, if photographs are good visuals, then video must be even better.

Video résumés are catching on in a big way. In fact, many job seekers see video résumés as a powerful tool to help them distinguish themselves from the crowd. According to Phillip Thune, chief executive officer of HireMeNow.com:

> The video résumé idea has been around as long as video. It's not really a new idea. What's changed is the technology. If you have a cell phone or a digital camera that has video, certainly a Webcam or camcorder, you're good to go.[3]

One of the primary advantages of a video résumé is that it streamlines the process—for the company and the candidate. Thune says, "The last thing an interviewee wants to do is get dressed up and travel to the company and have someone decide in maybe the first 30 seconds that you are not right for the job." At HireMeNow.com, applicants have a place to post their video résumé, as well as their written résumé and profile, so that the information about a potential candidate for a job is "robust." Thune continues:

> There aren't really a whole lot of places to post a video résumé that's professional, especially for younger applicants. If you go to YouTube or MySpace and type in video résumé, you'll literally see thousands of video résumés, and it's our strong opinion that those sites are just not a very smart place to send an employer. So if you send a cover email and you tell the employer, "I would really like to apply for your job and, by the way, check out my video résumé at YouTube/whatever," people can put comments under your video at YouTube, and you might not want an employer to see that.

Nick Murphy, operations manager of WorkBlast.com, concurs. He does not see the video résumé as a replacement for the written résumé or face-to-face, but the real advantage is "to get the hiring manager to pick up the phone and say, 'I wasn't necessarily sold on you, but now that I've seen this [video résumé] I am and I want to talk to you.' The point of the video résumé is not to get rid of the face-to-face interview but to put across to the employer your unique selling point."

When Meghan Gonyo, a recruiting and sales account manager at Creative Group, was asked whether she had viewed any video résumés, she said her company's computer system is unable to "view rich media." Thune of HireMeNow.com said this is still an "issue" at a lot of companies, because access to Macromedia's Flash Player is necessary and "even though Flash is a free download, the bigger companies may not allow their employees to view it. The network guys may have blocked Flash."

But that doesn't mean that the video résumé will languish in some obscure corner of the hiring landscape. Thune says:

> Younger folks are pretty much going to drive the trend, especially college kids. If you think about today's college kids, they've grown up having their parents pretty much recording everything they do. It's second nature for them to post things on YouTube and take videos of themselves and their friends, so they don't really have a fear of the camera. So it's very easy for them.

Thune added, "We think it's going to become a tipping point because if you're out there competing for a job and you don't have a video résumé and everyone else does, you're going to feel a tremendous pressure to do one."

Nick Murphy of WorkBlast.com says newcomers to the job market aren't the only ones using the new form. He said WorkBlast.com has many "golden-years candidates, who are in touch with the technology and the trends." He says many of these videos are actually more targeted than a younger job seeker's video because the older candidate has such "phenomenal experience." He notes, though, that his company does "target young professionals because they have the most need for it. They haven't done a whole lot yet, but they still have a lot of intangibles."

HOW TO CREATE A VIDEO RÉSUMÉ

Unless you are planning a "two-minute Hollywood feature film," according to WorkBlast's Murphy, you can normally handle creating your own video résumé. If you are looking for a professional touch, a no-frills, basic video can cost you between $100 and $150. But most hiring managers are not interested in full-scale productions.

Both Murphy and Thune also recommend that the video résumé should not run longer than one to two minutes. Thune says, "Hiring managers, especially those at Fortune 500 companies, are pressed for time."

And you must get across to the employer why they should pick you for an eventual face-to-face interview. Advises Murphy:

> Just keep in mind there are dozens of people applying for the same position. Be personable. Be yourself. If you're a computer programmer and you're kind of a geek at heart, then be that. If you're enthusiastic, with lots of energy, be you. What you don't want to do is get on the video and

be just a talking head and say nothing special. Then you're going to get yawned off. Be professional and make that unique selling point.

Thune said that HireMeNow.com contains a lot of advice on the best way to proceed, but all you need is a digital camera (with video capabilities), a Webcam, camcorder, or even a cell phone, and someone with a "steady hand" to shoot it. He added, "We think that the right video résumé is typically the answer to the standard question in a job interview, 'So tell me a little bit about yourself and why I should hire you.'"

BY INVITATION ONLY

If you are concerned about who is watching your video résumé at HireMeNow.com, Thune reassures his clients that all the employers on his site are invited. He said:

> We don't allow employers to just come to our site and start searching for people. . . . So if a candidate has put all that stuff on their HireMeNow profile, they have to have a link to an employer, with a pass code. (We call it a viewing code.) That's the only way the employer can see it. We give the candidate a lot of control over the code, so if, for instance, you send a link to an employer and you don't want them to check you out anymore, you just deactivate them and change the code and that person can't get into the system anymore.

One of the reasons it is so challenging to get a face-to-face interview at a company is that job interviews are time consuming for the hiring manager. The video résumé acts as another tool to zero in on the right applicant. Thune said:

> I view the HR chat boards just to see what people are saying, and there seems to be a misconception that video résumés will replace the résumé. We don't agree, especially with big companies. A lot of times, how they narrow down candidates is through a key word search. You obviously can't do a key word search on a video résumé.

With all the emphasis on video, you may be wondering what happened to the strict policy of never sending a photograph with your résumé. Many human resources departments are forbidden even to view a photograph because of discrimination laws. Will the transparency of video résumés hamper their eventual adoption by hiring managers?

Thune offered this explanation:

> In talking to employment lawyers, I think the legality of video résumés—whether it's going to be used for discrimination—is different. From a photograph, I can see if you're white, what your age is, what your size is (which, according to the Labor Department, is a huge area of discrimination), but a photograph doesn't add to your qualifications; it doesn't tell me if you're qualified for the job. Even though a video résumé lets you see a person's race, sex, and all that other stuff, it also shows your energy, your enthusiasm, your communication skills, how you would dress for the job, how you present yourself—and those are all valid criteria by which to judge someone you want to hire. So will people use a video résumé in a discriminatory way? I'm sure they could, but they probably could do the same thing in a face-to-face interview.

When Aleksey Vayner, a Yale student, "submitted his video résumé, titled 'Impossible Is Nothing,' to investment bank UBS last fall" his karate-chopping antics gave Wall Street a good laugh and made his video résumé a "YouTube classic."[4] It also got people's attention in another way. "But another funny thing happened: Vayner's vanity creation awakened recruiters and job seekers to the possibilities of marrying the video CV to the Internet—and that may just revolutionize the job-search process as we know it." Even if Vayner's video résumé became a lesson in what not to do when creating this hiring tool, it still provided impetus to this medium.

And Vayner wasn't the only one who sent ripples through the media and online crowd with a video résumé. The *New York Times* reported recently that "Sean Combs, known as Diddy, is looking for an assistant [and] . . . the star is accepting only video applications uploaded onto YouTube." Diddy posted his own videotape of a help-wanted ad on the website and said, "It's a new age, new time, new era. Forget coming into the office and having a meeting with me and being all nervous."[5]

Looks as though Generation Y is already making an impact on the hiring environment. Maybe the time is right for those seasoned professionals out there looking for a second career to stop shooting video of the kids and start rehearsing their own "So Tell Me about Yourself" video résumés.

*"Be prepared to give specific examples of experience you have
that relates to the position and requirements noted in a posting."*

Amy Moers Reeves
Director of Corporate Staffing, SYSCO

CHAPTER 9

Three Fortune 500 Hiring Professionals Critique a Résumé

Even with the best qualifications and skills, job applicants need to know how to tailor their résumés so that hiring managers pull them out of the pile. That often means recasting your skills and accomplishments to fit a specific job description.

I asked three Fortune 500 hiring professionals to critique a sample résumé. Host Hotels & Resorts Lisa Whittington, Kindred Healthcare's Donna Campbell, and Jabil Circuit's Heather McBride (now with Fiserv) offered their comments and suggestions for improvement. To summarize their recommendations: Accomplishments—with verifiable numbers—speak volumes. So does progressive responsibility. Many job seekers can stay in the same job for ten years, but hiring managers are practiced at recognizing those who steadily progress throughout their careers. Those are the job applicants who catch their attention.

Make sure your résumé reflects your true accomplishments and job progress. If you do that, you increase your chances of not floating around in the unemployed pool for too long. Before reading the comments from the Fortune 500 hiring professionals, review Theresa Smith's résumé (Figure 9.1) and see if you can spot the areas that need improvement.

FIGURE 9.1 *Theresa Smith's Original Résumé*

THERESA SMITH
100 East 10th Street, #10E, New York, NY 10000
(212) 674-1000

EXPERIENCE

1999–present   **Alexandria International Finance Corporation,** New York, NY
Director, Corporate Communications
- Work with senior management to develop and implement communications strategies and programs to support the company's business objectives.
- Serve as editor of monthly internal publication, managing content development, writing, editing, design, and production.
- Write speeches, memos, and other communications for senior executives.

1992–99   **Shearman & Sterling,** New York, NY
Marketing Manager
- Planned, wrote, edited, and oversaw design for firm's first annual review, working with partners in offices around the world.
- Developed strategies and materials for presentations and proposals to multinational corporations, investment banks, and governments.
- Developed new materials for firm practices and regions, including Latin America and Asia.
- Served as editor of the internal newsletter, managing content development, writing, and editing.

Media and Communications Specialist
- Worked with partners to write articles for business press.
- Assisted director in developing and implementing communications plan.
- Wrote and edited press releases and fielded calls from the media.

1991–92   **United Nations Development Programme** and **The Economist Group**
Consultant for Latin American projects

1990-91   **Senie Kerschner International Housing Ltd.,** Moscow, USSR
Deputy General Director, Joint Venture Rosinka
- Served as first Moscow-based representative for Western partner in U.S.–Soviet joint venture in construction sector.
- Conducted meetings with Soviet partner, international and Russian banks, international construction companies, and potential clients in the business and diplomatic community.
- Participated in negotiations with Soviet government officials.

1988–90   **Philip Morris International,** New York, NY
Business Communications Specialist, International Planning Dept.
- Wrote/edited presentations for senior management. Projects included president's five-year business plan for board of directors and vice chairman's presentation for securities analysts.
- Summarized international business for president's monthly written report to board of directors.

1984–88   **Business International Corporation/The Economist Group,** New York, NY
Editor, Business Latin America and *Senior Analyst/Latin America*
- Analyzed the impact of economic, political, regulatory, and financial changes in Latin America.
- Planned and edited a weekly newsletter.
- Traveled to region on fact-finding missions, conducting interviews with government officials, economists, executives, and bankers.

1981–84   **Whitney Communications Corporation,** New York, NY
Managing Editor; Senior Editor; Editorial Assistant

1980–81   **Marsans International,** New York, NY. *Administrative Assistant*

1978–80   **Inlingua Idiomas,** Barcelona, Spain. *Language Instructor*

EDUCATION: New York University, Master of Arts, Latin American Studies. **McGill University,** Bachelor of Arts, English. **LANGUAGES:** Fluent Spanish; proficient French; rudimentary Russian
CITIZENSHIP: United States, Ireland

General Feedback from Jabil Circuit

Job seekers often spend too much time formatting the résumé and less time with the actual content. You want the résumé to look clean, but you should spend most of the time figuring out how to market your experience in a way that recruiters and hiring managers see how it relates to the job he or she is trying to fill. I have many versions of my résumé. I always start with the job posting that I am applying for and then I adjust my résumé to draw attention to the requirements that the company is looking for.

Positive Feedback

- Theresa has chosen to highlight her professional experience by placing it first. Because she has had a great deal of professional experience, this is the ideal place for it. Had she been a recent graduate, placing her education first would have been more desirable.
- Theresa was also able to keep her résumé to one page. This is desirable—as long as she is able to emphasize why her experience qualifies her for the job to which she is applying.

Areas for Improvement

- Always place your email address on your résumé. Recruiters like myself find it is sometimes easier to make contact with candidates via email rather than playing phone tag.

- Think about placing a list of accomplishments or professional achievements inside your résumé. Your résumé is simply an advertisement about you, a quick list of why you are better than your competitors is a classic marketing ploy. For example, if Theresa had been able to increase sales by 10 percent by creating a marketing plan at Shearman & Sterling, she should definitely place that in her résumé. If the communication strategy she developed at her present employer resulted in winning a $100 million contact, that is also something she wants to mention. Numbers always talk; if you can relate your accomplishments to dollars, your résumé will get more attention from recruiters.

- Computer skills: In the electronic era, almost all positions require knowledge of Microsoft products. Knowledge of SAP, Peoplesoft, and other operating systems is also very desirable. Without that information on your résumé, you might be overlooked by someone who has a little less experience but lists experience in the operating system the company uses.

Heather McBride
Senior HR Generalist/Recruiting Manager, Jabil Circuit

Positive Feedback from Kindred Healthcare

- I liked the candidate's use of past tense when referring to past positions and present tense when referring to her current job.
- Overall, a good résumé.

Areas for Improvement

The résumé, in this case, should have been expanded to two pages. This would have made it appear less "bunched up" and would have allowed the bullets under each position to be indented, giving a more readable look overall. It would have also enabled the candidate to add some useful information, such as the following:

- An objective, which gives the screener an idea of the candidate's purpose in applying
- A line stating nature of the business for each employer (really important)
- A section listing technical familiarity/capabilities

- The heading could have been expanded to include an email address and alternate phone numbers, if applicable.
- Candidate should have shown the dates of the two positions held at Shearman & Sterling.
- The position at United Nations Development Programme should have been better explained. What kind of projects?
- Perhaps the two earliest positions (Administrative Assistant and Language Instructor) could have been omitted, as they are quite dated and don't tie in to recent experience.

Donna Campbell
Manager of Recruiting Services, Kindred Healthcare

Positive Feedback From Host Hotels & Resorts

- I like that the résumé is on one page—easy and quick to review.

Areas for Improvement

- I like to know what phone number is listed—work or home— so I know if I need to be discreet when I call.
- I like it when a résumé has an objective listed first; that way I know what the person is looking for and whether it matches our objective.
- I would probably remove the earlier work history, as it's really not relevant to her current experience and the assignments have short tenure.
- I would remove the citizenship information if the applicant is applying in the United States, unless the employer is requiring it be included for security purposes, for example.
- I would recommend moving the employment dates to the right side of the résumé, especially if there is a short tenure with some employers, so they aren't the first thing the person reviewing the résumé sees.
- For some specialized positions, it helps to include the type of business that the former employer conducted, especially if the names aren't easily recognizable.
- My last recommendation would be always to include a cover letter that tells the prospective employer why you are looking for work and why you are the best person for the position for which you are applying. I often have multiple openings and don't know which position people are applying for if they just send their résumé without a letter.

Lisa A. Whittington
Vice President, Human Resources, Host Hotels & Resorts, Inc.

THE REVISION

Lisa Whittington and Heather McBride both liked that the résumé is on one page but then asked for additional information, including an "objective" or list of "accomplishments" and technical skills. Also, Donna Campbell thought it looked too "bunched up" and requested an expansion to two pages. Therefore, the revised résumé (see Figure 9.2) has been expanded to two pages to accommodate the additional information.

It's important to add more white space—to give the text a less bunched-up look. At this point, you can see what space you have to work with to add the other features that the Fortune 500 hiring professionals requested. It's essential today that an email address be part of your contact information, so as suggested, this has been included in the contact section.

All three Fortune 500 hiring professionals requested a focus statement so that they understand precisely which position the candidate is seeking. The professional objective that begins this résumé now binds the key information together. The most recent position in a résumé usually is the most important one, so the job description for the first job listed was expanded. The candidate also added results, something emphasized again and again by most of the Fortune 500 participants.

Moving the employment dates to the right was Lisa Whittington's useful suggestion for those who have short tenure at jobs. Dates were further de-emphasized by putting them in roman typeface rather than bold.

Experience dating back more than 15 years is often considered irrelevant by many (but not all) hiring professionals, especially if it is unrelated to the position you are currently seeking. The suggestion to remove the last two positions is taken, but because the new professional objective now emphasizes the international focus, the candidate's experience in Spain is reconfigured in the language section. Removing the last two positions also provides the candidate an opportunity to highlight her progressive responsibility at Whitney Communications.

A description of the type of business was given in each position held. If you struggle for the language to describe your business, go to the company's website to find the wording you need to describe briefly what your company does. If your former employer is a smaller company, make sure you mention somewhere what type of business it is. For larger, well-known companies, it isn't necessary to mention the type of business, as those employers need no description. One of the rewards of

FIGURE 9.2 *Sample of Theresa Smith's Revised Résumé*

THERESA SMITH
100 East 10th Street, #10E
New York, NY 10000
(212) 674-1000 (H) TS100@ att.net

PROFESSIONAL OBJECTIVE
Senior Corporate Communications position with an international organization
that will benefit from my executive and employee communications experience,
knowledge of international business, as well as finance and leadership skills

EXPERIENCE
Alexandria International Finance Corporation, New York, NY   1999–present
Director, Corporate Communications

- Work with senior management to develop and implement communications
  strategies and programs to support business objectives of financial services
  organization with offices in 25 countries.
- Write speeches, memos, and other communications for senior executives,
  including Chairman, CEO, CFO, COO, and CIO.
- Work with senior executives on presentations and memos to the Board.
- Write, edit, and oversee production of 20-page monthly internal publication;
  working with executives to provide coverage of all subsidiaries' business initiatives;
  internal programs, such as Six Sigma; and major industry developments.
- Write sections of annual report and edit entire document.
- Oversaw redesign of internal newsletter, improving quality of content, graphics,
  and design while reducing costs; conducted readership survey that indicated 94
  percent of employees find it a valuable tool for staying abreast of business.

Shearman & Sterling, New York, NY   1992–1999
Marketing Manager, Corporate Communications   1994–1999

- Planned, wrote, edited, and oversaw design for international law firm's first
  annual review, working with law partners in offices around world.
- Developed strategies and materials for presentations and proposals to win
  business from multinational corporations, investment banks, and governments.
- Developed marketing materials for firm's areas of practice (such as securities, law,
  and mergers and acquisitions) and regions, including Latin America and Asia.
  Helped increase business by 20 percent.
- Served as editor of monthly internal newsletter, writing, editing, and producing
  publication and working with partners in all offices to develop ideas.

Media and Communications Specialist   1992–1994

- Worked with law partners to write articles for placement in business publications,
  including the *Wall Street Journal* and the *New York Times.*
- Assisted director in developing and implementing communications plan.
- Wrote and edited press releases and fielded media inquiries.
- Served as editor of monthly internal newsletter, writing, editing, and producing
  the publication and working with partners in all offices to develop ideas.
- Recruited to join the firm's newly created Marketing Department after two years
  and promoted to Marketing Manager.

FIGURE 9.2 *(continued)*

United Nations Development Programme and The Economist Group   1991–1992

- Wrote a brochure on procurement best practices for division of United Nations.
- Wrote articles for *Business Latin America;* edited a Latin American research report; helped organize Latin American finance seminar for The Economist Group, a provider of business information and analysis on international business and world affairs (and a former employer).

Senie Kerschner International Housing Ltd., Moscow, USSR   1990–1991

Deputy General Director, Joint Venture Rosinka

- Served as first Moscow-based representative for Western partner in U.S.–Soviet joint venture in construction sector.
- Conducted meetings with Soviet partner, international and Russian banks, construction companies, and potential clients in business and diplomatic community.
- Participated in negotiations with Soviet government officials.

Philip Morris International, New York, NY   1988–1990
Business Communications Specialist, International Planning Department

- Wrote/edited presentations for senior management at Fortune 500 company. Projects included President's five-year business plan for Board of Directors and Vice Chairman's presentation for securities analysts.
- Summarized international business for President's monthly written report to Board.

Business International Corporation/Economist Group, New York, NY   1984–1988
Editor, Business Latin America and *Senior Analyst,* Latin America

- Analyzed impact of political, regulatory, and financial changes in Latin America.
- Planned and edited *Business Latin America,* a weekly newsletter.
- Traveled to region on fact-finding missions, conducting interviews with government officials, economists, executives, and bankers.
- Promoted to Editor and Senior Analyst after two years.

Whitney Communications Corporation, New York, NY   1981–1984
Managing Editor

- Promoted after one year to Managing Editor for monthly consumer magazine.
- Promoted after two years to Senior Editor.
- Edited, proofread, researched, and handled administrative work for Editor-in-Chief.

EDUCATION

New York University, Master of Arts, Latin American Studies
McGill University, Bachelor of Arts, English

LANGUAGES

- Fluent Spanish (worked as Language Instructor at Inlingua Idiomas, Barcelona, Spain)
- Proficient French; rudimentary Russian

CITIZENSHIP	**COMPUTER SKILLS**
United States, Ireland	Word, Excel, Lotus Notes, CMS

working for a large corporation, according to Carol F. Nelson, second vice president of staffing and relocation services at TIAA-CREF, is that candidates who have worked for "large or nationally recognized employers" usually catch her attention. Many HR hiring managers think it is easier to transition to a large company if you already have experience at a large corporation.

Finally, promotions were highlighted. Companies want to see your career progress. Donna Campbell's suggestion to provide a date for the first position at Sherman & Sterling was taken, but the promotions are also re-emphasized in the bulleted material. One- and two-page résumés cannot fully do justice to your contributions, so listing your promotion(s) allows hiring professionals to see in a nutshell that your former employers valued you as an employee.

It's essential that the hiring professional doesn't have to work too hard when reading your résumé. Overall, the new résumé is more results-oriented and precise, and it highlights the candidate's qualifications and strengths in a more readable format. Once you have the basic information on a résumé, revisions are not time consuming, so take another look at your résumé and make sure it does justice to your skills and accomplishments.

Part II The Job Interview

"Be prepared to talk about your work in detail and sound like you really want the job."

Audrey Goodman
Vice President of Organization Development
Medco Health Solutions, Inc.

CHAPTER 10

What the Second Survey Tells You About the Job Interview

Even if applicants have spent weeks or months priming their résumés and cover letters for targeted jobs and have made hard-won inroads at companies, they still have to ace the interviews—whether it's the first, second, or third time they have met with someone at the prospective company. For many, the final stage of the job search is the most daunting, simply because each job interview differs from the last and the desired result—an offer—depends on so many variables.

So how do job seekers prepare for an interview? I conducted a second survey about the job interview process in 2003 in which 25 Fortune 500 hiring professionals shared their views on the job interview process at their companies. The results formed the basis of my second book, *You've Got the Interview . . . Now What?* These HR professionals were asked what separates the average candidate from the job applicant who gets the offer. The results were surprising.

You have probably heard about "the right fit," but what does that phrase mean? The Fortune 500 hiring professionals surveyed will give you an understanding of what constitutes "fit." But here is the first clue: it goes beyond skills and qualifications. In fact, it has more to do with who you are as a person—the inner substance that drives you—than the degree you may have from a university. Think integrity, accountability, energy, and initiative, and you will be closer to the crux of "fit."

To ace the interview in today's hiring territory, you have to know how to articulate that inner stuff. One of the aims of the second part of this book is to provide you with the language you need to answer those delving questions and also to give you an inside look at how America's corporate giants arrive at their hiring decisions.

The Fortune 500 hiring professionals said it best: the more you know about the job and company, the better the results. Follow their suggestions and you may find that perfect job—a job that taps into your talent, strengths, skills, and qualifications.

THE RESULTS OF THE SECOND SURVEY

To pry the doors open at a Fortune 500 company, you need good skills and qualifications. You won't get an interview without them. But what you probably didn't realize is that your personal values also play a key role in whether you will be hired. These values form the core that drives the offer. Without a doubt, those last two promotions listed on your résumé got you in the door, but it's your integrity, drive, enthusiasm, accountability, positive attitude, and team orientation that often seal the deal. At least that was the theme of a survey of 25 Fortune 500 hiring professionals.

The respondents of the second survey—Fortune 500 managers, directors, and vice presidents from human resources—said they want candidates who fit both the job and the corporate culture. How they decipher "fit" depends on many factors; everything, in fact, from skills to personality to attitude. The 25 questions on the survey were formulated to reveal a more complete picture of the interview process at large corporations; the responses were particularly illuminating in the realm of personal values, attributes, and personality. In fact, a new set of desired capabilities seems to be emerging. So what exactly are the expectations of hiring managers?

Of course, problem-solving, organizational, and communication skills rose to the top of the list of personal attributes, but so did a strong work ethic, team orientation, respect for people, and accountability—qualities that are hard to evaluate within the normal one-hour time frame of an interview.

Perhaps that's why the trend is to interview and then interview some more. Today it's rare to jump on board after meeting only once with a prospective employer. Instead, multiple interviews with three, four, and five people are commonplace—especially for senior-level positions. In fact, you may be scrutinized for hours before an offer is made.

IT'S ALL ABOUT THE Q&A

The most incisive tools interviewers have at their disposal are the questions they ask candidates. The problem is that "Describe your strengths and weaknesses" has morphed into questions such as "Describe what safety means to you as a personal value" or "What is your strongest criticism of yourself?" or "Describe your most challenging work environment and how you dealt with it" or "Describe a project that failed" or "What is your biggest regret?" These questions can throw you off balance. After all, you came into the interview prepared to tell the employer how extraordinary you are. What's all this talk about difficulties and setbacks?

Brian Little, a group director at HSBC, said questions like the ones above "generally give the interviewee a chance to show introspection and also how he or she deals with adversity." Although most job interviews are conversational (for instance, "How long did you work in that capacity at XYZ Corporation?"), behavior-based questions ("Give me an example when you . . .") are now standard forms of inquiry that are interwoven into the "conversation." Interviewers want to know what makes you tick, so they probe, and then they probe some more. You may be thinking that hiring professionals may be watching too much *CSI*. Actually, there's a good reason to evaluate prospective employees carefully.

For one, replacing employees is costly. Figures vary, but the average cost for replacing an employee is $14,000 (and thousands more for senior levels—generally up to a third of the salary). Many of the Fortune 500 companies surveyed have 40,000 employees or more, so managing turnover is a priority. To compound matters, about 35 percent of new hires quit after six months, so HR departments want to make sure they take their time to find the right people.

That's one of the reasons why the questions asked at job interviews are becoming less routine and more thought provoking. Not only do interviewers want to know why you left your last job, but they also want to know how you would handle multiple deadlines, ethical dilemmas, and challenging work environments. In other words, prospective employers really want to know what you're made of before they hire you.

It should be mentioned that the second survey was conducted in the aftermath of Enron and WorldCom. In 2003, when this survey was conducted, corporate scandals were daily fodder for the evening news. Company reputations were taking a beating—in the public eye and in the marketplace. And instead of waxing poetic on wealth building and profit margins, everybody started talking about corporate governance and transparency. As a result, companies were forced to reevaluate their priorities. It was no surprise when the new corporate mantra became, "Companies are only as good as the people who work for them."

That is where your personal values and attributes play into the equation. Employers will always value expertise, but ever since that corporate scandal heyday, a premium has been placed on candidates with strong values—ideally those who are energetic, ambitious, hard-working, positive, efficient, professional, credible, and trustworthy.

And companies are eager to employ individuals who already exhibit these characteristics, because these qualities are next to impossible to develop in people who are resistant to them. In other words, you can go to all the management classes in the world and still act like a brute if you refuse to learn the lessons.

THE FACE-TO-FACE

The face-to-face interview ultimately determines who makes the cut at most Fortune 500 companies. That's where HR professionals decide who fits and who doesn't. If you have made it to the interview stage, congratulations. But now you want an offer, and to get it, you need a good understanding of the new requirements. Otherwise, you may blow that one-hour opportunity that took you three months to create.

Generally, it takes one to three months for a Fortune 500 company to fill a position. In fact, only 20 percent of the respondents said it "depends" on the position or it takes longer. PSEG is proud of its record in "averaging 40 days"; and Jabil Circuit makes a special notation that it has a "relatively quick turnaround" at 30 days, as does HSBC, but there are definitely no overnight successes. Filling positions is, in fact, a labor-intensive process, so a lot of care and planning goes into it.

Nearly unanimously, the Fortune 500 respondents agreed that a successful interview lasts about an hour. That does not mean, however, that you are in and out—with or without an offer—in that time. That may be how long it takes for the first interview. Then it's another half-hour for the next, and maybe another hour for the one after that, and then . . . You get the picture. Unless you are subjected to a panel interview, at some companies, you can expect to meet up to seven or eight people before an employer offers you the job.

But some Fortune 500 companies have turned the process into a science. Deb Palmer, a manager of staffing at Thrivent, said, "Our interview process is broken into multiple sections. The first on-site interview typically is 30 to 45 minutes with HR and 1 to 1.5 hours with a hiring manager or interview team."

A good first question to ask when you schedule an interview with a representative from human resources is, "How does the process unfold at your company?" In other words, what's the routine? It differs significantly from one company to the next.

When the respondents were asked how many interviews they conducted to fill a position, 28 percent said they conduct five or more, 8 percent said they conduct four interviews, 24 percent said they conduct three interviews, and 24 percent said they conduct two interviews. However, two company representatives said the two interviews are panel interviews, which means you still meet quite a few people before you're hired.

Rocco Mangiarano, the director of human resources at Engelhard, said he normally conducts two interviews, but ten or more people may see the candidate before an offer is made. Nearly 16 percent of the respondents said the process depends on the level of the position, and according to Bill Vlcek, manager of strategic staffing at International Truck & Engine, the higher the level, the more interviews.

Sometimes a candidate is escorted from one interview to the next the very same day. In fact, 52 percent of the respondents said this is normal procedure. But 36 percent said it depends on the position, because making the necessary arrangements on the spur of the moment is often impossible. Robert Moll, a senior human resources generalist at TIAA-CREF, said it "depends on the availability of hiring managers. Sometimes it is prearranged; occasionally, it happens spontaneously. Most often HR screens a few candidates for the hiring manager to see." Sheri Lamoureux, a director of human resources planning at Energy East, said that following one interview with another is not typical:

> We have variations as far as hiring practices. Some departments will have group hiring, where everyone interviews the candidate at the same time. What's more uncommon is that a candidate will go from one person to the next person. Hiring managers like to actually hear what the responses are to all of the questions together.

There can be other variables as well. Anne Foote Collins, a director of recruiting and services at Office Depot, said the process "depends on the position and whether or not the applicant has had to travel for the interview." Only 12 percent of the companies said they do not follow one interview with the next—ever—on the same day.

Besides the level of the position, another factor is how eager the company is to scoop you up—or how dire the company's problem is that needs to be resolved. Regardless of the process, candidates should make the job interview the primary objective of the day. If the first interview goes well, don't squelch the potential employer's enthusiasm because you have another obligation that prevents you from meeting the next person in line.

RED FLAGS AND GREEN LIGHTS

When asked to rate red flags—tardiness, unsuitable attire, lack of eye contact, poor communication skills—52 percent of the respondents said that all of these flags are equal and any of them would set off alarm bells. But 28 percent of the respondents ranked poor communications skills as the number one alarm, whereas 4 percent said tardiness and the other 8 percent said unsuitable attire. The good news is that every red flag can be turned into a green light with a little effort.

Follow the basics of a good first impression: be on time, wear neat and pressed business attire for job interviews, maintain eye contact (no matter what), and do your homework to ensure that your communication skills are up to speed during the Q&A. Don't knock yourself out of the running for a great job just by assuming that the rules of the game apply to everyone but you.

Two respondents added that the red flags given in the survey were not inclusive enough. Barry Martin, a director of staffing and development at Timken, said the most glaring red flag for him is "talking too much without listening." Engelhard's Mangiarano added, "All of the red flags mentioned, but what is particularly off-putting to us is someone who doesn't answer the questions directly and tries to control the interview rather than letting the interviewer take control."

The survey addressed one red flag in more detail in a later question. In an era of casual dress, some candidates assume that they can show up at a job interview for a corporate position in less than their Sunday best. According to all the Fortune 500 respondents, not wearing a suit (or the appropriate business attire for your profession) is a bad idea—even at a high-tech operation like Jabil Circuit, where some people would assume the environment is more casual. For the most part, men are expected to arrive in a suit and tie (or blazer and khaki pants) and women are expected to show up in business attire (either a dress suit or pants suit) for a job interview. There are exceptions, of course. John Garofalo, an enterprise staffing and resource manager at PSEG, said, "For professional and managerial positions, it is business attire. Bargaining-unit candidates are expected to wear the clothes they will wear on the job." But, again, do not neglect the basics: neat and pressed is the order of the day.

Some people assume that certain businesses or other areas—fashion, academic, entertainment—call for a more creative approach toward business attire. According to one Fortune 500 participant:

It's very important to ask, 'What is appropriate to wear for this interview?' That's not a question to be ashamed of asking. That's a question that shows . . . [the candidates] are thinking . . . [and] interacting. They want to do the right thing versus making an assumption.

Another requirement when you go to a job interview is to bring several copies of your résumé. This was a unanimous response by the Fortune 500 hiring professionals. Every respondent said you should bring extra formatted résumés (not the plain text version). Each hiring manager you see that day needs to have a copy. Not unanimous were opinions as to whether a candidate should bring a list of references. Only 36 percent thought a list adds a touch of professionalism. The remaining group said they have various other protocols when it comes to references. For instance, at PSEG, John Garofalo said, "We have introduced an e-reference report," and Engelhard's Mangiarano said his searchers handle all reference checking. However, play it safe: bring a list of references. Many companies request candidates fill out application forms in addition to submitting a résumé, so you may need your reference information when you go for the face-to-face interview.

None of the respondents disqualify candidates because they haven't been personally thanked for their time, but distinguish yourself and write a thank you note to each and every person you meet with that day. If you can craft a note that helps you to stand out above the competition, it will further your cause. Creative Group's Gonyo said, "Email is appropriate for a thank you note. Very few people write handwritten thank you notes. But I just think it's the classiest thing. I love [a handwritten note]. It makes a great impression."

HOW'S YOUR TELEPHONE MANNER?

The first contact that candidates have with a prospective employer is often through a telephone screen. Nearly 52 percent of the respondents said they always use the telephone screen to decide which applicants are suitable. That doesn't mean you won't get a call from the others: 28 percent of the respondents said they use a telephone screen "sometimes"; only two respondents said they never use a telephone call to screen out applicants. This means that job seekers must sell themselves as good candidates immediately and should be prepared to be quizzed in this initial conversation. What interviewers are primarily interested in hearing during the telephone screen is whether you handle this call professionally. Often you are expected to give a brief overview of your qualifications and skills. The more delving questions are usually reserved for the face-to-face.

Here's what one Fortune 500 hiring professional said about the telephone screen:

> We do telephone screening 80 percent of the time. When I first came here, there were a lot more face-to-face interviews. Since the growth in our company and general turnover in the industry, what I found is that it's very ineffective to just look at a résumé and invite someone in. You can't understand from [the résumé] whether the person is going to be at the price point, whether the candidate has any flexibility in the price point, whether he or she can work in different locations. There are so many things that I think are important to establish. Does the person have an issue with the title change? We probably do a 20-minute telephone screen.

Discussing salary during the telephone screen is not unusual: 20 percent of Fortune 500 companies talk about your salary expectations. Usually, they are just trying to decide if you fall within their range—specifics will come when an offer is made. That's why you should know a rough estimate of what you are worth in the marketplace. Maybe you sent a résumé to a big corporation more than a year ago and a position requiring your exact skills just opened. Always know what your skills are currently worth in case an employer calls you unexpectedly. You can get a base salary range for free at Monster.com or Salary.com. (A base range does not take into consideration the amount of experience you have or specific expertise.)

DISCOVERING WHAT'S REQUIRED

You may also need to prepare for a test or technical interview. Respondents said tests are usually administered in human resources in 40 percent of the companies surveyed; 16 percent said tests were administered in the departments in which the candidate will work. Forty percent of the companies said they give no tests whatsoever to applicants (not including the technical interview for IT professionals); but one company reported that the department gives the test, two companies reported that a third party administers it, and one company reported testing can take place in either HR or in the department. It is your responsibility to find out whether a test will be required for the position you are interviewing for. It could be a typing test, a basic skills test, a spelling and grammar test, a logic test, a writing test . . . depending on the position.

In some fields, testing is standard practice; in others, it is not. At PSEG, all entry-level candidates must be tested before they are considered. Testing requirements are usually posted on the company website. If you are uncertain about the requirements, ask the interviewer if this is part of the interview process.

One Fortune 500 participant said the idea of testing discourages a lot of candidates who may apply for the open position just for the sake of applying but are not especially interested in working for the company. So instead of receiving 500 résumés for one open position, the HR department can eliminate up to 400 of them with a testing requirement. If you are serious about an open position, do not be discouraged by a test requirement. By all means, prepare for the test and take it. If you do well, your odds of getting an interview are actually better than if you applied to a job that 500 other candidates were seeking.

ANSWERING AND ASKING

Survey respondents were creative when asked about interview questions. Breaking this aspect of the interview into percentages and numbers just doesn't work. But 100 percent of the respondents said that candidates should always ask questions—but not just any questions. You have to ask the right questions—questions that flow organically from the conversation and pertain to the job or company. Timken's Martin said, "They should reflect genuine interest and be related to the position or the industry, not be gratuitous or textbook questions."

How many questions should you ask? Sherri Martin, a director of human resources at Deere, said there is no limit, but you have to be "reasonable and not take over the interview with too many questions." Energy East's Lamoureux said, "The amount depends on the rapport" between interviewer and interviewee. Art Calderon, a director of human resources at Phelps Dodge Corporation, said, "The candidate should always be respectful of the interviewer's time and schedule."

An interview, ideally, is a 50-50 exchange of information. The employer is evaluating you, and you are evaluating the company. Engelhard's Mangiarano called the interview process a "dance." Some career experts call it a "blind date." Whatever you call it that one hour is loaded with information, emotion, reflection, and, with some good luck, satisfaction.

According to the respondents, their top priority in hiring a candidate was the following: qualifications (28 percent), skill fit (16 percent), experience (12 percent), and "all of the above" (32 percent). A few respondents, once again, have a few priorities of their own: Office Depot's Anne Foote Collins said she looks for leadership in addition to skill fit. Barbara Morris, a vice president of human resources at Baxter

International, looks for a solid track record. Deere's Martin looks at a candidate's education in addition to experience. PSEG's Garofalo said, "We hire the most qualified candidate for the position. This is a combination of education, experience, an electronic reference report, performance evaluation (for internal candidates), attendance, interview, background, and medical." Thrivent's Palmer looks for team fit in addition to skill fit. HSBC's Little likes team players, too, but adds that applicants with a professional attitude toward work are also desirable.

All of these attributes are probed during the face-to-face. As already mentioned, the interview may start as a pleasant conversation, but you can expect behavioral questions to be lurking in the background. Hiring managers are determining your workplace fitness, so it's necessary for them to quiz you on many levels that go beyond your skills and qualifications. Prepare yourself to be grilled in a (hopefully) friendly way. Allied's O'Leary said candidates often stumble on "behavioral questions that ask for specific examples. Many struggle to the point that they can't give any specifics; only less valuable generalities."

Many Fortune 500 respondents disclosed that this question typically creates discomfort in applicants: "Why are you leaving your current job?" Know the answer to this question—but here's a clue: do not say you are leaving your old job because you dislike your boss or even the job. Instead, here are some suggestions to answer this question:

- You have always wanted to work at XYZ Company, and this seemed like the perfect opportunity.
- You want to broaden your experience.
- You want to gain knowledge in a particular field because it aligns more closely with your interests.
- You are interested in companies that develop their employees.

You get the idea. The point is to steer clear of being negative and focus on the positive, which means you never trash your old boss, you never complain about your old job, and you avoid blaming your company for your low salary. Instead, present your interest in a new job as an interest in career advancement.

Employers today are looking at the whole package. Therefore, your personality matters. Only two respondents said that other factors are more important than personality. A large majority—52 percent, in fact—felt the personality of the candidate is important, and 24 percent felt it is "extremely" important. One respondent said fit within the company is more important, and another respondent considered job-related competencies more important. Of course, defining personality is a loose science, but one thing is certain: your skills and qualifications are not the only criteria being evaluated at a job interview. This also works both ways, because you don't want to work in a place that makes you feel like an oddball.

HOT TOPICS

Behavioral questions aren't the only stumbling blocks for many candidates. If there is a gap in a résumé—whether from a layoff, from having been fired, or even because of a criminal record—candidates often squirm. The Fortune 500 respondents thought candidates should be brief but also honest. You would not have been called in for an interview if they weren't interested—in spite of the gap. And so much depends on your attitude—of seeing what good came out of a difficult situation. Focus on what you learned, how you grew, what kind of contingency plans you came up with. Allied's O'Leary advised candidates to "be honest, with a positive spin on learning experience. Be able to provide positive references as a balance." And Deere's Martin said, "Never claim to be a victim. Admit to a shared responsibility but not too much detail beyond a basic explanation."

Another hot topic of conversation is salary. Overwhelmingly, the respondents agreed that this topic should be initiated by the interviewer, not the candidate. You need to pay attention to the signals, though, because this discussion can occur at various stages of the interview. Twenty percent of the respondents said they initiate the topic of salary in the telephone screen, 40 percent said they talk about money at the first interview, 8 percent reported the conversation begins during the second interview, and 8 percent said it is not brought up until an offer is made. Pay attention to the subtleties. Even if an interviewer brings up salary in a telephone screen, it may not be appropriate to discuss specifics until the offer is made. Don't think a mention of salary warrants an effusive negotiation. Pay attention to the clues. Hiring managers want to see first and foremost that you are interested in the job; money should be handled as an afterthought (even though it probably is not an afterthought to you).

The survey reveals that preparation for the interview is the single best strategy a candidate can use, so research and then research some more. The more you know, the better your interview—guaranteed. The following chapters should arm you with the information you need to ace the interview, but you still need to know the specifics about the job, the company, the industry, and, most importantly, yourself.

CHAPTER 11

Getting to Know Your Work-Self

Maybe you assumed that once you sent your résumé to a few companies, you were finished with your research. Nothing could be further from the truth. To ace a job interview, you have to know the particulars of the company and a good deal about yourself.

This chapter asks you to set aside some time for contemplating—and planning—your next career move. You may be asking yourself what this has to do with a job interview. You already have the coveted meeting next week, so you want to hear about how to handle questions or negotiations, what to do in a face-to-face with HR, or whether it's appropriate to jot down some notes. What's the point of additional research when you are so close to landing a job?

Interviews are made up of questions and answers. In their simplest form, the interviewers ask you questions and you answer them. Then you ask the interviewers a few questions and they answer them. There are times, especially in behavioral interviews, when you have to think on your feet and talk about something completely unrelated to the position, but the research you do now should still form the basis of most of your questions and answers.

Everything revolves around knowing what you want to do and how you can offer your skills and services to an employer. According to Richard Bolles, the author of *What Color Is Your Parachute?*,[1] the best interview is a 50-50 exchange of information. It is all about the give-and-take. In a job interview, you are being evaluated, but you are also finding out if the job is right for you. Research, and then research some more. You are building a career and a reputation—not settling for just anything that comes along.

SETTING YOUR EYE ON THE TARGET

Even though your livelihood has a direct impact on your personal happiness, most people never fully address their career prospects. In *The Rhythm of Life: Living Every Day With Passion and Purpose,* Matthew Kelly, an Australian author and lecturer, wrote that when he surveyed 40 graduating seniors, only one had a specific plan for achieving his goals. The remaining 39 students told Kelly about their vague wants and befuddled desires—and didn't have a clue how to go about implementing these fuzzy ideas.[2]

Obviously, since you are reading books about the hiring process (at least you're reading this one), you are developing a strategy for achieving your goals. Try not to rush past the preliminaries. One word the Fortune 500 HR professionals used consistently was target—and you cannot hit the bull's-eye without perfecting your aim. You improve your chances tenfold of finding a job that is personally and financially rewarding if you know in detail what you want and what you can offer a particular employer. Sorry, but homework is required.

HOW TO START

It is all about research—the material you put in your job file when you were creating a résumé and now the information you gathered on this particular company. In a digital world, access to a prospective employer has never been easier. Every Fortune 500 company that participated in the two surveys for this book has a comprehensive website that provides job applicants an inside look. You can find out everything, from whether a company offers a tuition reimbursement program to whether it offers a 401(k) plan.

But before you even look at the career page of a company website, it's a good idea (especially for newcomers to the job market) to assess your skills and study your industry. And to make a good match, you need to know something about yourself as well as something about the job market. At this point, ask yourself a few of these questions: Do you know what skills you prefer to use throughout the course of a day? Do you know what contribution you want to make on a day-to-day basis? Do you prefer working for one boss at a small company or are your skills going to be most appreciated in a team-oriented atmosphere at a large corporation? Do you want to work for a service-oriented nonprofit or are you zeroing in on a Fortune 500 company?

If you already know the answers that relate to your own skills and strengths, what about your industry? Do you know what the average salary range is for someone with your experience? Do you know how much education is necessary to meet the requirements of the job? Do you know what skills are necessary to perform the job for which you are applying? Do you know the latest trends in your industry? Do you know which technology skills are most valuable in your profession?

Perhaps you answered these questions even before you wrote your résumé and cover letter. If so, that's a good indication that you're on the right track. If these questions stumped you, then you probably are not ready to go on a job interview. Sherri Martin, a director of human resources at Deere, said this is the question that applicants stumble over most often at a job interview at her company: "What provides you with job satisfaction?" It seems a simple enough question, but it's one you won't be able to answer convincingly if you haven't given it some thought and done some research.

COLLEGE CAREER CENTERS

Nearly every college and university has a career services center devoted to setting its students on the best career track. These centers provide assessment tests and help students gather information, develop résumés and cover letters, and even participate in mock interviews. According to Chrystal McArthur, associate director of career services at Rutgers University, it's not unusual for job seekers to overlook this valuable resource. She claims that almost "50 percent of students don't know what their next [career] step will be."[3]

You may have taken advantage of this type of resource at college when putting together your résumé and cover letter, but according to McArthur, the career process is more complex. Counselors at Rutgers Career Services prefer to work with students during the entire course of their studies so they can build a solid relationship that will help students discover all their options. McArthur explained:

> Throughout the four years, there are different issues that crop up. Some students come in and say, "I don't know what to major in," or some students say, "I need help getting an internship," or some students say, "I need help with my résumé." We get a lot of students who come in senior year who have not thought at all about what they want to do when they leave. In addition, the people who are even more challenging are those

who have had no pre-professional internships. Maybe they have worked at McDonald's or The Gap.

Even if you have some catching up to do, don't be discouraged. McArthur said that much "depends on the person." She explained that students who are "diligent and self-reflective in this collaborative process" can discover their strengths and skills fairly quickly through a variety of tools available in the career center. One student, a business major who came in requesting help with her résumé just before she graduated, discovered after four sessions that she was better suited for a nonprofit organization than for corporate America. After taking an assessment test and talking with her counselor about her interests, favorite classes, leadership skills, grades, and strong commitment to service, the student shifted her job search significantly.

Career centers have many tools at their disposal to help students discover and identify their strengths and skills. The Holland Self-Directed Search or assessment test (McArthur prefers to call it an "assessment instrument" because there is no such thing as a right or wrong answer) operates on the concept that "birds of a feather flock together." She said that Dr. John Holland's "research has shown that people have certain likes and dislikes. If you're in a work environment where your values, skills, and interests are fairly consistent with the group's, then it's more likely that you'll like your work."

Although the service for students is free at college career centers (usually extending for three months to a year after they graduate), alumni can also benefit from these career centers. Rutgers charges $40 an hour for personal career counseling. At the University of Nebraska–Lincoln, an Alumni Advisory Network encourages alumni to assist, coach, and support other alumni, both professionally and socially. Not only does UNL Career Services have a "Husker Hire Link" that connects employers and alumni, but it also offers a "lifelong career assistance" program.[4]

Some colleges and universities even offer for-credit classes to juniors and seniors that help familiarize them with the realities of the current job market. At Bowling Green University, Jessica Turos, career center assistant director, teaches a class that helps students with their résumés and cover letters, prepares them for interviews, and uses other techniques to aid students in building their skills and confidence.[5] There are also countless workshops, such as the ones offered by Career Services at the University of New Mexico, where topics such as "Dining Etiquette," "How to Work a Career Fair," and "Network Skills with Reception-Mixer" are covered.[6]

What if you are not a student or alumnus? Just go online and explore the websites at several colleges and universities. You won't get the personal attention students or alumni would, but these websites still provide invaluable career guidance. In fact, a plethora of information is available—everything from worksheets that aid you in identifying your transferable skills to questions you should ask at an interview. Even more importantly, research on these sites furthers the "self-reflective" process: you actually start to think about your individual skills and strengths, which helps you to develop a mind-set that comes across as focused and prepared in a job interview.

STATEWIDE EMPLOYMENT SERVICES

CNN columnist Anne Fisher wrote, "The federal government is about to embark on a hiring spree . . . and 193,000 jobs will open up between now and 2009."[7] Because not all of these jobs are located in Washington, DC, it makes sense to visit your state employment website. In addition, these websites offer training and placement as well as industry trends in a specific area. For instance, on the Massachusetts Division of Career Services website, you can find a wealth of material on organizing your job search, identifying and learning to talk about your skills (scripts are even provided), finding new sources for job leads, preparing for job interviews, and tips on how to decide if a job is the right fit for you.[8]

Why would you explore these websites if you already have garnered an interview? Because the more you know about what you want to do, the easier it is to convince an employer that you can actually do it. In addition, to make a persuasive pitch, you need to know the language of the place where you want to work. Think of it this way: every time you research these sites, you subconsciously pick up the words and phrases that are apropos to the current work environment. You find out what skills are in high demand, and you figure out how you can transfer what you already know to what is required at the prospective job.

Employers have an expectation that you know how to navigate the Internet with ease. According to one Fortune 500 hiring respondent, the most egregious mistake a candidate can make when interviewing is to lack information about the company. One HR director said, "In this day and age, if you don't have access to the Internet, well, where do you come from? The moon?" Set aside some time to go to the library if you don't have access at home.

Many of the HR professionals who participated in this survey said you should "be yourself" at a job interview. Obviously, that doesn't mean showing up at an interview in your comfortable clothes with a laundry list of requests and demands—even if that's an authentic version of your real self. Rather it means knowing who you are as a worker and what you can offer the company.

TRANSFERABLE SKILLS

It's time to clarify any fuzzy goals you may have. That means knowing exactly how to translate strengths and skills into *quantifiable* (a word frequently used by the Fortune 500 respondents) results. This is especially important for people switching careers. In *What Color Is Your Parachute?* Richard Bolles said, "There is a total misunderstanding of what the word [*transferable*] means." He further explained, "By understanding the word, you will automatically put yourself way ahead of most job hunters." Bolles calls your transferable skills "the most basic unit—the atoms—of whatever career you may choose."

So what are transferable skills? Remember when you created your résumé and used that list of "active verbs" to describe yourself (for example, *organized, structured, researched, managed, supervised, mentored, programmed, streamlined, administered, persuaded*)? Those verbs describe the skills you have acquired—not just at your last job but in all your activities. If you went to school, you researched, wrote, and edited reports. Those are skills you bring to the workplace, where, most likely, you will be expected to research, write, and edit. Even if you are one of those "challenging" students who has little "preprofessional work experience" other than waiting on tables at the neighborhood restaurant, you still developed transferable skills because you *juggled* multiple orders, *provided* excellent customer service, *built* a loyal clientele, *coordinated,* and *delegated* tasks. In fact, you can turn practically all of your life experience into transferable, marketable skills once you learn how to identify them.

Newcomers to the job market or those who are changing careers usually have the most difficulty identifying their skills, because they have not yet adopted the language of their new profession or they are still uncertain what transferable skills they have to offer a new employer. That's why research at this point is invaluable.

For instance, if you had to decide how your club was going to spend the money it raised at a recent benefit, that activity would translate fairly easily into "resource management skills." If you helped everyone in your dorm hook up to the Ethernet, then that demonstrates a useful technical skill.

You already have an interview, so why bother? It's simple. Even though you wouldn't have been asked to come in for an interview if you didn't match the company's skill fit, the ability to communicate these skills effectively to the employer at the interview is essential. In fact, Allied's Kathy O'Leary suggested that at her company, you should prepare notes on your relevant experience so you can address this topic at the job interview.

If you have spent some time in the workforce, identifying your skills is somewhat easier as most companies periodically review your performance. The language for identifying your skills, in other words, is already in place. In "Keep Track of Your Value to the Company," Anita Bruzzese, a business columnist for Gannett News Service and the author of *Take This Job and Thrive*, said a "performance evaluation can also serve as a chance for employees to tout successes, showing their value to a company and how they met or exceeded goals."[9]

It's a good idea to keep a hard copy of all your performance reviews and then take a look at them before you go to a job interview. That way your accomplishments will be fresh in your mind (maybe you forgot about the $14,500 you saved your department when you streamlined its accounting procedures two years ago). That goes for any variation of the performance review, whether it's a 360-degree review or a simple memo your boss sent to her boss the last time she secured a salary increase for you.

Other useful materials that address specific skills and competencies also add value to your interview. Bill Vlcek, a manager of strategic staffing at International Truck & Engine, said his company's standard interview questions are based on the Lominger 67 core competencies, part of Lominger's Career Architect®, an HR tool for developing leaders.[10] Vlcek said there are "a set of questions that each competency comes with." They were developed to decipher the qualities necessary for leadership. International Truck & Engine chooses eight to ten competencies and applies them to specific positions. How do they apply to you?

67 Core Competencies

Action-oriented	Fairness to direct reports	Personal disclosure
Approachability	Functional/technical skills	Personal learning
Boss relationships	Hiring and staff	Perspective
Building effective teams	Humor	Planning
Business acumen	Informing	Political savvy
Career ambition	Innovation management	Presentation skills
Caring about direct reports	Integrity and trust	Priority setting
Comfort around higher-ups	Intellectual horsepower	Problem solving
Command skills	Interpersonal savvy	Process management
Compassion	Learning on the fly	Self-development
Composure	Listening	Self-knowledge
Conflict management	Managerial courage	Sizing up people
Confronting direct reports	Managing and measuring	Standing alone
Creativity	Managing diversity	Strategic agility
Customer focus	Managing through systems	Technical learning
Dealing with ambiguity	Managing vision and purpose	Time management
Dealing with paradox	Motivating others	Timely decision making
Decision quality	Negotiating	TQM/Re-engineering
Delegation	Organizational agility	Understanding others
Developing direct reports	Organizing	Work/life balance
Directing others	Patience	Written communications
Drive for results	Peer relationships	
Ethics and values	Perseverance	

COMPANY SPECIFICS

Once you have determined who you are and what you have to offer an employer, then you are ready to move to the second stage: investigating the company you want to work for. Because you already have an interview scheduled, a large part of your research time between now and then should be spent on the company's website—and not just the career page. Sheri Lamoureux, a director of human resource planning at Energy East, said that one of the most egregious mistakes an applicant can make when interviewing at her company is to display a "lack of knowledge [about the company]." Lamoureux asserted that positions are offered to individuals who demonstrate "proactive orientation." She explains:

> We have some people who interview and they did not even take the time
> to go on our website to get some basic information about our company.
> That just tells me that they are lacking initiative—a competency we look
> for in candidates.

Most companies today have extensive websites brimming with information, so a good way to begin the second stage of your research is by looking at the career posting for the particular job you are about to interview for—even if you found out about the job through a classified advertisement or from a close friend who works at that company. There's more information contained in a brief job posting than you may think.

Take, for example, this job posting for a dividend specialist at Morgan Stanley[11]:

> Analyze, research, and resolve differences resulting from dividend pro-
> cessing. Monitor and reconcile dividend house accounts and control
> receivables and payables. Assist management as required with daily pro-
> cessing, client queries, and ad hoc projects and assignments. Document
> formal procedures. Skills required: Dividend subject matter expertise
> encompassing standard processing routines, including DTCC, SIAC,
> and Euroclear. Understanding of interim accounting, fail and stock
> loan tracking, claims, etc. Sound end-user computing skills. Ability to
> operate independently and back up the section manager when appro-
> priate. Proactive individual who can handle multiple projects and ad
> hoc assignments; interacting with colleagues at, above, and below this
> level. Desired: Understanding of U.S. tax reporting (e.g., 1099s) and the
> implication of dividend processing on same. Ability to create workstation
> solutions to replace manual processes.

Parse the job posting so you understand every word it contains. For instance, the applicant should have some data on the companies the posting mentions (DTCC, SIAC, and Euroclear). In addition, before the interview, applicants should think about the kind of "workstation solutions" they created at their last job. Applicants should certainly think about their interaction with colleagues "at, above, and below" them at their last job. They should also think of past situations in which they were proactive, independent, and adept at multitasking. If certain skills are mentioned in the posting, then you're guaranteed these skills will surface during the interview. Finally, it is fairly obvious that a few soft skills are also required—someone loyal, calm, analytical, and capable of taking direction from a supervisor. These are skills that applicants want to emphasize at the interview, even if questions about them are not asked directly.

Once you discover everything you possibly can about the position, then you should explore the entire career site of the company you want to work for—and don't forget to take notes. You don't want to ask a throwaway question about whether the company has a tuition reimbursement plan if it is already explicitly described on its website. Your questions at the interview should be delving and incisive, not requests for a rehash of information readily available elsewhere.

Many company sites provide invaluable recruitment information. Some even provide detailed information regarding what to expect at a job interview at their particular company. For instance, take a look at "Preparing for Your CarMax Interview" on CarMax's career page for useful guidelines that are applicable at almost any job interview.[12] The Alltel career page, which is also comprehensive, actually gives applicants a step-by-step rundown for the interview process[13]:

> The first interview may be conducted by phone, in person, or by videoconferencing. It may be conducted by a recruiter, hiring manager, or a group of hiring managers. Once the first round of interviews is completed, the top candidates are scheduled for a second interview. Some of our positions may require only one interview, while others may involve three to four interviews.

In a column by Nick Corcodilos, "Ask the Headhunter," Corcodilos likened the job interview to an "open-book test."[14] This is an apt description of how you should consider—and approach—your interview. Obviously you are going to gather more information than you could possibly use at an interview, but this information gathering is a testament to your preparation skills and should convince the interviewer that you are indeed serious about the company. Know as much as possible about the position and company before you shake hands and introduce yourself.

Heather Otto, an employment manager at Jabil Circuit, advised that an applicant's research should include general information about her company. Job applicants should "look at the customers, number of employees, locations, etc." Although you may not always get an opportunity to display everything you know about the company or the industry, this basic information should be on the tip of your tongue in the event that one of the interviewers at the prospective company asks a question such as, "Why do you want to work at this company?" If you respond with hard facts to this question, rather than "Because Company Z has great benefits," then your chances of getting an offer improve exponentially.

For more in-depth information about a company, go to the investor relations page on its website. Many times, the company will send you an annual report just for the asking; on some company websites, you can view the complete annual report. What can you find out about the company in an annual report? Because an annual report is written for investors, much of the focus is on the company's financial position, but you can also discover a company's recent business developments, who the division executives are, its market share, and what new products are being developed.

Another useful link for online annual reports is *www.irin.com,* the Investor Relations Information Network (IRIN) site. IRIN offers "a single point of reference" for accessing electronic annual reports. If you want a hard copy of an annual report, IRIN will forward your request to the company. If you are researching multiple companies, this link will save you some time, although once you have garnered an interview, you still want to go directly to the company website to get additional information specifically about that company.

PULLING IT ALL TOGETHER

You should review your notes on the targeted company prior to the interview. Use the following checklist to make sure you have covered the basics:

- ❏ Products or services the company offers
- ❏ Size of the company
- ❏ Names of the company's competitors
- ❏ Company's rank in the industry
- ❏ Information about the industry
- ❏ Company type (public or private)
- ❏ Key people
- ❏ Relevant information pertaining to your particular position

Art Calderon, a director of human resources at Phelps Dodge, asks applicants to describe their "wow factor" to him at an interview. What are the components of "wow"? One part enthusiasm and one part knowledge about what kind of work you want to be doing at that particular company—and the confidence that you can succeed.

INFORMATIONAL INTERVIEW

At an earlier stage in the job search, you may have arranged an informational interview. Perhaps you sat down with an old friend at XYZ Co. to ask her some pointed questions about the marketing department, or perhaps you contacted your mother's former boss at ABC Corp. to quiz him about the pharmaceutical industry. If any of those informational interviews helped garner a formal interview, then don't hesitate to contact the person with whom you originally spoke.

Assuming you had intermittent contact with this person during the course of your job search—you sent a thank you note or perhaps a friendly email apprising the person of your progress—now would be a good time to reconnect to ask for additional advice. Don't expect another face-to-face meeting, but a brief telephone conversation or an email exchange may give you an edge by providing you with a more detailed scoop regarding the company culture. Once again, put on your best professional face when you make this telephone call. Creative Group's Meghan Gonyo said, "Be prepared when you call. . . . You have to conduct yourself in a professional manner." That's true even if this person is a friend of a friend.

At your informational interview, you quizzed the company insider by asking some preliminary questions about the company or the industry. If you subsequently get a formal interview at this company, your knowledge of the company is already deeper because of this informational interview. You have done your research. All you are missing is some nitty-gritty details. Don't be afraid to ask your original contact to provide you with further information. Consider asking the following questions: Do you know the people with whom I will be interviewing? Do you know the people to whom I would be reporting if I got the job? Do you remember what your interview was like at this company? Will my three-piece suit make a good impression, or should I wear chinos and a blazer? Do you know anything about the job I'm interviewing for that wasn't in the job posting? Have there been any recent business changes that I may not have come across during my research?

Don't be afraid to ask for guidance. According to a Purdue University publication, "Generally, most people enjoy sharing information about themselves and their jobs and, particularly, love giving advice."[15] Nurture these relationships. Regardless of the outcome of the job interview, you have made this individual a part of your network, so be grateful to those who help you—and then return the favor when you are in a position to do so.

Knowledge—about yourself and the prospective employer—is the number one strategy for getting an offer. Some will dispute this ranking; after all, nothing beats connections and networking, right? No doubt connections and networking are helpful, but inevitably success comes down to what you know—not whom you know—at the interview.

If you don't have a friend, relative, or associate working at the company, consider getting temporary or contract work there. Not only does such work experience give you an inside view of the company, but according to Gonyo:

> It's tremendous because . . . you are introduced to a community and exposed to other freelancers who work in the same field. Provided you do a good job, work will come to you. It also shows a future employer your adaptability.

And many companies consider temporary workers potential permanent employees. In addition, if you are short on certain qualifications, a temporary or contract job is the way to go. Usually a company's expectation of temporary help is lower than that of permanent employees. Once you get in the door, you can quickly pick up the company's computer system or the other skills that you were lacking.

One Fortune 500 hiring professional offered this advice:

> Never turn down an opportunity to interview . . . even if it's not exactly what you are looking for. A face-to-face exposes you to a hiring manager, and maybe there's another job in the company that's perfect for you but not open at this point. Hiring managers call people back and tell them about the job. And never turn down an opportunity to work on a temporary basis. I started as a consultant at my job. It gives the company an opportunity to check you out, and you get an opportunity to look at it.

Should you go on an interview to merely practice your interview skills? No. That's a waste of time for both parties. But if you have interest in working at the prospective company, by all means jump at the chance to interview. It's one of the best ways to see if the job and company will fit.

"We sometimes bring up the issue of salary in a phone screen because you come across candidates who are very good, very interesting, and their salary is just way out of the ballpark, so we don't even bother to interview them."

Sheri Lamoureux
Director of Human Resources Planning, Energy East

CHAPTER 12

The Dress Rehearsal

For each open position you have targeted, assume that a slew of applicants are going after the same job. Although the prognosis for future hiring is encouraging—forecasters are calling the economy "solid"—the overall job market is still competitive. So how do you distinguish yourself? Aside from the extensive research you have done, there are still a few more bases to cover.

Lisa Whittington, vice president of human resources at Host Hotels & Resorts, maintained that job applicants should always "think before they speak." Even if you are habitually thoughtful, sometimes a telephone call from a prospective employer can catch you off guard. Ask yourself what you would say this minute if a prospective employer called you. Are you ready for that call?

In the Fortune 500 survey, 52 percent of respondents said they always screen applicants by telephone first. Once you send the news out that you are looking for a job, you should be prepared and ready for a telephone call from a prospective employer. That may mean that it's time to change your telephone message. Your "Yo, this is Rocky B. I'm out with the guys" will not score any points with an HR recruiter, who expects you to be nothing less than the ultimate professional—even at this stage of the game. Creative Group's Gonyo said, "If your voice mail message has music playing in the background or something else that is inappropriate, I think it shows that you are not a professional looking for a job. I may not leave you a message."

Most likely, your contact information on your résumé included either a cell or a home telephone number. Fortune 500 respondents said they will honor your request and call either the cell or home as indicated, but it still is wise to make sure that both messages are straightforward and upbeat. "Hello, this is John Byrne. Please leave a message," works just fine.

Because the average job search is three months—sometimes longer if the market is especially tight—you might have forgotten that you sent out a résumé to ABC Corp., in which case being prepared for the telephone screen can be a tricky matter. That's why it's a good idea to think specifically about what you want to say if and when an employer calls. Gonyo added, "You need to be able to take the call and not have the toilet flush in the background."

You might also rehearse a few key sentences and repeat them to yourself periodically. Your tone should be cordial and professional. Consider the following exchange and see if you can come up with responses that are natural for you:

> INTERVIEWER: Hello, this is Myles Smith from XYZ Company. I'm calling because you expressed an interest in our company.
>
> YOU: Oh, hello. I've been looking forward to your call.
>
> INTERVIEWER: Did I catch you at a bad time?
>
> YOU: Not at all. I would be happy to speak with you.
>
> INTERVIEWER: I understand you have six years' experience working in the sales department at ABC Company. Why do you want to leave?
>
> YOU: As much as I like my current work, I think I'm ready for a more challenging position. ABC is a small, family-owned business, and, frankly, I am eager to test my skills in a bigger arena . . . .

Notice that the hiring manager referred specifically to the applicant's experience. Most recruiters and HR professionals review résumés prior to the telephone screen, so your work history is fresh in their mind. In fact, they may be looking directly at your résumé as they speak to you. That's why it's essential to know every detail listed on your résumé. The best way, then, to handle the telephone screen is to refresh your memory periodically—going through the details of your complete work history—so that all of your skills and qualifications are easily recalled. It's entirely possible that the interviewer is taking notes, and this information may be addressed later in the face-to-face interview.

MORE THAN ARRANGING A TIME AND PLACE

Think of the telephone screen as a mini-interview with the prospective employer. If there are 20 applicants for one open position, then the hiring manager's job is to whittle away candidates at this stage of the game. The telephone screen is a perfect vehicle for doing this: in a day or two, the hiring manager can reduce the pool of 20 applicants to about four. The hiring manager has already identified the skills required for the open position, so it's your responsibility to convince that person that your experience and skills are the right fit for this job. Be prepared to talk about your qualifications in this conversation.

In addition, some recruiters and HR professionals may quiz you on the cultural fit. If the work environment is highly stressful and long hours the norm, you may be asked if an erratic schedule is amenable to you. If the atmosphere is low-key and conservative, a recruiter may try to ascertain if you will blend in well with the rest of your team. Don't be surprised if you are expected to answer a few questions regarding your work habits: Is your schedule flexible? How do feel about working overtime? How do you react when you are faced with multiple deadlines? Do you prefer working in a structured environment? Do you function best in a team or independently? Do you prefer to lead or support projects? Which of your skills do you prefer to use regularly?

Barbara Morris, a vice president of human resources at Baxter International, said it was important to her that applicants "understand the jobs they are applying for." Knowing specifics ahead of time about the prospective position is difficult, especially if multiple job leads are being pursued simultaneously, but try to keep some notes about the jobs you have applied for.

You should also know what the position you are applying for is worth and your own salary range. Many Fortune 500 respondents said they use the telephone screen to make sure that they are in the same "ballpark" as the applicant. However, don't bring up this topic unless the question of salary is initiated by the interviewer. Salary negotiation differs from one company to the next. Sometimes it is determined (in a general way) during the telephone screen, and sometimes this topic is not discussed until much later in the process.

Rocco Mangiarano, Engelhard's director of human resources, asserted that salary negotiation doesn't take place until the final stages of the process. "You can never negotiate anything that's not offered," he said. Instead, Mangiarano asks his "searcher"—that is, his recruiter—to ascertain that the applicant's salary range falls in line with the company's range during the telephone screen. No exact figures are negotiated until the job is offered to the applicant. The important thing to remember is that you must research what the job is worth as well as what you are worth (in terms of experience and skills). Then, if the matter comes up during the telephone screen, you have a starting point, but you should also stay as flexible as possible. The best time to negotiate salary is when an offer is made.

Engelhard's Mangiarano added that, depending on the level of the job being filled, he allows a recruiter, or searcher, to conduct the telephone screen:

> If we use a recruiter, then we expect him or her to do the telephone screen. And I only work with recruiters with whom I have worked for a significant period of time . . . the reason being that I like to build relationships with recruiters so they get to know me and they get to know what I'm about. They also have to understand what Engelhard is about. By the time the recruiter screens candidates, they can screen them as well as I do to make sure they will be a good fit.

During a telephone screen, don't be overly concerned about what the company can do for you. In the early stages of the interview process, you make a much better impression if you focus on what you can do for the company. Before you speak with a recruiter, you need to think about what you will bring to the table.

Sherri Martin, a director of human resources at Deere, said she expects candidates to be articulate. In fact, "poor communication skills" is her primary red flag for disqualifying candidates. Because fluency with the language of the workplace does not come naturally to everyone, especially newcomers to the job market, rehearse some responses as soon as you begin to apply to jobs. Look over your résumé and talk about it—to anyone who will listen. You should be able to talk for one minute about every strength you list on your résumé.

Remember to listen actively as well as respond during a telephone screen. Don't hurry to get to the sought-after time and place of the face-to-face interview. Allow the evaluation to unfold naturally. Whittington of Host Hotels & Resorts said that "in my initial contact, I'm just trying to get a feel for how applicants conduct themselves and why they are interested in the job and how they heard about it." In the telephone screen, don't be shy about selling your interest in the job and company. Then, by all means, sell your qualifications and strengths.

Some career experts recommend you request to call the employer back so that you can retool your brain, but if you are fairly confident that you can speak coherently without being interrupted, then seize the opportunity and express your interest in the job. Don't delay unless you are literally jumping on a train or burning the stir-fry. If that (or a similar scenario) is the case, then politely ask the employer if you can call back at a scheduled time. Host Hotels & Resorts' Whittington said:

> If I have a scheduled time to talk to the person and he or she asks me to call back, I'm OK with that as long as it's something urgent that came up suddenly. It if happens more than once, I'll probably move on to someone else.

At many companies, telephone screens are always the first point of contact between employer and job seeker. Treat this opportunity seriously. Expect to answer standard questions and remember the interviewer is comparing what you say with what the other candidates have said. Do not get too discouraged if you don't make it past the initial phase. According to Deere's Martin, applicants should "realize that not every position you interview for will be the right fit." Host Hotels & Resorts' Whittington added:

> I will tell an applicant during the phone interview that I think he or she is not a fit for the job. Sometimes something big comes out that immediately eliminates someone, and I will go ahead and tell [that person].

Regardless of the outcome of this conversation, remain cordial and professional. If you are told that you are not the right person for the job, ask to be considered for other opportunities as they come along. Occasionally, interviewers say that they need to call you back to let you know if you qualified for the next round. Stay positive. Not only do interviewers want to see if you can think on your feet, but they are also interested in how you handle the process.

QUESTIONS TO ASK

Every job interview is a give-and-take—and your questions are as important as your answers. The telephone screen is not the exception. Consider this an opportunity to discover whether this job is right for you. Here are a few sample questions to ask at this stage: When do you expect to fill the position? Is this a newly created position or am I replacing someone? Can you give me a little more detail about my day-to-day responsibilities? How would you describe the work environment at your company? What computer technologies (or systems) will I be working with on a daily basis? What level of expertise do you expect me to have? How soon will you be conducting on-site interviews?

Take notes. Depending on how the conversation unfolds, you may be able to glean valuable information that you can use at a later stage of the interviewing process. If you cannot take notes during the telephone conversation, jot down some thoughts afterward, trying to pinpoint what the interviewer thinks is important about the open position. Chances are the interviewer's thoughts and values are a good reflection of the company's—one more example of why it's so important to be an active listener.

PRACTICE YOUR TECHNIQUE

If the conversation goes well, the date and time for the job interview will be set. Your research is complete and directions to the corporate office are exact. What do you do next? Practice.

Without a doubt, there is a learning curve when it comes to job interviews. The more often you interview, the more adept you become. However, if a recruiter calls and asks you to come in for a face-to-face and you realize at that point that you have no desire to work at that company, then be honest. Resist agreeing to a site interview. Time is precious. An actual job interview is not the place to practice your interviewing skills. But if you are interested in the company, then by all means go on the interview, even if you are currently employed and not quite ready to move to another position. You never know what might turn up at a later date.

To get ready for an interview, a good plan is to sit down in a quiet place and talk into a tape recorder. For those who are not old hands at talking comfortably to relative unknowns, speaking at a job interview can be an enormous challenge. For some, culturally, it is awkward to sing your praises in public, not to mention that our everyday language is full of fits and starts—stalling techniques ("um"), unfinished thoughts, and inarticulate transitions ("like")—that prevent us from clearly expressing who we are and what we want. That's why it's a good idea to practice with a tape recorder. A few recording sessions can help rid your speech of language tics and also help you formulate your ideas in a confident, cohesive manner.

Why should you do this? One reason is that your skill as a communicator is being evaluated during a job interview. Aside from personality or a good fit, 90 percent of the Fortune 500 respondents said "poor communication skills" (in conjunction with other factors) may initially disqualify a candidate. Office Depot's Anne Foote Collins asserted that poor communication skills are one of the red flags that "would potentially be cause for pause in the hiring process." Lara Crane, a manager of staffing at Alltel, said:

Many positions at Alltel are customer-facing (both internal and external). If a candidate can't communicate clearly or would not be able to build relationships among different department members, then the demands of the position will not be met as easily.

American business is geared primarily toward service—and every business has a customer—so a company's bottom line depends on the ability of its workers to communicate clearly and effectively. Even newcomers to the workplace are expected to demonstrate this skill. In regard to recent graduates, Energy East's Lamoureux said, "The expectations for new entries is that they are not going to have a ton of experience other than potential internships, so you really are looking at their future potential. Obviously they need to have good communication skills."

You probably have heard this emphasis on communication again and again, but you may be wondering how you can improve your communication skills immediately—or at least in time for the interview. You can improve your communication skills immediately by researching the position and company—and then talking about it. Become a subject matter expert about the job you are seeking as well as what you have to offer.

Start by examining your résumé, then use the tape recorder to talk about your skills. Listen to what you say—objectively. First consider the general impression. How do you sound? (Depressed? Positive? Nervous? Confident?) Where can you remove a "you know"? Where can you pause without losing the listener's attention? Should you slow down? Should you talk faster? Then ask yourself if you are conveying your skills in a coherent and logical fashion. Are you putting too much emphasis on your routine duties and not enough on your accomplishments? Are you speaking to the requirements of the prospective job? Can you easily recall how long you were with XYZ Company and your responsibilities there? Can you say why you are right for the job you are interviewing for?

Going on an interview is, in many ways, comparable to speaking in public. If that idea accelerates your heartbeat, you are not alone. Most people—not just the shy among us—would prefer standing in line for two hours to speaking publicly about their own strengths and weaknesses. That's one reason why rehearsing for an interview is so important. The better prepared you are, the less likely you will become tongue-tied and faint of heart.

Practice with the recording session as often as possible before the scheduled interview and measure your progress. After a few rounds, you'll notice improvement.

Maybe you went from mumbling to speaking clearly. Maybe you got rid of the more tiresome "ums" so only a few are left. Maybe you added some heft to your normally whispery voice. In addition, your delivery of your work history is now fresh in your mind. You have all the facts at your disposal.

Engelhard's Mangiarano said, "You would be surprised by how many people are not prepared for an interview." Surprised? Yes and no. It was once a common assumption that you graduated from school, went on a job interview, and then worked at the same company for a good part of your life. In fact, many people thought it unnecessary to develop job interview skills as the opportunity to use those skills came only once or twice in a lifetime. Today, though, the climate has changed dramatically. According to the Bureau of Labor Statistics, "The average person born in the later years of the baby boom held 10 jobs from age 18 to age 38."[1] That suggests you may change jobs every two years. (Other statistics indicate that members of this generation change jobs every 18 months.)

Practicing your interviewing skills is an investment in your future. The practice session can be friendly and informal. Grab a friend and ask that person to sit down with you and playact the interview ritual. Office Depot's Anne Foote Collins advised:

> Spend time up front preparing for the interview; research the company (via the Web or, in our case, by visiting a store); have someone "mock" interview you so you're comfortable—especially if it's been a period of time since you last interviewed.

Now that you have mastered the recording session, what's next? Take a look at the innumerable questions listed in this book—questions that you might be asked when you sit down for your face-to-face. Write out five or six questions and then hand them to your mother, brother, spouse, aunt, or friend—anyone who's objective and willing to help—and request that person ask you a few questions so that you can practice your interview skills.

As you did with your own résumé, examine the job listing and specifications section and pull questions from them. If you are even more ambitious, you might videotape this Q&A session. You can see for yourself where you stumbled and squirmed. Learning how to present yourself in a convincing manner is never a waste of time. Instead, think of it as adding another transferable skill to your briefcase or lunch bag. Talking about your strengths in this manner does not come naturally to most of us, so you need to practice. There is no way around it. Remember, though, that the payback will certainly be worth the effort—within and outside the workplace.

SOME SOFTER SKILLS

Many Fortune 500 hiring professionals interviewed for this book said they always open up an interview with small talk. Engelhard's Mangiarano said, "I have a very formal interview process and I have about 15 questions that I must get through, but the first thing I do is try and put the applicant at ease." He continued, "Typically, the first thing I ask him or her is, 'How was your trip? Was everything OK? How was the hotel?'" Neil Bussell, a group manager of business solutions at PepsiCo, commented:

> The first thing you do is make the applicant comfortable in the setting. I generally do small talk to start—usually about the weather or about getting to the building. I let them settle in. Generally I start with the softer stuff.

HSBC's group director, Brian Little, said, "After the usual warm-up questions, we get to the point and ask what piqued their interest in knowledge of the company and why they are a good fit."

Your small talk should be positive—even if you are asked about the weather and you are still shaking off the snow from your overcoat—or at least be diplomatic. Good business is about good relationships, so everything about you (even the small talk) should say that you know how to have good, positive relationships.

"My experience has been that people of both genders tend to push the envelope nowadays. . . . I think even if you were going to interview at a retail organization or a creative design firm, I think you should really look to the old ways of dressing yourself and grooming yourself for the interview. I think that makes a very positive impression."

Rocco Mangiarano
Director of Human Resources, Engelhard

CHAPTER 13

The Big Day

The primary purpose of a job interview is to get an offer, but an equally important purpose of every meeting with a prospective employer is to discover whether the job is indeed a good fit for you. The interview has to operate on both of these levels for the match to produce good results. You could say that the successful interview is a meeting of minds—with a hundred variables thrown into the equation.

You already jumped several high hurdles to secure your interview. In fact, you did a heck of a lot of work to get it. One way to maximize this opportunity is making a good first impression. What are ten variables affecting first impression?

1. You arrive on time.

2. You are dressed professionally.

3. You are well rested and alert.

4. You are respectful of everyone you meet throughout the day.

5. You are honest and coherent.

6. You can express clearly your qualifications for the job.

7. You show interest in the job and the company.

8. Your responses to the questions are specific and informed.

9. Your questions are relevant.

10. Your personality fits in well with the team and/or organization.

With the exception of personality, nine out of the ten preceding variables are entirely within your control. Yes, you have to research; yes, you have to practice for your interview; yes, you have to be qualified; yes, you have to show up on time and in your best attire; yes, you have to be a decent human being. These are up to you. Perhaps the personality factor is beyond your control, but remember the fit works both ways. At Jabil Circuit, a Fortune 500 company, high energy is one of the top attributes the company looks for in an employee. Heather Otto, an employment manager, reported that "Jabil is a very fast-paced environment. If the candidate lacks energy, this is an indicator that he or she may not be successful in our environment." But who knows. Depending on how flexible and teachable you are and how much you want the job, you may choose to change a few things about yourself.

INTERVIEW PRELIMINARIES

You have heard it a hundred times: show up at the job interview neatly groomed and wearing your best business attire. This is a simple direction, but it's also often ignored. Engelhard's Rocco Mangiarano said female applicants wearing "halter tops and miniskirts" or male applicants sporting "ponytails and earrings" are not going to "fit" at his company.

Your individual style needs to take a back seat to your professional image when you are looking for a job. Depending on your profession, invest in an outfit to wear on interview days. *All* of the Fortune 500 hiring professionals who responded to the survey said the expectation at corporate interviews is a suit and tie for a male applicant and a suit (either pants or skirt) for a female applicant. For corporate jobs, that is the appropriate attire. For positions where a suit is not required, your appearance still matters, and your clothes should be neat and pressed. Don't forget to ask, if you are unsure of the appropriate attire for an interview. And regardless of the industry, err on the conservative side.

It may seem obvious, but several HR professionals mentioned that applicants occasionally show up at interviews insufficiently groomed. Granted, some events are beyond your control—maybe you have to catch three buses while a nor'easter saturates you at every transfer—but it is a testament to your problem-solving skills if you have a contingency plan to ensure that you are putting your best foot forward (even if that means a change of clothes).

A word to those who smoke: it shouldn't come as any surprise that attitudes have changed. A friend recently reported she was one step away from getting a job offer when she was introduced to the CEO, who promptly disqualified her because she smelled of tobacco. At Weyco, an insurance benefits company in Okemos, Michigan, a no-smoking policy under which employees who smoke off the job are fired has been put into place. Howard Weyers, the president of the company, told employees, "They had until January 1, 2005, to quit. Mandatory testing would begin after that, and anyone who failed would be fired."[1] Given the current atmosphere, make sure to wash your hands and pop a breath mint before showing up.

DEALING WITH INTERVIEW NERVES

Some anxiety before a job interview is natural. You put a lot of effort into securing this meeting, and you don't want it to be derailed because of a case of nerves. What can you do to ensure that you present yourself in a confident and convincing manner? As already mentioned, feeling prepared is one of the best antidotes, but you can also realign yourself so that you are in the best frame of mind. Here are some suggestions to consider:

- Make sure you get a good night's rest.
- Go easy on the caffeine before the meeting.
- Repeat positive affirmations to yourself.
- Listen to calming music on your way to the interview.
- Look at the job interview as an opportunity to shine.
- Breathe.
- Exhibit interest in the job instead of trying to be interesting.
- Stay focused and positive.

The face-to-face interview with a prospective employer is what you have been hoping for all along, so act accordingly. Smile. This is exactly where you want to be. The prospective employer is eager to meet you because you are, after all, solving a problem for the company, so hiring managers want you to succeed. Rest assured that they will make you feel comfortable because it is not in the employer's interest to distress you. In fact, most hiring managers are adept at helping you feel at ease. This means you have to be courteous, interested in the job, groomed, and prepared. It does not mean you have to be best friends with everyone you encounter that day. Don't overdo it.

WHAT TO BRING TO THE INTERVIEW

If you secured this interview by sending your cover letter and résumé electronically, bring approximately ten copies of your formatted résumé to the interview. These are the résumés that are printed on your finest stationery and neatly placed within your briefcase or padfolio.

Why so many résumés? Because many Fortune 500 respondents answered that once the candidate meets with human resources and if HR believes the applicant is a good fit, then the applicant sometimes moves right to the next interview with the hiring manager without another day being scheduled. That's why it's important to have extra copies of your résumé. Rocco Mangiarano said that at Engelhard, applicants often go through a whole day of interviewing in which they can meet with up to ten people.

Energy East's Lamoureux concurred: "You never know who else is going to be in the room during the interview, so you want to be able to provide one [a résumé] if requested." Jabil Circuit's employment manager, Heather Otto, added, "Bring a few copies of your résumé. You never know when another manager may be pulled into the interview." Mangiarano said:

> Typically, the way the interview works at Engelhard is that you have the first round, which is an intake process. And again, depending on the level, that may include me for fit, the hiring manager, maybe the hiring manager's boss, and some peers. If it's a senior-level job, then the second round may include a couple members of our senior leadership team. And if it's a very senior-level job, like a corporate vice president or group vice president, then I would have the applicant meet with our CEO. We can generally get through six or seven interviews crammed into one day. And for technology people, R&D, and Ph.D.s, we have them do a whole day of interviews separate from this process, where the applicant gives a technical presentation in front of the community of R&D scientists.

Another item to bring with you to an interview is a list of references, even though most Fortune 500 respondents said they usually don't ask for them at your interview. Just in case, it's a good idea to have three or four references with complete contact information (including email addresses) on a separate sheet of paper from the résumé. (Try to put it on the same fine stationery.) Always alert your references that you are seeking work and they may receive a call. Also, try to ascertain if your references are in the position to return the call (or email) promptly. (Perhaps they plan to be away on vacation for several weeks.)

Your references should be current. If you cannot pick up the telephone and make contact with your references that day or the next, then that's a pretty good indication they should not be on your list. In addition, if you bring a list of references to your interview, wait until you are asked before providing them. Sometimes the employer will ask you to send them by mail, fax, or email after the interview. Follow the instructions, even if your neatly typed list is screeching for attention in your briefcase. According to Timken's Martin, "I would say we are flexible about references. If the candidate brings them, that's fine. If we go further in the process, then we certainly will ask for them. But not having a list is not a deal breaker."

At every stage of the interview, follow the protocols of the company. At PSEG, references are handled differently because the process is electronic; you receive an email from PSEG with a link that opens to a Web page. This is where you enter information regarding your references. You then plug in all relevant information, including the name, email address, company, professional relationship, and length of the relationship. Once the information is entered, you submit this information and launch the e-reference process. Emails are then sent to your references, who are expected to fill out a survey consisting of competency-based questions (numeric scoring) with additional space for comments. If your references don't respond, they get an electronic reminder. (You may have to get on their case, too.) Once all the references respond, a report is formulated and sent back to PSEG.[2]

References are an important component of the evaluation process at PSEG, but in the whole scheme of things, references are not the primary reason you are offered the job. Most employers figure your references will sing your praises—regardless of your actual work history. As Englehard's Mangiarano said:

> I have never talked to a reference who wasn't glowing. That's why I have the searchers do it: because they can probe more deeply than I can. It would be silly for an applicant to ever give you a reference that's going to challenge his or her good standing or good name.

But it is equally important to understand that even your best reference may stumble and inadvertently blurt out inaccurate or damaging information. That's why it is imperative that you have recent contact with your references. Make sure both of you are on the same page in terms of your qualifications, skills, and work habits.

If you are applying for a position that involves fiscal duties, a company may run a credit check on you—with your permission. The Fair Credit Reporting Act allows credit reporting agencies to furnish your credit information to the employer.

Occasionally companies request credit reports, regardless of the nature of the position. Why? The rationale is that your financial stability (or instability) can affect your performance at work. (Stealing or embezzlement is less likely if you are solvent.) This practice makes some employees uncomfortable (with hints of "Big Brotherism"), but the emphasis these days is on transparency. If you are not an open book, some employers may assume you are hiding something. You should make sure your credit report is in order. If you don't know how to interpret your report, go to your bank and ask for your FICO score. If it's not very good, review your credit reports. There may be misinformation that you can correct.

In an age when negligent-hiring lawsuits are becoming commonplace, more and more employers are conducting background checks on prospective employees. What will a background check tell an employer? It tells an employer where you worked and when; where you went to school and what degree you earned; whether you've been in trouble with the law (misdemeanors are often omitted, but felony convictions are not), and if you have a criminal record (but not your juvenile record). If you have an interview scheduled next week and some noisy skeletons are keeping you awake at night, you might want to conduct a background check on yourself.

Electronic court records can be checked by employers, so do not try to hide anything serious. If, however, the topic does not come up during the interview process (and you are not required to fill out an employment application, which usually addresses this subject), then do not bring up any convictions that may be in your background. If the topic does come up during the interview, address it honestly—and briefly. The survey participants stressed again and again that honesty and integrity were important attributes in prospective employees, so use your discretion but tell the truth.

Other materials to have available the day of the interview are work samples. For instance, if you are applying for a position in corporate communications, recent samples of your best writing are required. Some hiring managers request samples before the interview; others ask for them during the face-to-face. But the request for samples is not confined to creative positions. Energy East's Lamoureux said it creates a favorable impression when applicants

> provide samples in a nice and neat way and bring them up in a timely manner during the interview. To give an example, during the interview we may be talking about the candidate's experience with Equal Employment Opportunity training, and the candidate would show a sample of the training he or she created.

So whether you have a massive portfolio, a simple brochure, or neat folder documenting your past activities or accomplishments, concrete samples add impact.

Finally, most interviewers will not request your business card because they already have your contact information, but it is acceptable to ask the interviewer for a business card as the meeting concludes. If the person does not have a business card to give you, make sure you jot down all necessary information so that you can compose a letter or follow-up note to thank the individual for his or her time. This is especially important if you are on a second or third round of interviews and the contact information has changed. Again, be sensitive and follow the signals of the interviewer. If, for some reason, you don't catch the names of the people with whom you interviewed or don't know how to spell their names, try to stop by the receptionist's desk and ask on your way out. Once you have interviewed for a job, it is your responsibility to address all future correspondence with specific individuals (rather than "hiring manager"), so make sure you have the correct spelling of their names as well as their titles.

A FEW MORE PARTICULARS

Many career experts agree that it's a good idea to arrive 15 minutes before your scheduled interview. Some say that it's an indication of the applicant's enthusiasm; some say it allows the interviewers to move things along if the preceding interview ends earlier than scheduled or abruptly; some say it gives the applicant a chance to get a feel for the lay of the land. However, it's probably best to arrive five minutes early or exactly on time. It can be disruptive to a department head if the receptionist calls 15 minutes before your scheduled appointment announcing that you are there. In addition, spending a prolonged period in the waiting room does not normally calm those pre-interview jitters. Ultimately you must decide what works for you, but the important point is that you must not be late for your appointment. Tardiness is a red flag to employers. If something truly out of the ordinary occurs and you are delayed, make sure to call the contact at the company to explain that you are running late.

When you are first introduced to the interviewer, smile, make eye contact, and shake hands firmly—and wait for direction before you barge into anyone's office. You are a guest. As already mentioned, be prepared for some small talk. You may be asked if you want something to drink. Unless you are completely comfortable in this setting, politely decline. A cup of coffee or a soft drink will just get in the way. A job interview is not a social occasion, so instead stay focused on the business at hand: winning an offer. You will have plenty of time to share a cup of java when you land the job.

The style of most interviews is conversational, but don't let this sidetrack you. Most interviewers want to know primarily if you can do the job—not your political opinions. Once you are in the office and asked to take a seat, sit up straight and listen carefully. One of the most glaring red flags to Fortune 500 hiring managers is a "negative or complaining attitude," so refrain from complaining about your former job or boss. Stay positive, throughout the entire interview. Hiring managers are interested in your experience or, as Barbara Morris of Baxter International called it, your "track record."

Let the interviewer initiate the preliminary conversation. Ideally, the interview will be a 50-50 exchange of information: you respond to questions and ask your own. Try to keep this balance in mind, but don't feel compelled to take charge. Let the process unfold naturally.

BACK TO THE FUTURE

Technology is making an impact on the hiring process as well. Take, for instance, the videoconference. When an organization or institution initiates a nationwide or international search for a candidate, videoconferences are sometimes the method of choice for interviewing (especially at academic institutions). When asked about the new technology for the interview process, however, most Fortune 500 respondents said they rely on standard methods (flying in candidates to interview face-to-face). But several Fortune 500 companies surveyed do use videoconferencing, so you may be interested in what's involved.

Videoconferencing provides a simulation of a normal face-to-face meeting by enabling people in distant locations to interact (via computer) just as if they were in the room with you. The interviewer asks a question and the candidate responds in real time (sort of). Several technical problems can arise. For instance, the sound/video is often delayed, which makes conversation a little awkward. Then there is the issue of setting up the equipment correctly so that full-face, eye-to-eye contact is maintained. Companies do save on candidates' travel expenses, but for those not completely comfortable in front of a camera, the videoconference can be an ordeal. As always, you must treat this meeting with an employer in the same professional manner as a real face-to-face, so wear business attire (think of your friendly TV anchorperson when choosing a suit) and be prepared to ask and answer questions.

Those Fortune 500 respondents who use virtual interviews suggested it was, at best, a cost-saving alternative to the face-to-face. TIAA-CREF's Robert Moll noted, "We do occasional videoconference interviews for distant candidates," and Sherri Martin of Deere said they use videoconferencing in "very limited instances." Another Fortune 500 participant agreed that videoconferencing can be useful, but the cultural factor must be taken into account. Her prior experience at Sony led her to believe that many candidates' level of discomfort was so significant that this method was rendered unsuitable. But Deb Palmer, a staffing manager at Thrivent Financial for Lutherans, said, "Since we have multiple locations, we very frequently use videoconferencing for interviews. This helps reduce travel costs for candidates and/or hiring managers."

What normally occurs when a videoconference is arranged is that you either go to a prospective employer's branch where videoconferencing equipment is set up or you contract with an outside service. Kinko's, which has a 150-site network, also provides this service and charges a few hundred dollars per hour to videoconference. A few kinks still need to be ironed out, but as the technology improves, you can expect videoconferencing to become a more common means of interviewing. If you are asked to proceed in this manner, find out all the particulars ahead of time by completely familiarizing yourself with the process before the big day. Also, it is perfectly acceptable to ask the individual in human resources for additional information regarding videoconferencing. One Fortune 500 participant said you should always ask questions if you are not familiar with a company protocol; a question regarding procedure is a testament to your "professionalism."

BE YOURSELF!

Fortune 500 respondents emphasized again and again that applicants should be who they authentically are to make a good match. The fit has to work both ways, so it doesn't make sense to say in an interview that you thoroughly enjoy writing HTML all day when, in fact, you prefer spending a good portion of your time on the telephone pitching the latest project. Try to keep your responses sincere—even if you think the interviewer may want to hear something else. Art Calderon, the director of human resources and strategic programs at Phelps Dodge Corporation, advised, "Be yourself! Anything else is unfair to both yourself and the prospective employer."

Bill Vlcek, of International Truck & Engine, made the same point. He said, "You don't want to put something over on the company, nor does the company want to put something over on the applicant, because then when the work relationship starts, it's not going to be what either party expected." The temptation, of course, is to win an offer every time you interview. Many of us are programmed to win, but taking a job that is not right for you can be a Pyrrhic victory. As much as you may want to get an offer, an unsuitable job can be tedious or even torturous.

And it may cost you, too. According to the *New York Times,* "Human resources professionals and labor lawyers say that more companies are compelling employees to sign employment agreements that hold workers responsible for repaying training, tuition, and relocation costs if they leave their jobs within a specified period."[3] Usually that means you have to stay at the job, which is not a good fit for you, for at least a year. But it also means that the company should present itself in an accurate light as well. Neither party benefits when filling the position or winning the job takes precedence over a satisfactory match. International Truck & Engine's Vlcek told a story to illustrate the point:

> There's an HR director who gets hit by a bus. Then she finds herself at the Pearly Gates, and Saint Peter says, "You know, we don't know what to do with you because we never had an HR person up here before. So I'm going to give you a couple of days to check this place out, and then I'm going to send you downstairs so you can check that place out as well." So the HR director is upstairs in Heaven for a couple of days, sitting on a cloud doing Angel things. But there are a couple of really slow days, and she complains to Saint Peter that there's nothing for her to do. Saint Peter tells her to go back to her cloud and keep doing all those Angel things.

> At the end of three days, she says, "This is nice, but let me try the other place." Downstairs is beautiful, and she sees all her friends and there's a whole lot of stuff going on. The three days down there pass quickly. She goes back upstairs to Saint Peter, and he says, "Okay, it's your choice now. Are you going to stay up here or are you going to go downstairs?" She answers, "Well, you know, I really like it up here and it's so nice and peaceful and calm and beautiful, but downstairs is more fitting to my style—the activity, the friends, and so on," so down the elevator she goes.

> She gets off the elevator, and now everything is just the dregs of the world. She finds the devil, and says, "Hey, this is way different than it was these last three days. What's going on?" The devil answers, "Those last three days we were recruiting. Now you're staff."

CHAPTER 14

The Gatekeeper

"Gatekeepers" are the individuals who escort you to meet your prospective boss and peers, yet so much hinges on your encounter with the person in human resources. HR people are practiced at sizing people up. They usually get a good reading on job applicants in about five minutes. They have already reviewed your résumé, so they know your qualifications and general skills. Thus, at the initial face-to-face, you are more or less being evaluated for your ability to communicate and fit in. Even though HR professionals are capable of giving a fairly accurate quick once-over, protocol still requires they spend more time with applicants to ensure that their gut hasn't steered them in the wrong direction.

Hiring professionals don't ignore their instincts, but they are also committed to the entire process—interviews, background checks, recommendations, and tests. Generally, these matters take time; in fact, the larger the company, the more likely the hire will move at a slow pace. As Cydney Kilduff, an HR director at Kellogg, said, "Big wheels move slowly." Regardless of your sense of urgency around finding new employment, keep in mind Murphy's second law: "Everything takes longer than you think." Be patient. Hiring professionals are evaluating the whole person (not just your curriculum vitae). Your personality is as important a factor as your work history, so let the process unfold slowly.

According to Engelhard's Mangiarano, "We are all go-getters here, but we hire nice people—people we want to work with and with whom we share a fairly common set of values." It is fairly evident, then, that as much as your credentials may glitter, you won't get a shot at performing your duties unless you also have the potential to work well with others at the company. Every corporation or organization expects applicants to fit its corporate culture, and HR professionals are especially adept at knowing what it takes to fit in—both professionally and culturally.

Exactly what does *fit* mean? It means you have the skills required for the job. Equally important *fit* also means you will blend in well at the organization—with your superior, peers, and coworkers. Companies resemble families in many ways, so the dynamics—low-key versus high energy, fast-paced versus sedate, team-oriented versus mavericks, thin-skinned and sensitive versus thick-skinned and blustery—are important.

Again, it goes both ways. As much as you are in need of new employment, look at interviews as a discovery process. Yes, you are being evaluated, but you also are doing your fair share of assessing whether this position is indeed a good match for you. Your research reveals a lot about how a company works, but you, too, must trust your instincts in the interview. No matter how much your ego is flattered, if the job doesn't feel right, then continue searching until you find something that is comfortable for you.

AFTER THE FIRM HANDSHAKE

There is no denying that a good first impression is crucial to interview success. And ensuring that this impression is favorable is relatively easy. You dress appropriately. You are neatly groomed. You show up on time. You smile and look in the interviewer's eyes as you shake hands firmly. You chat amicably until you are seated.

The rest of the interview depends on how well you pay attention to the signals and, more importantly, answer questions as well as ask your own. Clearly your responses to the questions matter, but don't forget that you are gathering information as you move through this process. In other words, you should be responsive to what you have learned along the way—taking mental notes and paying attention to what the people who work at the prospective company are saying. Partly you need to be sensitive to what insiders think is significant, and partly you need to address those issues that are important to you (concerning the job at hand, not necessarily the benefits and perks).

Robert Moll, a senior HR generalist at TIAA-CREF, advised that at the initial interview, job applicants need to "be prompt. Be neat. Be personable. Be prepared. Know your own background, accomplishments, dates, and something about the company and job you are interviewing for." Barbara Morris, a vice president of human resources at Baxter International, acknowledged that after the initial introduction, mistakes that immediately hit her radar screen are "no energy, or the applicant did not find out more about the company." So don't assume your work is done once you show up for the interview. You are still on a fact-finding mission. Stay alert.

BUILDING RAPPORT

Every interview unfolds in its own way. As much as companies try to standardize the process, a lot depends on the rapport between the interviewer and the job applicant. Try not to get too caught up on what you are going to say next. Instead, pay attention to what's going on at that moment. If the HR professional seems distracted or harried, it may be time to ask a question. If you notice that the questions on her notepad are being checked off in a routine manner, try to rescue the exchange by bringing focus to your most outstanding accomplishments. Occasionally there is absolutely nothing you can do to avoid disqualification. The HR professional obviously knows something you don't, so trust that the decision will inevitably be the right one in the long run. This is not the right job for you.

Your first encounter with human resources may be with an HR generalist. In many companies, the generalist is responsible for staffing, training, communications, and employee relations. Generalists are thoroughly familiar with the company's HR policies, procedures, and strategies. You may have spoken to a generalist during the telephone screen. Generalists can answer any questions you may have regarding the organizational design or overall workforce of the prospective company. Generalists often provide your first inside look at the company. If you have questions regarding the infrastructure of the company, a generalist can probably answer them. However, some of the Fortune 500 companies surveyed for this book have more than 40,000 employees, so keep this in mind when you begin to delve into the specifics of a particular job. Generalists know the overall requirements of the job for which you are interviewing, but for a more detailed description of your daily responsibilities, you may want to reserve a few of your questions for a hiring manager or department head.

Your first meeting with a representative of human resources is your introduction to the company, so the give-and-take will most likely open with the general and close with the specific. Keep your focus on the job being offered, and by all means allow the employer to do the steering. No matter how confident and qualified you are, the home court advantage belongs to the employer. Don't take over the interview.

For the most part, even at Fortune 500 companies, the interview is conversational, even though standard questions are often asked of each applicant. Although the style varies from one company to the next and depends on the size of the company and the level of the position, the Fortune 500 respondents said that generally their interviews are a mix of standard questions along with open-ended inquiries (behavioral-based questions). Many respondents said they want to see if applicants can "think on their feet."

What does this mean in regard to the interview? It means your input at an interview should not be a memorized script, nor should you rely on stock answers. Your intuitive and analytical skills are required, so your answers must be thoughtful and meaningful. You can discover much about the company by the questions the hiring manager asks. Your questions should be formulated from the information that you have gathered along the way as you speak with HR professionals and hiring managers. In other words, you are expected to be responsive to the interview. Even good questions can seem irrelevant if you ignore what you have learned thus far at the interview. TIAA-CREF's Robert Moll added that candidates should:

> Ask about four or five questions. It shows interest and preparation, but they should not ask about basic, readily available information. Instead, they should ask about the specific job, department, duties. Don't ask for the sake of asking.

By the time a job applicant interviews at Timken, Barry Martin knows a good deal about the applicant's qualifications, values, work habits, and level of communication skills as well as the way the applicant thinks.[1] "The road into Timken is not the standard résumé. [Applicants] must go online and create a candidate profile in the company's new candidate relationship system." Candidates typically visit the company site twice and interview with seven to ten people. Candidates show up for a face-to-face at the site after they have "answered multiple screening questions based on the specific roles they are interested in. We probably already did a telephone screen." For senior-level roles at Timken, "general manager or above, we actually have an additional set of questions that we mail to the applicant that requires quite a lot of lengthy information—anywhere from 8 to 12 questions."

On many levels, the interview process has begun even before the candidate shows up for a face-to-face at Timken. Martin said that this process was implemented primarily because "not only does this allow us to see the breadth and depth of the applicants' experience, but I also get to see how they think and how they communicate." Even though the "candidate relationship system" at Timken may be time-saving and cost-effective, the real purpose is to find the most qualified candidate. Sometimes Timken can fill the position after interviewing one or two candidates but not always. He said, "We just recently filled a chief learning officer position, where we ended up interviewing, either on-site or through a teleconference, probably 30 people."

You may be wondering what is left to cover at an interview at Timken when the screening process is so extensive. According to Martin, what he is trying to discover at a face-to-face are, in fact, two essential elements of every successful interview:

> Number one, we are trying to give the candidate a good exposure to the kind of company we are and the specific responsibilities of the job, along with the kind of people with whom they would be working, so that the company and the job are a good fit from their perspective. We also want to make sure they have the kind of interpersonal skills—communication skills—that are a requisite for the job.

You may say to yourself that you are the premier expert in blue-laser diode development and would much prefer to spend your time working on the commercialization of blue lasers to honing your communication skills for a job interview. Shouldn't the company be more interested in your development of next-generation, high-volume optical discs than how well you can express yourself to mere mortals? Yes and no.

Employers recognize talent—even if you get a little tongue-tied when introducing yourself to nine scientists sitting in on your presentation. But there is still an expectation at companies that you will be able to communicate your ideas and visions in a coherent, accessible manner. It's all about good, working relationships (for which communication is key). Add to this equation the electronic revolution—the necessity to use email on a daily basis—and the need to express your ideas clearly and concisely gets ratcheted up a notch. As is evidenced by the Timken evaluation, you need to speak and write well before you are even considered a contender for many positions.

Regardless of your expertise—whether in blue lasers, mutual funds, depolymerization, HTML, or Lotus Notes—you need to communicate clearly, so attack this skill with everything you have at your disposal. In fact, commit to lifelong learning on this front. Take classes on writing or volunteer to do telemarketing for a charity—and read. Find the language you need to be an expert at your job. Communicating effectively is one transferable skill that has a life of its own.

In an era when the skill set changes as quickly as a traffic light, good communication skills never lose their edge. As William Zinsser, author of *On Writing Well,* said, "It's a question of using the English language in a way that will achieve the greatest clarity and strength. Can such principles be taught? Maybe not. But most of them can be learned."[2]

ATTITUDE ADJUSTMENT

One of the primary reasons many candidates are disqualified for jobs at Fortune 500 companies is a negative or complaining attitude.

You might be wondering what you should do if you have a tendency to wear your melancholy on your sleeve. As the Fortune 500 respondents asserted, be yourself at an interview, but make sure it's your best self. Figure out what it takes to do the job being offered and be willing to adapt yourself to your job and your surroundings. It doesn't require a complete overhaul of your personality—just a willingness to be flexible. Investigate the underlying currents in your personality so you can make an informed decision about a job offer: a decision based on who you are, what you have to offer, and how well you could (if you wanted to) fit into the company.

A study by Right Management Consultants and cited by Anne Fisher, the workplace columnist for *Fortune* magazine, said, "About 35 percent of managers who change jobs fail in their new ones and either quit or are asked to leave within 18 months." Anne Fisher said, "Most managers who blow it have fine technical skills but stumble over the softer side—fitting into the culture, navigating the political landscape, and forming the kind of friendships that help get things done."[3] Your personality matters. Translate Mangiarano's "nice" people into those who are capable of building and maintaining solid relationships. Success inevitably comes back to good relationships.

Besides fit and communication skills, another theme that cropped up repeatedly in the Fortune 500 survey was a candidate's "integrity." Corporate scandals at individual companies have had an across-the-board impact. When Timken's Barry Martin was asked about this newfound emphasis on a candidate's moral fiber, he replied:

> We are a 106-year-old company that is known for its ethics and integrity, but . . . a lot of these scandals have made companies more aware about the kind of company they are keeping. I am sure [hiring managers] ask about these issues with considerably more frequency than they have in the past.

Your ethics may in fact become a topic of conversation at a job interview, so if you haven't thought about how your integrity impacts your job performance, maybe it's time you did. Engelhard's Mangiarano said that after he asks job applicants his standard questions, he usually ends the interview with precisely this type of question:

> I ask them to explain to me a situation where their business or personal ethics were challenged. And I ask them to describe that and how they responded to it. If they tell me that their personal or business ethics were never challenged, then I know they are lying to me.

Allied's O'Leary said the best way to handle these difficult questions, such as being fired, is to "be honest but with a positive spin on it as a learning experience. Be able to provide positive references as a balance." If you can't avoid addressing your own personal skeletons at a job interview, then manage them honestly and diplomatically—and as quickly as possible. Answer these questions, if you can do so honestly, by focusing on what you learned and how you grew.

On the flip side, a new study sponsored by 24 leading U.S. companies analyzing the responses of 7,718 American workers (the "New Employer/Employee Equation Survey") states that 54 percent of workers question "the basic morality of their organizations' top leaders and say that their managers do not treat them fairly." Resist using the third degree, but by all means ask the hiring manager questions about the company's policies: Would you characterize the workforce at XYZ Company as diverse? How does this company resolve a personality conflict between a manager and a subordinate? Are your employees generally dedicated and loyal? Do employees generally feel passionate about their work at this company? How are decisions made?

You don't want to find yourself among the "substantial numbers of employees [who] feel dead-ended and are seeking changes at work or new jobs altogether."[4] The interview process must go both ways for a good match to be made. Working for a company with high standards should be a priority for you as well.

A FEW OTHER THINGS TO KEEP IN MIND

All job interviews are uniquely challenging. The employer may sit at the computer during the entire interview, throwing out questions without even looking at you. Or your shoes may squeak loudly as you walk down the hall because you just came out of the rain. Lots can go wrong—and you still may get the job. One way or the other, you're going to have to deal with it. Lara Crain, from Alltel, said she prefers candidates who exhibit an "ability to adapt and grow." Show you can adapt, no matter what the circumstances.

Pam Hill, a staffing and planning director at CarMax, recommends that job candidates apply the four Es when interviewing:

1. **Energy.** Show good energy during the interview. Don't slouch, do sit up straight, walk at the pace of the interviewer, and so on.

2. **Enthusiasm.** Show interest in the position and company, even if it is not your top choice.

3. **Eye contact.** Maintain eye contact with all interviewers throughout the interview.

4. **Examples.** Use specific examples of past employment and performance to answer the questions.

"I always ask open-ended questions, so that it's rare

that I get a one-word or two-word answer."

Neil Bussell

Group Manager

PepsiCo Business Solutions Group

CHAPTER 15

The Inner Circle

You made it past the gatekeeper in human resources, and now you are about to be introduced to the people with whom you will be working—provided that you, once again, prove that you would be an asset to the company. Although many Fortune 500 respondents said they don't always immediately follow up one interview with another, you should be prepared nonetheless to meet with more than one person after your initial face-to-face interview. In fact, at large companies, you can expect to meet up to seven or eight people, depending on the level of the position.

Assume that the more senior the position, the longer the interview. But generally, and according to 76 percent of the Fortune 500 respondents, an interview lasts about an hour. Remember you may be asked to proceed immediately to your next interview with a department head or for a technical interview. If so, the interview process can last more than two hours—sometimes even a whole day (in some cases, maybe even two days). The HR representative usually gives you an idea of how long the process will take, but don't hesitate to ask if this is not addressed.

Try to keep your interview day clear of other obligations. When you go on a job interview, your primary purpose is to get an offer, so you don't want to rush through this process because you have an important meeting or obligation later in the day. Take the day off from your other job if possible—or at the very least mention the time frame for which you are available prior to meeting for the face-to-face. You don't want to have to excuse yourself from an interview that is going well because of a prior commitment.

TECHNICALLY SPEAKING

Many jobs require that you exhibit technical proficiency. Sometimes HR administers the test and sometimes you must go to the department in which you will work to take the test or give a technical interview. The test may be given at your first face-to-face, but sometimes you must return to the site for another visit. Obviously, the process varies from company to company and from one position to the next. What's important to remember is that you observe all interview formalities. If you are asked to return and take a test, make sure you are dressed appropriately—just as if you were meeting for the very first time. The job interview is a formal process, from start to finish.

The technical interview gives the employer insight into how you think and process information. Unlike other phases of the interview—where interpersonal skills play a major role—the results of technical interviews or tests are quantifiable. Either you know your stuff or you don't. But that doesn't mean you can't prepare for a technical interview or test. For instance, at PSEG in Newark, the PSEG Career Guide is on the company's website. The guide provides a sample test that the company gives to all entry-level applicants. This test ensures that employees have the basic knowledge necessary to perform their jobs well at this particular company.

If you are being considered for a job within BellSouth, you will be informed of what selection screens are required for that job. Each screen has a study guide associated with it. Study guides describe the selection screen and provide information (TIPs) that may help candidates perform well.

Knowing ahead of time what to expect on the test will make the entire interview go more smoothly.

These tests occasionally require you to use skills that may be a bit rusty (geometry, for example). The turmoil of being unprepared can wreak havoc on your demeanor for the rest of the interview, so know what's expected and brush up ahead of time. Usually you are given advance notice of a test requirement and you have a chance to prepare, but occasionally there is no notice. Try to find out ahead of time.

Other professions may require even more grueling testing—the kind that puts your expertise on the line and makes you sweat. Technical interviews at Microsoft are notorious for stumping programmers. Microsoft's tech interview supposedly is crammed with tons of tricky questions regarding data structures, algorithms, and logic puzzles. In fact, some techies actually sell information on the Web about their failed attempts at Microsoft interviews.

Even seemingly nontechnical industries have test requirements. At newspapers and magazines, for instance, copy editors take a test. One way to review for that test is by taking a look at the 50-page "Editing Booklet" from the American Copy Editors Society (ACES)[1] as well as by reviewing applicable stylebooks, such as *The Associated Press Stylebook*. Bill Walsh, author and founder of TheSlot.com, advises copy editors to "memorize the AP stylebook and a good list of the most commonly misspelled words and you'll out-test 90-something percent of the competition, no matter how much experience they have. If you can test well and interview well, you're in."

At the corporate communications department at Verizon, Peter Thonis, senior vice president of external communications, said some applicants are given an hour or two to write a sample press release.[2] Thonis said, "We want them to do a press release just to make sure they can do it. And you can tell a lot by just the way someone writes a press release what kind of writer he or she is." Thonis said he prefers this type of testing to relying solely on the candidate's writing samples because he is primarily interested in seeing how well and how fast the candidate can write. He explained:

> Sampling is an interesting thing because very often in this business whatever you have written has already been edited, so I really don't know how good a writer you are. What I'm looking for is somebody who is a good writer but, even more important, a good writer who is fast. When I look at samples, I don't know whether it took the person 10 minutes or 15 days. What I really want is someone who can write something quickly.

MOVING UPSTAIRS

Once you have discussed your qualifications and skill set with the initial interviewer, the focus begins to shift slightly from you to the prospective job and company. Neil Bussell, a group manager with the PepsiCo Business Solutions Group, maintains that by the time he meets with a candidate, he has already prepared for the interview by reviewing the candidate's résumé.[3]

As noted earlier, you can usually expect some small talk to open the interview. Bussell said, "The first thing I do is make the applicant comfortable in the setting. I generally do small talk to start." Even though the purpose of this soft introduction is to make you feel at ease, try to keep your own comments pleasant and positive (or at least neutral). Your interpersonal skills are being evaluated at every encounter in the interview process, so don't assume that an exchange about the weather cannot be a loaded topic of conversation if you are griping about the snow. At all times during the interview process, you want to give the impression that you are an easy person to be around and that spending eight hours or more in your company will not be an endurance test.

Remember that a job interview is not just all about you. Expect to get a detailed briefing about what the company does and what the specific job entails, especially if the business is esoteric and difficult to assess from initial research. The interviewer wants to make sure that the candidate is comfortable with the nature of the business or can make the necessary adjustments if the type of business is new or a stretch. Your comfort level is important.

Once you progress to the second interview, interviewers are often trying to assess whether you have the right chemistry to work in the department. However, another layer of questioning may be directed at your level of interest in the job and the company. As you have already met with human resources, you have picked up some information along the way. Don't ignore what you have learned. You want to exhibit a level of interest that suggests you have paid attention to the information that was given to you by the human resources professional. By the time you get past the gatekeeper, the department head or second interviewer expects that you have some grounding in the business (besides what you discovered in your own research). Provided you like what you see at this stage, Cecilia McKenney, of Pepsi Bottling, advises you to "sell yourself."

Bussell said that when he meets with candidates, his primary purpose is to "review their experiences with them and their roles on [former] projects." Your responses should show that you are a solutions-oriented, can-do individual—someone who is able to offer verifiable results and specific instances where you achieved your goals. Highlight your career accomplishments without appearing arrogant or brash.

At this point, Bussell likes to ask candidates, "What would your manager tell me about you?" It's his favorite question:

> It's great to hear what people say or how they think they are perceived. Then I ask the same question about their business partners or internal clients or external vendors. If the role happens to be someone who is going to manage a vendor: "What would the vendor most often say about you?"

Make sure all of these topics have been given some thought, but don't sound as though you are repeating a memorized script. Bussell thought a good answer to these questions "indicates the candidate's ability to think on his or her feet."

As preparation for this stage of the interview process, you might want to review your work history with the following topics in mind: your past relationships with your boss and coworkers; your respect for the values of others; your ability to meet deadlines in a timely fashion; your ability to rally support for a project; your value-oriented approach to problem solving; your efficient use of time; your ability to multitask, especially in cross-functional aspects of a project; your initiative; your commitment to continual learning; your thorough knowledge of the industry; your ability to adapt to your surroundings as well as to the personalities of those with whom you work; your ability to remove obstacles.

After the introductory small talk, focus on the job you did and the job you want to do. Don't be tempted to go off on a tangent—unless you are specifically asked to speak about your extracurricular activities or interests. Also, do not be overly preoccupied with what you said or what you are going to say next. Stay in the moment. Bussell said:

> I try not to make any snap judgments as I am going through. It's very rare that I would end an interview early based on an answer or even a series of answers, although I have done that once or twice. The vast majority of time I give them the benefit of the interview.

If your strength lies more in the realm of technical knowledge than with people, don't immediately count yourself out of the running. According to Bussell:

> I don't judge a technician solely on his or her communication skills, because good technicians are as hard to find as good communicators. There has to be a certain level of communication; the person has to have a minimum of social graces. For instance, not doing inappropriate things at an interview, certainly not using foul language, but basically there has to be a culture fit. If the person is a little bit shy, that's not going to be a negative. I came up through the technical rank and I can still talk enough tech to make the person feel comfortable in an interview.

NOW IT'S YOUR TURN

A lot of what transpires at this point revolves around what the company has to offer you, such as the type of work environment, the kinds of projects you will be involved with, the type of people you will be reporting to or managing, or the type of culture the company projects. You are free to ask as many questions as you see fit, but according to Sherri Martin of Deere, "The interviewee should not take over the discussion with too many questions." When it comes to interpersonal skills, listening is just as integral as talking. Bussell, on the other hand, said he never gets impatient with questions, which mean "the candidate is interested and engaged. It's great answering questions. It shows the person listens, especially when he or she can connect to what I said and then ask further questions."

A PLURALITY VOTE

The panel interview can be intimidating: three, four, five people sitting at a table looking you up and down. Not only do you have to make eye contact, but now you have to make eye contact with everyone in the room without favoring one person over another. Essentially what's being evaluated in a panel interview is your skill with groups, or how well you interact with individuals in a group setting.

On many levels, a panel interview makes perfect sense. A business environment is a group environment. No one works in isolation. As an employee, you'll be expected to deal with key players in various organizational units on a daily basis, so your interpersonal skills are of primary concern to a prospective employer. You may be outnumbered in a panel interview, but the good news is that a panel interview can work to your advantage as well.

Instead of meeting with three, four, five people throughout the day, you meet with the panel. Ideally, the panel gives you an opportunity to meet with several representatives of varying levels at the company. It is likely that every member of the panel provides a different point of view or reference regarding the company, so the information you receive tends to be more balanced and thorough. Rest assured that a serious comparison of notes transpires after the interview, but at least the panel is evaluating you while you are at your best and not at the end of a grueling day.

Every organization and company handles the panel interview differently. Sometimes the panels are small (three or four people); sometimes they are large (eight or nine). The real challenge lies in building a rapport with the various interviewers.

At Verizon, panel interviews are not unusual. Verizon's Thonis said his company is a "very flat organization," which means there are not a lot of layers of bureaucracy between the applicant and the job. Thonis tells a representative from human resources that he needs someone to fill a certain position, and then he puts out feelers to find that person.

> HR is involved in the sense it knows about our need, but that department doesn't contact the applicant. We contact the person. We would never hire someone inexperienced, so we usually find them by virtue of somebody in the business who knows of somebody who is looking. That person says to us, "You know, you should really look at this person," or, "I know this person is interviewing," and then we go after him or her. There is no HR at this point.

In a recent panel interview, Thonis said three members of his department interviewed three candidates for an open position. By the time the applicants showed up for the interview, the panel had already determined all three were qualified. "First of all, I know from the résumé whether he or she is a viable candidate," Thonis said. Although Verizon has more than 200,000 employees, Thonis said the corporate communications department recruits talent like a "very small, high-level, intimate shop."

But the senior vice president of external communications said there is nothing intimidating about a panel interview in his department. Most recently, three people—the person the candidate is going to work for, his boss, and Thonis—composed the panel. "We basically don't sit there and conspire on the questions. We really have a conversation." In fact, he said the atmosphere is relaxed and he gets the candidates to open up by "engaging them in war stories."

The people who compose the panel already understand what skills are necessary to perform the job. In fact, the members of the panel are all on the same page as to what it takes to succeed in the corporate communications department at Verizon. What Thonis tries to gauge is whether candidates possess the necessary traits for the particular job. Many Fortune 500 respondents said the same thing. They try to discover if a candidate has certain personal qualities that are not only integral to performing the job but also predict the person's ability to get along with others in that particular corporate culture.

> I am looking for some very specific traits, and those traits I'm going to find out in the conversation. I'm not going to find them out by grilling them about what they know about the business. I want to make sure they

are intelligent because they are not going to be experts in telecom, especially if they come to us from outside the business. But I do expect them to know what they are doing in terms of media relations.

Because most of the candidates Verizon hires for this department have solid reputations in the business, the panel can jump right in and start to delve and dig. Don't forget that the underlying question running through every hiring manager's mind during a job interview is, "Can I work well with this person?" To get the conversation going, Thonis asks questions such as, "I hear you worked in XYZ's office. What's the most fun you've had? What's the most stressful thing you've done? What are you most proud of?" Thonis said he keeps the dialogue as informal as possible "so that people are just acting naturally." This reinforces another theme in the Fortune 500 surveys. Hiring professionals advised job seekers to be themselves. In other words, the job interview should not be an Oscar-winning performance. You may win an offer with a performance, but your chances of making a good match are minimal.

MAKING THE CONNECTION

Building a rapport with the interviewer is essential. In many respects, rapport has a lot to do with fit—how well you fit the position, how well you fit into the corporate culture, and how well you fit into the department. When rapport is established, the interviewer can actually visualize you in the new position because in many respects you share many of the same ideas and values. Engelhard's Mangiarano drove home this point, and so did Thonis.

Hiring managers basically hire people very much like themselves. Rapport goes beyond skin color or race or gender or generation. Rapport has more to do with what's going on inside. Hiring managers want to know what drives the candidate. If it's the same as what drives them—energy, ambition, initiative, team orientation—then there's a fairly good chance they will recognize those characteristics in you and bring you on board.

Tight deadlines and breaking stories are commonplace in Verizon's communications department. The atmosphere is intense at this "shop," so the second characteristic Thonis looks for in a candidate is the ability to produce very good writing in a pressure-cooker environment. He makes the distinction between managing pressure and loving pressure:

People who thrive under pressure, not people who do well under pressure. There's a difference. There are people who do well under pressure but don't like it, and they will burn out. We like our people to love pressure. They take anxiety and channel it into productive energy. And that's the way I am. The more pressure I'm under, the better I do. And those are the kind of people I like.

That's when you have to decide if the job is right for you. If you hear you have to love pressure but you break out in hives every time you are under the gun, then no matter how much you think you can transform yourself, you're going to struggle in that environment. It goes back to what Sherri Martin of Deere said: "Realize that not every position you interview for will be the right job for you." You need to recognize what makes you tick—what brings you satisfaction, what gets your adrenaline going, what matters to you most in the workplace. That type of research you cannot do on the Web.

Thonis knows his own strengths and looks for the same qualities when building his team of communicators at Verizon:

If you look at me, for example, I'm a good writer. I am a very good fast writer, so if you say to me I need a five-page paper and I need it in one hour flat, I can write it and it will be good. Will it be excellent? It will be good. Somebody would say, "Oh my God, if you had five hours to write it, it would be excellent." It probably wouldn't be any better. I'm really good, really fast, but I'm not necessarily better if you give me more time.

When hiring managers evaluate candidates, they are asking themselves these questions: Do these candidates work like me? Do they value teamwork? Do they burn the midnight oil? Are they can-do people who know how to finish strongly? That's what the face-to-face is all about, and that's why it's so important that you pick yourself up and brush yourself off when you don't get the offer. You won't be happy if you work at a job or in an environment that doesn't challenge you, and you won't last long if you feel like an outsider in an atmosphere where everyone works weekends while you are constantly longing for regular bouts of fishing at a mountain stream.

RELATIONSHIP BUILDING

Thonis said the third characteristic he looks for in a candidate is the ability to build relationships:

And the third [characteristic] is being able to work through and with people. It's about relationship building. And it's about trust and integrity. And it's about the ability to get things done through other people. Because we are a very, very big business here with 210,000 employees and no one person has all the information. So you have to be able to work with people.

Whether you intend to work at a large organization or a small start-up, word spreads. Newcomers to the job market sometimes assume that the world is bigger than it really is. Industries are much smaller than they at first appear. You build a reputation at every job—and that reputation precedes you to the next level. Thonis continued:

They have to trust you enough to know that what you are doing is important enough to be able to drag them out of meetings at a moment's notice and have the person not say, "I'll get back to you."

This was a common thread throughout the surveys. John Garofalo, an enterprise staffing and outreach manager at PSEG, said:

We do assess candidates on job-related competencies relevant to the position. For example, a manager would be assessed through a behavioral-style interview on his or her honesty and integrity, building credibility and trust, accountability, decisive action taking, and emotional intelligence.

Hiring managers need the face-to-face interview—either in a panel or one-on-one meeting—to determine whether candidates possess these attributes

ARRIVING AT A DECISION

For those still dreading a panel interview, another advantage of this format is that a consensus is arrived at more quickly than if the candidate went on five individual interviews, because the comparison of notes often takes place immediately after the interview. Thonis said, "Usually, especially if the candidate is a person we happen to know, we make a decision right away. The last time, we [the panel] talked about it for 15 minutes, and we all agreed on the person. We moved."

The panel interview can cut the process time frame in half by eliminating several days of interviewing or, in some circumstances, several hours. When a cross section of staff is on the panel, the results of the interview are even more objective. Add to this the fact that members of the panel tend to put their best feet forward when they are among their peers, and you have a winning combination.

"We have seven guiding values at our company: respect for people;
speed, simplicity, and agility; relentless pursuit of quality;
communication; customer focus; innovation; and accountability."

Bill Vlcek
Manager of Strategic Staffing
International Truck & Engine Company

CHAPTER 16

Value-Driven Questions and Answers

In the second survey, Fortune 500 hiring professionals were asked what they value in an employee. Initially, it was surprising to see that honesty, integrity, and trust led the way, with communication skills next in line. Most likely, companies are still reeling from the corporate scandals involving cooked books, outlandish CEO perks, and insider trading. As a result, values have been pushed to the forefront.

So many Fortune 500 respondents emphasized that a company's success essentially depends on the quality of its business relationships. Because honesty, integrity, and trust are integral to good relationships, employees who share these values fortify the core of the company. Good employees, good company—it's that simple.

When describing Nucor's primary strength in *Good to Great,* Jim Collins had this to say:

> In determining "the right people," the good-to-great companies placed greater weight on character attributes than on specific educational background, practical skills, specialized knowledge, or work experience. Not that specific knowledge or skills are unimportant, but they viewed these traits as more teachable (or at least learnable), whereas they believed dimensions like character, work ethic, basic intelligence, dedication to fulfilling commitments, and values are more ingrained.[1]

As a result, values and personal attributes have been nudged into the limelight, and job seekers are expected to examine how those values function in their work life. Engelhard's Mangiarano said, "We all share a fairly common set of values, and we ensure everyone is highly ethical." In an interview, Mangiarano asks probing questions that compel applicants to think about ethical behavior in the workplace.

Although most job candidates can address their strong organizational skills or problem-solving abilities at a job interview, questions that delve into their character often throw them, because applicants generally don't consider how integrity or trust or accountability impact their job performance. Host Hotels & Resorts' Whittington will say to an applicant, "Tell me what you value," and Phelps Dodge's Calderon said candidates stumble when he says, "Describe what safety means to you as a personal value."

From the Fortune 500 responses, you can expect these types of questions. You should know what core values motivate you and plan to talk about them in detail if you are asked. According to Lamoureux of Energy East:

> We tend to use a lot of the behavioral interviewing questions. Candidates typically need more time to think before they respond to these types of questions. They are hard questions to answer, so the candidate should take his or her time.

QUALITIES IN A CANDIDATE

The Fortune 500 hiring professionals listed the most important personal qualities in a job candidate. With integrity and communications skills leading the way, a number of other qualities were also cited. Consider how the values they mentioned pertain to your own work history and how you can best address these qualities during your job interview.

No one—no matter how qualified and self-motivated—has all of these qualities. Some qualities would not be suitable for some positions, and some companies place more emphasis on certain attributes over others. The intention here is to provide a specific list so that you know what Fortune 500 companies value.

One way to ensure a good outcome at your interview is to answer the interviewer's questions thoroughly and insightfully. You may be wondering how you can prepare for an interview for a specific job at a specific company armed with the information you read in this chapter. In one sense, you can never be 100 percent prepared for the questions you will be asked. So much depends on the particular company and the nature of the job. Even if your interview opens with some general questions, eventually you have to address the specifics regarding how you are qualified for that particular job.

But you can get a fairly accurate sense of how you will be quizzed by looking at some of the questions that Fortune 500 hiring managers use during their interviews.

Integrity, honesty, sincerity, and trust	Communication skills
Customer service–oriented	Dedication and loyalty
Positive, friendly, can-do personality	Strong work ethic
Team-oriented	Initiative
Strong organization skills	Speed, simplicity, and agility
Decision-making ability	Respect for people
Drive, energy, ambition	Problem-solving ability
Focus	Result-orientation
Accountability	Relentless pursuit of quality
Innovation	Enthusiasm for the job
Flexibility	Diplomacy
Motivation in seeking the job	

Even when an interviewer runs out of standard questions, the conversation may not be over. When concluding an interview at TIAA-CREF, Moll asks candidates, "What haven't I asked you that you would like to tell me about?"

Think about how you would answer these questions at your interview and build your own responses. When you review the following list of the 25 most common interview questions from the Fortune 500 participants, think about your job, your work history, your strengths and skills, what personal attributes you can bring to a new position, and how you can make a positive impact at the new company.

1. What are you looking for ideally in a job?
2. Tell me about how you got to where you are.
3. We have a number of very talented applicants for this position. Why should we select you?

4. Tell me a little bit about yourself.
5. In what area do you feel you need personal and professional development?
6. Why did you major in X?
7. Why are you leaving X Company?
8. Tell me about a specific project you recently worked on.
9. If I talked to your manager, what would that person tell me about you?
10. What interests you about this job at this company?
11. What did you learn from one of the projects that you worked on that failed?
12. If you could recreate one cultural aspect from a previous employer and bring it here, what would it be?
13. Describe your "wow factor" to me.
14. Have you acquired a reputation for anything in your work?
15. What competencies would you like us to help you develop?
16. What leader do you admire most? Why? What have you learned from that person?
17. What have your accomplishments been in your current role?
18. What are your career aspirations in both the short term and the long term?
19. What influenced you to pursue a career in your particular area of expertise?
20. Why is this position your next right move?
21. Tell me about the qualifications and experiences/skills you can bring to this organization that will add value.
22. Why did you go to X College?
23. What is motivating you to consider another position?
24. Explain to me a situation in which your business and personal ethics were challenged. Describe how you responded to it.
25. Describe your leadership style.

Remember what PepsiCo's Neil Bussell said: "I've been interviewed more times than I care to remember . . . but you still have to put things in the best light." No matter how difficult the question, your replies must emphasize the positive and cast your work history "in the best light." Even if you have to account for a gap in your work history or a layoff, portray it in the best terms. Allied's O'Leary said, "Be honest about the gap, but explain how you took advantage of the time off."

Timken's Barry Martin said candidates often stumble when he asks them for a brief overview of their career ("People tend to talk way too much") so remember to be sensitive to the interviewer's time. Be clear, be thoughtful, and be confident. According to Lara Crane, a manager of staffing at Alltel, applicants would be wise to:

> Learn from the interview. Use this time to do a self-evaluation and set goals. Interviews often help you become more confident with your skill set and abilities. Examine what you have, what you want, and how you want to improve yourself.

The following responses to the questions reflect various professions, but they should give you a general idea of the direction you need to go. When you speak, try to keep the tone conversational and friendly at all times. Employers are trying to gauge your skills, but they are also evaluating whether you have the right personality to fit in with the group or department.

THE QUESTIONS AND ANSWERS

1. What are you looking for ideally in a job?

Reply (Computer Programmer). I have ten years' experience as a programmer analyst, so I have a good sense of my strengths and what I need from a job. Even though I am focused on data, working in a team environment suits my personality. Ideally, my coworkers will energize me. I like working on a team because it gives me an opportunity to learn different styles and next-generation technologies. In my last job, the team consisted of eight programmers. Each of us brought something different to the table.

After thinking about my next career move, I decided—after working for the two smaller companies I mentioned earlier—that ideally I want to be working for a large, reputable company. Affiliation has always been important to me. Your company has a stable, yet strong, market presence in Internet-based systems. Web hosting and data analysis are my strong points. The possibilities in this field are infinite, so I would like to work in an environment where my inventiveness is encouraged.

2. Tell me about how you got to where you are.

Reply (Sales Manager). As you can see by my résumé, I started at the bottom as a sales representative at GVBC. I did print advertising and conducted outside sales with the local businesses in the community. I did well, but there were periods of the month when I was hungry. So I created my own business doing promotion for local bars and clubs at night. It took off, and I managed to bring 500 to 1,200 people into those clubs on a regular basis. In fact, I built the company from the ground up, hired a few people, and was able to leave my day job. I also had enough extra revenue to finish my master's degree.

A few of my business associates suggested I go to ENT, Inc., because it was a fast-growing company with lots of opportunity. I think I was hired by that company because of my strong sales background and communications skills. I also have a knack for cultivating new clients and expanding territories. I have been with ENT for five years now. It's a good company. In one way, the growth at ENT reminds me of your company, but on another level, I think you offer something that ENT cannot provide: stability and more opportunity to advance. I also am eager to break into online ad sales. But back to ENT: I was promoted quickly. I continually exceeded expectations. In my first year, I won two of the four company-wide sales contests. I then won a top performer award in the fourth quarter. This moved me up to senior account executive the following year—in April actually. I just want to mention here that I achieved my sales goals 83 percent of time while at ENT. Last year, I was promoted again to sales manager, as I was ranked number-one East Coast salesperson and generated 21 percent of all sales in 2007. I am a go-getter, and I am very adept at listening to clients' needs so that good relationships develop. That's a quick overview, but basically that's how I got to where I am today and why moving on to online ad sales is a natural fit for me.

3. We have a number of talented applicants for this position. Why should we select you?

Reply (Magazine Editor). I have a diverse background with experience in many facets of production and content development. I have worked on both sides of the editorial process—as a writer and editor—so I am a better manager because I understand the process thoroughly. I also think I'm ready for another challenge. I have always been a reader of this magazine, and I admire its focus and content. As an editor, I have a good sense of emerging trends. It's something I have always enjoyed about this business—being a few months ahead of the curve. Another strength that makes me particularly suited to this position is that I am at my best when faced with tight deadlines. I am proud of the fact that in the five years I've been at BCD, I have never missed a deadline. You mentioned that the pace at this company can be frenetic. This is the type of atmosphere where I do my best work, as I prefer working in a high-energy environment. I am much more effective when there isn't too much downtime.

4. Tell me a little bit about yourself.

Reply (Accountant). After graduating from Kansas City State, I worked as an accountant at D&L, where I spent most of my time analyzing quarterly and yearly financial statement balances. Occasionally I worked on client portfolios and composed audit reports. It was my first introduction to the business and I liked the work, but I wanted more diversification, so I returned to school and got my M.B.A. in finance at the University of Delaware. I'm glad I spent some time at D&L before going back for my M.B.A. By the time I went to ARD, which was an interim step for me while I completed my master's, I had a good idea of what direction to follow. The telecom boom was at its height when I was at ARD, so I was knee-deep in daily client reports on telecom services and equipment. My reports focused on projections of equity prices. It was an exciting time for telecom—change was minute-by-minute practically. Oh, yes, at ARD I also constructed quantitative models for earnings and equity valuations.

With my background in sell-side equity research, I made a move to TDS, which was a significant step up for me. At TDS, I was a member of several four-person deal teams. We did a lot of due diligence, credit analyses, some negotiation of transaction terms, and loan documentations. I spent quite a bit of time with investors. I am very persuasive, and I was adept at convincing investors to jump on board several key initiatives. Two years ago, I was promoted to Transaction Manager. I currently have 13 accounts worth $600 million in the media and communications portfolio. Recently I negotiated two loan defaults of Argentine cable companies. The negotiation resulted in a partial receipt of interest payments and loan principal. The company—and particularly my supervisor—considered the negotiation very successful.

5. In what area do you feel you need personal and professional development?

Reply (Reporter). I move very quickly. I think it has a lot to do with working in this business for ten years—dealing with breaking news and deadlines. Where I may need some improvement is in my expectations that others will move as quickly as I do. I sometimes feel impatient when things must go through endless channels for approval. I don't let my displeasure show, but I am always wondering why things don't unfold at a much faster pace. Part of the problem is that I work project to project. I write one article, and I am on to the next, so I can be single-mindedly focused and not have enough understanding of those who are multifocused. This is an area where I could use a little more development—not so much for their sake but for mine. That way I won't be disappointed the next time someone tells me they will get back to me . . . in two weeks. On the other hand, I don't think I would be such a good reporter if I weren't so single-minded. But I would like to be more sensitive to the working styles of others when there are a lot of interests competing for their time.

6. Why did you major in X?

Reply (Biologist). The first semester I was at college, I was convinced I wanted to be a veterinarian. I grew up with two dogs, three cats, and an assortment of other small critters. So I took a lot of biology classes—on animal behavior, marine biology, plant systematics—and then I took a class on genetics that basically changed my whole direction. It may have had something to do with the professor, who was amazing, but suddenly I found myself more interested in human applications than in animals. I knew I had made the right decision after a few more classes with that professor. She actually helped me find an internship and also refocused my major. She was very influential. I consider her an important mentor for me while I was at school.

I know I'm just starting out, but I think I have a lot to offer your company. I am a strong writer, too, so I was hoping to use this skill in a multidisciplinary manner. Without totally getting away from clinical trials, running instruments, and other bench work that I got a taste of during my internship at YZ Pharmaceuticals, I would also like to work on reports with other scientists for, say, the Food and Drug Administration. I enjoy collaborative projects and I know the science already, so the technical background will have a real impact on my ability to communicate.

7. Why are you leaving X company?

Reply (Office Manager to Publicist). Actually, as an office manager, my intention was to round out my skills. At my first job out of college, I was an assistant director at an art gallery, where I utilized my background in fine arts. Although I enjoyed working with the public, writing press releases, and managing day-to-day operations, I discovered I needed to strengthen some of my other skills. That's why I went to DEF. There I was able to immerse myself in the technology that will further my goals, which is to represent artists and writers in larger markets.

At my current job, I develop and maintain databases and tracking sheets as well as grant-related tracking. I also manage the internal news/press cataloging system. I have become involved with website maintenance in recent months—a skill I have wanted to develop for a long time—by working closely with the CTO on technical support. He encouraged me to take an HTML night course at the community school, which I have just completed. I think this will help me when I deal with clients who need to know how to place the contents of the media kit on their website and thereby allow reporters to access the information instantly.

8. Tell me about a specific project you recently worked on.

Reply (Director of Systems). My last project involved supporting a large equity trading exchange. We had to provide a functional migration from a manually intensive method for brokers on the floor to express their trading interest to an electronic method. Before the migration, brokers on the trading floor verbally expressed their interest to the specialists, who had to manually enter that interest into a template at their workstations. This was time-consuming for a fast market. The new project, the migration, was intended to allow the brokers to express their interest electronically from their handheld terminals and have their quotes pass through our trading systems and arrive in the specialists' open-order books as orders to buy or sell. This streamlined the process considerably.

My role was to coordinate the planning, development, testing, and implementation activities across diverse groups within my company as well as to outside vendors. I had to raise and mitigate issues, report status to senior management, and develop testing methodologies. The major challenge was to ensure a coordinated development effort among these diverse groups and maintain a strict cutover schedule because the project was run under a BBB-mandated delivery time frame. Time-to-market was of the essence. This new functionality was needed to maintain the SSS's role as the leading marketplace for equity trading.

9. If I talked to your manager, what would that person tell me about you?

Reply (Marketing Director). He would say I understand niches well and that I am creative. In addition, my communication skills let me move effortlessly between the newsroom trenches and the boardroom. Those are my major strengths, but he would also emphasize that I know how to sell and also what salespeople need to close the deal. I recently developed highly successful publicity campaigns for our daily newspaper—plus five weeklies—that produce revenue from our niche markets. He would say I have a good understanding of the needs of these diverse markets. The audience for the weeklies includes Latinos, other immigrant populations, African Americans, artists, and young professionals. In addition, for the weeklies I provided writing, editorial, and creative concepts. Advertising pages have doubled in the last three months.

My supervisor would say that my leadership skills are excellent as well. I lead a team of eight writers and artists for the five weeklies—creative members notorious for following their own individual lead—yet we produce a cohesive and revenue-building lineup. To top it off, we consistently come in on budget and on schedule.

10. What interests you about this job at this company?

Reply (HR Generalist). I am a good fit for this position, and there are several aspects of this job that interest me. X Corporation is an international company with a diverse workforce. I am fluent in Polish and Spanish, so I think this fluency will be useful in day-to-day employee relations. I also hope to work closely with your global staffing and recruitment departments. I noticed this company provides many opportunities for advancement. And you mentioned your policy of promoting internally before you look outside the company to fill key positions.

I have a bachelor's degree in psychology, so this background should prove useful in your Employee Career Development Department, which directs many initiatives on training, safety, and counseling. I have excellent communication skills, and I am particularly adept at conflict management and problem solving.

In my last position in the personnel department of BDC, I was often called on to deliver presentations on various training modules, especially safety issues. And I certainly can be trusted with confidentiality issues. In addition, I noticed on your website that the position requires a familiarity with both Microsoft Office and PeopleSoft. I am thoroughly proficient with Microsoft and I did use PeopleSoft for expense accounts in my last position.

11. What did you learn from one of the projects that you worked on that failed?

Reply (Facilities Manager). I decided to put a full-scale ergonomics program into place back in 1997. Just as we were seriously considering the implementation, I started to receive a lot of literature from a small company that offered good prices and all-around service: evaluations, safety plans, and the like. The literature from this company intrigued me—the brochures, the regular correspondence, the press releases—and over the course of the next few months, we began to establish a relationship with this new supplier.

At first we ordered piecemeal, and I was quite satisfied with the products and services, and then we jumped on board for a complete installation of keyboard trays, height-adjustable workstations, and so on. The supplier was very enthusiastic, and he had worked with some large outfits.

As it turned out, the investment of time was considerable, and the supplier bit off more than he could chew. We had a contract, but there still were serious delays and setbacks. He was a nice guy and I sympathized . . . to a point, but then we basically had to rethink our whole program and supplement products and installations from a different supplier to meet all the specifications. Luckily the new supplier supplemented what the smaller company could not do within the time constraints. We eventually implemented a very successful ergonomics program after a few sleepless nights, but the experience with the initial supplier taught me a valuable lesson. I usually buy only from suppliers in which the relationship is a long-standing one—built after many years in this business. But comprehensive ergonomics programs that addressed the needs of the computer workstation were relatively new. I got caught up in the newness of it all and didn't recognize that the scope of this project was too large for a small vendor. Normally I would seek recommendations from other managers in my network, but in this instance I bought into the initial supplier's enthusiasm and was lured by the better prices, hard sell, and sleek marketing materials. I took full responsibility for the delays and am happy we could rescue the project. I manage risk well, but from that point on, I resolved to proceed with even more caution with new vendors and new practices, especially for large-scale projects without tried-and-true comparisons. The good news is that my company was one of the first to have a full-fledged ergonomics program in place. That risk I don't regret because our workers' compensation claims declined. We reduced workplace injuries considerably by putting the program in as early as we did.

12. If you could recreate one cultural aspect from a previous company and bring it here, what would it be?

Reply (Equity Sales Trader). The environment at Corporation X is rigorous. We work long hours, weekends even, and the standards are extremely high. But there is a real emphasis on teamwork and community focus. Regardless of the strong work ethic and high expectations at Corporation X, we are encouraged to participate in Community Team. In fact, last year I was given a week off to volunteer at the local Head Start Program. You tend to get caught up in the daily high-pressure responsibilities of your job, and the time off refreshed me and gave me a better perspective. I had to tackle different issues and reach out on a level that was way out of my comfort zone. I certainly learned how to communicate in the simplest terms—liquidity and supply/demand don't have much meaning to little kids. I felt good about the service I provided. I also appreciated the fact that a company as rigorous and demanding as X takes its responsibility to the community seriously. Even though the company donates significantly on a philanthropic level, it also moves beyond just dollars and cents. We invest our time in the community, and then the community gets a better idea of who we are. It's mutually beneficial.

13. Describe your "wow factor" to me.

Reply (Webmaster). This may sound odd, but functionality is a wow for me. If it doesn't work, I'm not interested in the fancy interface or Flash design. It's all about easy navigation. Many users are not yet completely competent when it comes to the Web. One "clickisode"—that's what I call a mistake made by a user—and the buyer leaves the site before completing the purchase. I also like the fact that Web design allows me to use so many skills. I troubleshoot, create, publish—all in the name of a multimedia experience. I am lucky because I get to use my right brain/left brain: problem solving, decision making, creative, analytical. It's a great mix for someone who thinks as I do. Lots of Web designers are excellent at user interface and lousy at navigation. That's not going to work for me—or in e-commerce. You need to be able to capture data, persuade users to view a lot of pages, help them stick around for a while by allowing them to navigate easily and ultimately purchase something.

14. Have you acquired a reputation for anything in your work?

Reply (Grant Writer). Yes, I am resourceful and I know how to build relationships with key players. It has a lot to do with my political savvy, but I am also known as an excellent project manager who can close deals in a timely manner. No detail is too small. If a contingency category holds up a transaction, it's important. In a recent $2.5 million deal, I recently acted as a liaison to several government agencies and a nonprofit organization. I created a business plan and grant to develop a for-profit business that enabled low-income residents to gain full employment. I did this by searching and developing the potential funding resources. I drafted an evaluation plan, prepared the documents for submission, rewrote the document to their specifications, and then followed through to ensure that the proposal met the guidelines. I never hide behind email or avoid difficult situations. People should not have to spend hours on the telephone getting a minor detail resolved. That's why I set realistic expectations from the get-go, and I develop relationships with people who are not excessively bogged down in bureaucracy and inefficiency. Sometimes bringing all the parties concerned together is a gargantuan task, but I am known to be highly successful at brainstorming solutions for divergent groups. I have a lot of repeat business, which attests to the high level of satisfaction my clients have.

15. What competencies would you like us to help you develop?

Reply (Customer Service Account Executive). Actually, I would like to develop two areas. First, I would like to build my technical skills. In my last position, I had many opportunities to use the new technology as well as teach it to customers—they called me the "bridge expert" because I could help anyone understand the basics—so I am very comfortable with technology. I noticed on your website that for management associates you offer an opportunity to pursue an M.S. degree in information systems that is available on site through XX Institute. I would like to pursue that program. I am an advocate of lifelong learning, plus one of my strong points is discovering gaps in data. I see myself excelling in this program. Another way I would like to develop is by learning more management strategies. While at X Company, I was the youngest woman promoted to management in the North Jersey District, so I believe I have real potential, but I think I need better methods for getting others to jump on board an action plan.

16. What leader do you admire most and why? What have you learned from that person?

Reply (Account Manager). I just read *The Miracle of St. Anthony* about Bob Hurley and his coaching tenure at St. Anthony's.[2] I just finished coaching my daughter in basketball, and now she's moving up to the high school level, which is probably why I can relate to the book. Hurley coaches basketball at a small high school in Jersey City with 11 classrooms and fewer than 200 students. Hurley has mainly dysfunctional kids. About 50 percent of the students come from homes that are below the poverty level. During his basketball coaching tenure, Hurley has had 800 victories, 22 state titles, and two national championships. The school doesn't even have a gym it can call its own. The book is about St. Anthony's undefeated 2003–2004 season.

Hurley accomplishes his goals by instilling discipline and having high expectations—regardless of the fact that a lot people would have looked at the numbers and written off these kids long ago. Hurley has gotten a lot of offers to coach elsewhere, but he's dedicated—and he knows he's effective in that environment. I admire this man's compassion, code of discipline and optimism, and standards of excellence. I am also impressed that he has sent every one of his kids on to college.

Whenever my direct reports give me a hard time now, I tell myself that if Hurley can get his team to achieve—time and time again—then managing my group is really painless by comparison. I just have to keep my standards high, lead by example, and provide a specific framework in which my direct reports can achieve their objectives without micromanagement. My group is attuned now to what our primary purpose is.

17. What have your accomplishments been in your current role?

Reply (Vice President/Sales). I am particularly proud of the fact that I was able to build a $600 million open-system business from scratch in five years. In addition—in fact simultaneously—I increased sales productivity 50 percent and generated more than 70 percent of this business from new accounts. Part of this success was due to the economic boom, but I also managed 2,000 people who were motivated to move wholeheartedly beyond the momentum.

I was also a member of the operations committee, which approved product directions, set marketing strategies, determined corporate expense plans, and partnered investment. This was the major steering committee at DGA, so its impact was substantial.

And I successfully managed a budget in excess of $1 billion, which covered P&L, credit, technical support, account management, training, advertising, and promotion. Another accomplishment was the complete restructuring a few years back of field function to integrate VARs, OEMs, ISVs, telesales, teleservice, agents, subcontractors, integration channel partners, major accounts, and end users.

18. What are your career aspirations, in both the short term and the long term?

Reply (Account Executive/Retail). I make resolutions every year, and I try to stick to them closely. Each year, I review where I want to be the following year—both professionally and personally. So I have a one-year plan, but I also have a five-year plan. Professionally, my one-year plan is to spearhead international expansion. I have already increased my company's overseas market presence by 25 percent. I am especially interested in the new Chinese marketplace. I just came back from a trip to Beijing and it was unlike anything I have ever seen before. It's an enormous emerging market, and I was so enthusiastic about the customer base that I even considered signing up for a language class in simple Chinese, even though I know fluency in this language would definitely fall into my five-year plan—maybe even my ten-year plan.

Just recently, I teamed with other senior executives and played a key role in diversification of our product line by introducing new products to existing clients and marketing new brands to third parties. My one-year goal for sales growth of this line is 25 percent. I am almost there, and there are six months still left to the year. I intend to come as close to meeting these goals as possible, even if I am offered a position with your organization in the near future.

My long-term plan, five years from now, is to continue to work hard and advance. As I already mentioned, I am particularly focused on the new market in China. I would welcome the opportunity to expand your presence there and become a business pioneer in that new marketplace. It's the fastest-growing economy in the world.

19. What influenced you to pursue a career in your particular area of expertise?

Reply (Paralegal). I have a bachelor's degree in history and am a diehard history buff, but I realized my career options once I graduated were limited, unless I chose to teach, so I became a certified paralegal. Research and fact gathering appeal to me more than teaching. When you study history, your main objective is to make sense of complicated situations by looking at cause-and-effect. The answers are not always evident, so you need to look closely at how one thing is related to another. Because I'm good at examining cause-and-effect, I asked myself in what field I could use this skill and earn a living. It seemed a natural fit to gravitate toward law. The law interests me—historically and otherwise—and working as a paralegal allows me to use the research, investigative, and writing skills I picked up as a history major.

20. Why is this position your next right move?

Reply (Media Planner). I actually think I am the right candidate for the job, but I am equally attracted to your company. I have worked in all mediums—television, print, guerilla marketing—so I know this background will be useful in your media marketing initiatives for national brands. Your media lab is a hotbed of creativity, and I would fit in perfectly there. I see enormous potential for growth in wireless, instant messaging, broadband, and gaming. Your company is positioned best to take advantage of this.

I also like the work atmosphere here. You mentioned that brainstorming and team initiatives are the rule rather than the exception at X Company. This suits me just fine. My background suggests that I work best in a collaborative environment. The digital video documentary I worked on in 2004 required that I write, edit, produce, and even direct, but I had to work closely with a team of about ten other people to make this joint effort as successful as it was. I think I should mention that I am cost-conscious, but I would like to work for a company that has enough resources to put a multimedia plan in motion.

21. Tell me about the qualifications and experiences/skills you can bring to this organization that will add value?

Reply (Administrative Assistant). I have good skills overall, but I excel when a lot of detail is involved. I am an excellent proofreader. Reports that require a high degree of accuracy and technical knowledge showcase my talents well. I went to school at night to finish my associate's degree, so I bring a high level of proficiency to my other responsibilities as well. I was continually chosen to develop and work on specialized safety reports and also highly protected risk reports that require accuracy and technical know-how. I am also adept at multitasking. My computer skills are more than up to speed. I am proficient in Word, Windows, Flow Chart, Excel,

WordPerfect, and Lotus, and I am very good at Internet research. Customers have commented on my friendly and cordial manner on the telephone as well. I noticed that your job posting emphasized organizational skills. Well, my organizational skills are well tuned.

22. Why did you go to X college?

Reply (Engineering). College X is far away from my home base, but I thought that would be a good thing. I come from a small town, and I think you tend to get a narrow view of the world after spending 12 years in one school system. Also, as you already mentioned, X College has an excellent program in engineering. The professors in that department are respected—and some even internationally renowned—throughout business and industry. I participated in the 3/2 engineering program, which allowed me to put off deciding the specific area of engineering to pursue until my fourth year of college. For three years, I studied physics. That turned out to be a good option for me, because initially, I thought I wanted to be an electrical engineer, and as you can see, I ended up becoming a mechanical engineer—without any backtracking. The 3/2 program also gave me a broader background than I would have gotten otherwise.

23. What is motivating you to consider another position?

Reply (Systems Analyst/Senior Manager). I have spent the last eight years at AB Company, and I feel as though I need more challenge and diversification. I am very good at what I do, but my primary responsibilities are not allowing me to grow sufficiently. I fulfill all the requirements of the job and even exceed expectations, but every time I lobby for a different role, I am told that I am doing such a great job as a senior manager in charge of the BARAMIS and AVPS systems that they don't want to rock the boat and upset everyone. I have been promoted from manager to senior manager, so I know they appreciate my ability to get a job done, but I need to be challenged on a more regular basis. I have experience with all the development lifecycles and many program management methodologies, and I would like to manage enterprise-wide programs.

24. Explain to me a situation in which your business and personal ethics were challenged. Describe how you responded to it.

Reply (Advertising Manager). That's a hard question. Let me think about it a minute. Okay. The company was losing tons of money, as were many others when the market went flat. The CEO became very anxious. After weeks of rumors, he told a group of his executives he was going to send around an email to everyone in the company the following week announcing he would lay off one person in each department. Morale was already bad because of the company's fiscal uncertainty.

I knew the most recently hired ad exec was going to be laid off. The problem was this ad exec had told me the day before she was about to turn down an offer from a competitor. She was going to decline the offer as soon as the guy came back from his business trip. This was not a large company, and everyone was on a first-name basis, so I went to the CEO and told him that if he was intent on sending out that email and firing people in a few weeks, then he should just bite the bullet and get it over with because morale was already so low. I suggested he send out his email immediately so we could move forward. I did not want to betray anyone's confidence in this matter. The CEO sent the email out the next day; the woman preempted her layoff and accepted the offer at the new company. I felt I handled that dilemma well.

25. Describe your leadership style.

Reply (Financial Adviser). I have 18 years' experience at old-line companies, so I have managed large groups. I know how to create good outcomes primarily because I manage people well. First, I am an excellent communicator. I clearly state our goals and objectives to the group and delegate responsibilities. When I first started in my career, I had difficulty delegating. I thought no one could do it as well as I could. Then I realized it's more important to sacrifice a little perfection and instead get everyone involved. At the end of the day, the group accomplishes more than I ever could. On a recent global revenue plan, we had several new hires working on key sectors, so instead of reassigning the work to some already overburdened managers or doing it myself, I taught the new hires what they needed to know. They made a few mistakes, but we corrected it immediately. I like to teach now. It's important the company isn't so reliant on the expertise of one person. It makes the company stronger as well as the group.

THE NATURE OF THE QUESTIONS

Title VII of the Civil Rights Act prohibits employers from discriminating against candidates based on their sex, race, religion, age, or national origin. Even though this federal law has been in place since 1964, it still does not entirely prevent employers from asking illegal questions. If you are asked a question that suggests some form of subtle discrimination, do not react defensively by spouting off the telephone number of your lawyer. Occasionally these questions are asked by the interviewer in innocence. Sometimes the questions are so well disguised that even interviewers don't recognize the illegal nature of their inquiries. Be tactful. If you don't feel comfortable answering the question, either change the subject or suggest that you don't think the interviewer's question is relevant to the requirements necessary to do the job. If the question is exceedingly intrusive, then think twice about pursuing the job.

And what is sensitive territory? Anything that deals with age, alcohol or drug use, conviction record, citizenship, credit rating, disabilities, height or weight requirements, marital or family status, membership in an organization, military service, national origin, personal appearance, political affiliation, race or color, religion, sex, or union affiliation. Under certain circumstances, it is legal for employers to ask sensitive questions, but you should know the basics. Look online at the *Washington Post* website for "38 Illegal, Sensitive, and Stupid Interview Questions . . . and How to Respond" by Ronald L. Krannich for a better understanding of uncomfortable situations that might arise in an interview.

YOUR QUESTIONS MATTER

Once you answer the prospective employer's questions honestly and thoroughly, you get an opportunity to ask a few questions of your own. Ideally, your questions should grow organically from the Q&A that just unfolded. The interviewer said something that piqued your interest, and you made a mental note to ask for more information about it. Usually, but not always, you have an opportunity to ask your questions at the end of the interview. Occasionally, you get an opportunity to ask questions as you move along. Watch for cues from the interviewer. At Engelhard, where an applicant may meet up to ten people, Mangiarano said, "I ask them to let me get through my interview, and then I would be happy to respond to any questions they may have." If explicit directions on how the interview will be conducted are provided, then follow those directions to the letter.

Always have extra questions geared toward specific departments. Mangiarano explained:

> I find it off-putting when candidates don't ask me questions because it tells me that they haven't done any homework on us or about the job. And when a candidate comes to me third or fourth in the process and he or she says to me, "Well, all my questions were already answered by the other interviewers," I challenge them with, "Well, I'm the head of HR; if you've got questions about our business, things that we do, people issues, career path opportunities, development opportunities, I'm the person to ask." It surprises me that I give people the opportunity to ask questions and they decline.

Can you ever ask too many questions? Yes, according to HSBC's Brian Little: "A candidate should use the questions to show interest and, to a certain degree, to display their knowledge of the organization and position. Too many questions would indicate the candidate is unprepared." It's all about the right questions.

This chapter ends with sample interview questions that point you toward the types of questions you should ask. Each company has its own protocols, but you probably will speak with several people from the new company before you are hired. Ask relevant questions based on the person to whom you are speaking and on the phase of the interview process. Don't ask the HR generalist, "What are the most critical goals in the next three months for the department?" Save that question for the department head. Verizon's Thonis added, "We ask people to ask us questions because their questions tell us how they react and respond to us—and it's a sign of their mental vitality."

The questions should be organic to the "discussion" you are having. Fred Kavali, a retired engineer/businessman, who recently donated $75 million to ten scientific research institutes, spoke about his first job in Los Angeles after getting off the boat from Norway in 1956. He didn't know much about sensors when he was hired at a small company, but two years later he started his own company. Kavali said, "In America, you don't have to know anything. You just have to ask the right question." He sold Kavlico for $340 million in 2000 and now spends his time endowing scientific research; three of the eight 2004 Nobel prizes for science went to scientists affiliated with Kavali's institutes.

Write down a list of questions that are organic to doing the new job. This should be part of your preparation for the interview, but don't memorize stock questions and answers. If you perceive an opening to ask your own questions during the Q&A

segment of your interview, then make sure those questions are in response to the topic at hand. For instance, if the interviewer spends time detailing the new email marketing offering for which you would be responsible, you may want to ask a specific question regarding whether you would be determining new methods or fine-tuning existing campaigns. An organic question—one that specifically relates to the information being exchanged—indicates that you understand the requirements of the new job.

When you look at the sample questions, use them only at the appropriate interval; don't just ask for the sake of asking. As Trang Gulian, a human resources manager at Fannie Mae, said, "Come prepared with well-thought-out questions, [but] have your listening hat on" as well.

Questions to Ask About Development and Advancement

- What is the normal interval before someone is considered for promotion?
- Do you assess employees' roles regularly?
- How do you develop people at this company?
- How do you help improve skills in teams?
- Do you provide cross-training?
- Do you provide cross-assignments?
- What kind of outside training opportunities do you provide to heighten skills and teach new knowledge?
- What happened to the person I am replacing? Did that person receive a promotion? Move to a different department? Leave the company?
- Is this company proactive in offering advanced training to develop personnel?
- Can you tell me something about the corporate culture?

GAPS IN WORK HISTORY

What do you do if you have to explain a work gap on your résumé? According to Creative Group's Meghan Gonyo, "Legally an employer or someone who is interviewing a candidate is not allowed to ask about a gap like that. The correct answer always is 'family leave' or 'personal.' And that's it. You know, life happens." Much depends on the circumstances. The good news is that if you have been asked to come in for an interview, the employer is obviously interested in your explanation. Even though being laid off is traumatic, it's not that unusual. One Fortune 500 participant said two of the companies she worked for were downsized, and she even listed this information on her résumé.

Generally, the respondents to the Fortune 500 survey said that you should deal with a work gap—being laid off or fired or out of work for an extended period of time— as directly and honestly (and briefly) as possible. Everything comes out in the background check, so don't fudge. Fannie Mae's Gulian advised: "Provide enough details without sounding negative or bitter. Use the experience as a learning opportunity. Candidates should focus on adding value going forward, not backward." Host Hotels & Resorts' Lisa Whittington said to keep your responses "short and to the point." Barry Martin of Timken suggested that applicants who have been fired from a previous job should provide only the most relevant details: "Only as much as requested by the interviewer. If the particulars are pertinent, the interviewer will ask for them, and the candidate should supply them fully and openly." Alltel's Crane said:

> I think the candidate should be honest. I understand personality differences and job fit can be contributing factors to whether or not a person is successful in a career. If the reason for being fired is not illegal, then they may still succeed in a position within our company.

As for sequencers, those who have made the decision to opt out of the workforce to raise a family or take care of an elderly parent, the same advice applies. Dwell on the positive transferable skills you acquired while you were attending to other matters. SYSCO's Reeves stated that "it is perfectly acceptable to take time off or work part-time. Just tell the truth." Often individuals on family leave are involved in volunteer work or take less demanding positions. Lamoureux, a director of human resources planning at Energy East, said:

> People are always worried about providing an honest answer to why there is a gap in their employment if it's related to their family. . . . That being said, it would be helpful for candidates to demonstrate how they kept their skills up-to-date during the time they were off, especially because business is changing so quickly.

KEEPING YOUR SKILLS POLISHED

Several references have been made to keeping your skills fresh and up-to-date. By all means, take community college courses, enroll in certification classes, and investigate development programs. Many programs are inexpensive or even free. Even many state unemployment offices offer retraining at no cost. The Gateway Workforce Development Program, a Bronx-based employment services organization partnered with Columbia University, selects 20 candidates to attend class once a week in the computer lab at the university to obtain "on-the-job" experience in a real working situation. Other state and local organizations offer similar programs.

Questions to Ask About the Department

- Who is the primary client/customer for the services of this department?
- What problems do you anticipate I will face in my new role?
- Will I be expected to work on existing campaigns or will I be expected to create appropriate change when the time comes?
- If you could use one word to describe this department, what would it be?
- What are some of the unwritten rules of working in this department?
- Could you describe a typical day in this department?
- On a scale of 1 to 10, how important is teamwork in this department?
- Do you expect this department to grow in size and scope within the next year?

If you are currently raising a family or taking care of a disabled or elderly family member, commit yourself to keeping your marketable skills current. Plan ahead; investigate the programs in your area and sign up for a class as soon as possible. Although courses about gourmet cooking and Zen meditation may be good for the soul, it is especially important that you keep your computer skills current. The digital age is in full swing, and technology changes so quickly that you may need annual—or even semiannual—brush-up courses just to keep pace. Another advantage to freelance/contract work is that many of the agencies that handle this have on-site training. Creative Group's Gonyo said individuals can go to one of their nationwide offices and take training, without paying a fee. Gonyo adds:

> Highlight your knowledge of Excel, MS Office, Microsoft Word, PowerPoint. If you want to get up-to-date on that without spending any money, you can register at an [employment] agency. . . . The resources are there, and they are easy to obtain and they are usually free.

Student internships are also invaluable in providing marketable skills. In fact, these programs are so ubiquitous now that you may have to explain to a prospective employer why you did not participate in an internship during your college tenure. Even if the internship is only remotely connected to the new job, it is still valuable because of the real-world exposure it's given a newcomer. Because working in an office can be a shock to the system, employers prefer that you work out these kinks in an internship.

You may have reached a point in your life where you want to change things dramatically by embarking on a whole new career. A new direction obviously takes more planning, but the strategy remains the same. Find the company or organization or even your own business or profession that is a good match for the new you. Then develop the skills needed to enter and flourish.

Career changes usually begin by easing into the new business on a part-time, volunteer, or entry-level basis. For instance, if you want to become an interior decorator, work at a shop or business in that field, then get the necessary certification at night. If you want to fulfill your lifelong aspiration of becoming a painter or a playwright, volunteer at a gallery or a community theater. A second career can be as demanding as the first. Recently two friends made the change: one woman changed her profession as a gaming executive to become a firefighter; the other was a dentist who became a biology teacher at an inner-city school. Starting a new career or a new business can often translate into 60-hour workweeks. But at least you will love what you're doing—and that's the whole idea.

Questions to Ask about Your Management Role

- Who are the key stakeholders (customers, senior management, peers) who can affect my success or failure?
- Will I be able to read past performance reviews of the people in the group I am going to manage?
- How does this group keep metrics of its success?
- Is there someone in particular to whom I should speak regarding the department's consulting services?
- How would you rate the capabilities of the staff I am going to manage?
- Can you identify the steps I must take to maximize my success as a leader of this group?
- If the group had a personality, how would you describe it?
- Does the group normally meet its deadlines?
- Can you describe the projects in which the group had trouble overcoming obstacles? What were the specific obstacles?
- Can you describe some of the projects at which the group excels?

Every Fortune 500 respondent said applicants are expected to ask questions. How many depends on the level of the job and the rapport with the interviewer; however, be aware that most interviews last approximately an hour, especially if you are interviewing with a representative of human resources, where the interview is more structured than when you meet with a hiring manager or peers in the department. Thrivent's Palmer recommended that "the first thing a candidate needs to verify is the amount of time . . . permitted for questions. If . . . a specific amount of time . . . can be allotted to questions, [candidates] should ensure they do not run over that time limit."

That's one reason to keep your questions focused on the areas of particular interest to you. You probably won't have an opportunity to have all of your questions answered initially, so pace yourself. Be considerate of the interviewer's time and don't be tempted to pose a throwaway question just for the sake of asking something. Aim for a concise and equal exchange of information. Jabil Circuit's Otto agreed: "We encourage our candidates to ask questions and interview us just as much as we are interviewing them to see if it is a fit for both parties concerned."

Questions to Ask Your Future Boss

- How many direct reports are you responsible for?
- You have a lot of responsibility. How accessible are you to those you manage?
- How is conflict managed in the department? Do you resolve it, or do you expect the team to manage themselves?
- How often will you informally assess my performance?
- How do you help improve the skills of the team?
- What committees exist within the department?
- What types of measurement systems do you have in place within the department?
- What are the department's short-term and long-term goals?
- Are there any organizational obstacles that may impede you from achieving your objectives within the department?
- What are two major goals I would be expected to achieve this year?
- How do you see me fitting into the department?
- I just want to make sure I understand everything and we are all on the same page. Can you give me an idea of what you see me doing on a day-to-day basis?

CHAPTER 17

When the Offer Is Made

The interview was a success! The match has been made, and the new job fits you like your favorite pair of jeans. All signals are go that you are the answer to the company's dilemma. You want the new job, and the employer wants you.

Before you sit down to contemplate the company's offer, consider what really motivates you. For some, money may be the primary drive; for others, it's a flexible schedule; for many, it's engaging work. Decide what's important to you and then be prepared to do . . . more research. When you first started the process, you got a general idea of the salary range for someone in your profession. That information is easy to find just by searching various websites for salary ranges, going to career centers, or speaking to other professionals in your field. But now you have a specific offer in a specific town with a specific company—and it's time to crunch the numbers.

The topic of salary comes up at varying points in the interview process at Fortune 500 companies. The important thing to remember is not to mention salary until the discussion is initiated by the interviewer. You cannot negotiate anything until the topic arises, so be patient. You may knock yourself out of the running by demanding something the company is not yet ready to give, and protocol differs at each company. Some employers request that you state your salary range in your cover letter, some get a feel for your range in the telephone screen or first interview, and others wait until the final stages of the interview process—until they are absolutely certain that they want you on board—before they even mention dollars and cents.

You can do several things while you're waiting for the offer. First, consider several variables. Do you have to relocate (that's a negotiable item)? Do you have a particularly long commute (travel costs should be factored into your base)? Do you warrant top-of-the-range pay (your work history abounds with accomplishments, and you consistently exceeded goals)? Will you be working for a big company (with predetermined salary ranges) or a small company (where salary may be more flexible)? Do you have generous benefits (that's something worth negotiating as well)? Do you expect a signing bonus (ask if that's part of the deal)?

Anita Bruzzese, syndicated career columnist and author, advised:

> When you are negotiating salary for a new job, that's always the best time to get the salary you need. If you say, "Well, I'll wait until I get my foot in the door and then I'll ask for X number of dollars," it doesn't work that way.

Bruzzese added that it is much easier to be paid what you are worth when you negotiate at the starting point rather than to get big increases after you are at the new company for a while.[1] BCI Partner's Ted Horton added this:

> Candidates should always go in high. Big companies may have ranges, but smaller companies usually do not. At small companies, there are no hard and fast rules. It's all a function of where you begin. So the higher the starting salary, the better off you're going to be going forward. It's the only time you really have the leverage.

TIMING IS EVERYTHING

Some companies request that you state your salary requirements immediately, in your cover letter in fact. Ideally, you wrote in your cover letter that your salary was either "negotiable" or "competitive" and did not give a specific figure or range. It's normally not a good sign when a company asks for your salary requirements from the outset, because companies are basically doing one of three things: (1) eliminating candidates from the applicant pool based on salary, (2) determining what a phantom job is currently worth, or (3) revealing that the right price (rather than the right candidate) is its number-one concern. If you did put figures in your cover letter, preferably you gave a range that was wide enough to accommodate your needs (e.g., $50,000 to $60,000) but not so wide to render it meaningless (e.g., $55,000 to $95,000).

The same advice goes for salary history. Some companies ask for this information up front—in the cover letter or employment application. Trying to predetermine salary before the company gets to know you and you get to know the company is a fuzzy science. Avoid stating your salary history if at all possible. On the employment application that asks for a salary history, Nick Corcodilos suggests you write "confidential" and, in your cover letter, write "to be discussed at interview."[2] Corcodilos added, "When you provide your salary history, you give up your negotiating leverage." Remember, though, some background checks reveal salary data.

You could avoid this pigeonhole by neglecting to state your salary history altogether, but then you may risk losing the opportunity to interview. Keep in mind that if a company insists on a salary history, then negotiating more than a 10 or 15 percent increase in salary at your new job will be next to impossible.

If you decide to provide a detailed salary history before the interview, then put the information in a separate document (not in your cover letter). Make sure you state the starting as well as the ending salary to show your progression. Including some of the perks that went along with your current or former position, such as your 401(k) and vacation time, is also advisable. Companies that stipulate salary histories, however, are usually less flexible when negotiating pay in the final stages of the hiring process. If you expect a significant boost to your salary in your next position, then you may want to avoid applying for positions with companies that consider salary the number-one benchmark.

Going back to patience, avoid a discussion of salary for as long as possible. The best negotiating posture is after you have sold your interest in the company based on who you are and what you have to offer. You can win what you need when the employer is eager to have you on board, so the best time to negotiate—always—is when an offer is made. Why? Because at the initial stage of the job search, you are merely an anonymous entity, and midway through the process, there are still many viable candidates. By the end of the process, however, the choices have narrowed, and you have managed to persuade the employer that you are the perfect fit for the job and the company. The chemistry is in place. Finally, it goes back to what Engelhard's Mangiarano declared earlier: "You never can negotiate anything that's not offered. To talk about salary with a candidate at an interview is inappropriate until an offer is made."

Find out how the negotiation process begins or unfolds at the prospective company. If your best friend told you about the open position, probe further about the negotiation process (rather than about specific numbers). If a headhunter gave you the lead, ask the headhunter for full details about the stage at which you can expect this conversation to begin. If a salary base or range was posted on the company website, keep your antenna up when speaking to the interviewer to detect when this topic becomes relevant. At Engelhard, Mangiarano said:

> What I do is tell a searcher what my target salary is, what my range is, and what incentives or perquisites, if any, apply. And for somebody to come in and discuss that with me after he or she has been told all that information by a searcher is, in my judgment, quite bad taste because it's about the job and the fit. You have the opportunity to market yourself to me. And then it's about the opportunity for me to market the company to you. Until such time when we decide that we want to dance together, there's no real reason to put on the music.

Because recruiting software is dramatically altering the hiring landscape, your first contact with a prospective employer may be through the recruiting software on a company's website. If you apply electronically using the company's software, a salary base or range may be posted, but the figure is more of a guideline; negotiation is still an option. Kevin Marasco, director of marketing at Recruitmax Software, said:

> Our customers [the employers] typically utilize salary ranges (low/mid/high or low/high), leaving room for negotiation based on perceived value, experience, and so on. This information is typically displayed only internally, although they do have the option to show the candidate (rarely done, and a broad range when it is posted). Most customers also use an offer-approval process, where once an offer is extended, it has to be approved (as defined in the system's configuration but typically by a hierarchy of managers) before going to the applicant. Candidates can also accept/reject/negotiate the offer online (via the career site or email).

BCI Partner's Horton said that protocols will differ, depending on the size of the company.

> Again, are you going to General Motors or are you going to a private company that might only have 20 or 30 employees? You have got to know where your latitude points are. Who is more flexible? General Motors or IBM probably has everything labeled and tracked, so you probably are not going to have much latitude. But if it's a partnership or private company, I think you do have more latitude, and I think you can be a little more creative on your way in the door.

Even if you must discuss a range during a telephone screen, Bruzzese suggests you stall as long as possible before committing to specific numbers:

> What you want to do is say, "In my mind, it's too early to talk about salary. I would much rather discuss my skills in XYZ area. I see what you're saying here, but let me tell you about the time I saved my company $5 million because I caught an error . . ."

On the other hand, if the hiring manager is required to pin you down at this stage, make sure you are comfortable with the figures. There is no point telling yourself that you'll get the employer to jump up a hefty notch once the hiring manager falls in love with you. If the manager is determined to nail you down during the phone screen, then the likelihood of boosting the offer to a much bigger paycheck at a later stage may be nothing more than a pipe dream. You have to ask yourself, why waste your time or the employer's time? If the figures don't work for you at this stage, they won't work for you when you show up for your first day of work, either—unless you sell your house and your car and farm your children out to their grandparents.

But if the salary range discussed during the phone screen is slightly below expectations but not fiscally impossible, pause. Gently steer the conversation away from money for a moment and consider what you really want from your new job. Whatever you do, don't throw away the opportunity to interview just yet. Jeanne Sahadi, CNNMoney.com senior writer, advised that "another component to your compensation" is the following:

> Psychic income. Put simply, it's whatever rewards you derive from your job that can't be neatly quantified by a dollar sign. And those rewards can be just as important as a paycheck, although one without the other is like Abbott without Costello.[3]

When you don't have a lot of experience under your belt, salary requirements get tricky, because you can't base your new salary on what you were earning at your last job and you usually are short on the career accomplishments needed to leverage a better salary. That's why it is essential to spend a considerable amount of time researching the starting salary for someone in your field. A useful website for newcomers who are determining their worth in the marketplace is *www.salary.com*.

In addition, if your skills are particularly marketable—maybe you participated in several internships or you spent your evenings working in the college's computer lab—then factor those into the equation as well. All newcomers to the job market are not equal in terms of skills, so be realistic but don't shortchange yourself.

"You must show the employer how your participation led to success," Bruzzese said. That piece of advice applies to your college career, your part-time job, your internship, your fundraising for your sorority, or your role as a point guard on the basketball team. During an interview with Office Depot's Anne Foote Collins, the recruiting director gives newcomers an excellent opportunity to speak to this success. She said, "I ask about their college experience: why they selected the college they went to and their major. I find it's a question that puts them at ease, and it's a fun way to start an interview." This type of question provides you with an opening to differentiate yourself from the competition—and maybe even boost your starting salary.

Finally, decide what's most important to you at your new job. Perhaps the new company is a draw because you would be working with outstanding professionals who are capable of teaching you the ins and outs of the business. Maybe the opportunity to travel is attractive, or possibly the development and training the new company would provide are a priority. Whatever appeals to you, weigh that advantage versus potentially lower-than-expected pay. Then, negotiate the best salary you can. Whether a specific figure or a range is discussed, do everything in your power to keep the discussion open-ended. This doesn't mean you don't answer the interviewer's questions. But instead of committing to specifics, say, "Yes, I will consider that salary if . . .

- the work engages me because it is varied and challenging."
- the supervisor and my peers are people I can work well with."
- the company provides many training and/or development opportunities."
- the company provides room for advancement."
- the company is secure and diverse."

Fill in the blanks after the if: the tradeoffs are different for everyone. Perhaps on-site day care or a flexible schedule tops your list. Perhaps the reputation of the new company matches your need for affiliation. Perhaps earning potential is your bottom line. You have to know ahead of time exactly what factors are important. Naturally you are in a better position to talk about your salary after you have gone through all the rounds of the interview, but keep the following factors in mind when the topic of salary surfaces.

THE DOLLAR VALUE

A term that repeatedly surfaced in the Fortune 500 surveys was *return on investment (ROI)*. Job seekers who were scooped up quickly by prospective employers were those who could demonstrate quantifiably that they produced good results at their former or current jobs—either by increasing profit or eliminating problems. You may be saying to yourself that because you work in the law firm's library, it's difficult to quantify your contribution. Bruzzese said you may have to rethink that appraisal.

> I always suggest when you go into any kind of interview that you can recite chapter and verse the things you contributed to. "I worked on a $5 million project and my contribution was XYZ. They would not have found this obscure piece of research if it had not been for my searching for it." Everybody plays a part.

Knowing the exact nature of your contribution will make the negotiating process that much stronger. Bruzzese continued:

> You wouldn't be an employee if you did not play a part. If you're going to sit there and warm your chair, you're not going to last very long. Maybe you're not the project manager, but if you were on a successful team, then know what your role was and speak about it confidently.

Assert yourself, in fact. Tell the company about the ROI it will see as a result of giving you the salary you are asking for. If you set a tone of calm and reasonable negotiation, the company will usually return the favor.

Negotiation is a skill that you may not yet possess. If you haven't done so already, educate yourself quickly before your next salary discussion. Watershed Associates, a company that offers consultative negotiating training worldwide, has a recommended reading list for those interested in sharpening their skills. You might want to take a look at *www.watershedassociates.com* for further information. Ruth Shlossman, a director at Watershed and frequent speaker, offered advice during a recent business seminar on negotiating skills worth developing:

- Don't ask for something impossible and come across as hostile or immature. The important thing is to establish your credibility.
- Be assertive. If you start high, it gives you room to move.
- Go slow in negotiating. If the conversation becomes too emotional, step back, breathe, change thought patterns, and ask questions.

- Always think creatively. Consider what is valuable to the employer and won't cost you too much to give. You have to understand the employer's goals and values to make a good assessment.
- Don't answer a probe. Probe back. If you can't respond reasonably—one way or the other—silence is always effective.
- Never say yes or no during a negotiation. Saying yes ends the negotiation too quickly, and saying no puts the other person on the defensive. Instead say, "Yes, if . . ."
- If you are giving away concessions, let your counterpart know. But don't pretend to be making concessions if you aren't. Stay honest . . . your credibility is at stake.
- Listen attentively, especially if the situation becomes emotionally intense.
- When the relationship and the outcome are equally important, you need to negotiate. If the relationship is more important than the outcome, then don't negotiate every last detail. (In other words, don't haggle yourself out of an offer.)
- When you make a concession, get a trade.
- Always make a good case for why you are negotiating.

THE OFFER STAGE

Once the offer is made, you are in the best possible position to negotiate. You have determined that the company is the perfect fit for your skills and qualifications, and the company believes you are the answer to its problem. The hiring manager often speaks to human resources, and together they come up with a figure that fits into their salary range. Verizon's Thonis said, "We work very closely with HR on [salary]. HR will come back, and we'll know what we can offer. And we'll talk about a signing bonus or something like that. There are a number of things that we'll do."

Finally the moment you have been anticipating: the telephone rings, and the HR representative tells you that the job is yours. Once you express your interest, the representative then gives you the details regarding the whole package. Take notes if you can. You may have heard it a thousand times, but *everything* is negotiable.

Listen carefully to every word. Then reaffirm your interest in the job to the company representative. Politely tell the person you will call back tomorrow—or whenever you feel comfortable enough to speak about the specifics rationally. Sleeping on the information is good, but don't linger too long. Engelhard's Mangiarano said, "Do not delay in decision making. If an offer is made, either accept it or reject it. A company does not like to have its offer of employment leveraged against your current employer." Bruzzese said the appropriate time period for accepting an offer depends on the level of the position:

> I always think it's a good idea to sleep on it—at least 24 hours—and the higher you go, the more time you can take. . . . I've learned . . . to get up and walk away. I'm a real "Make your decision and go with your gut" person, but even I see the real value of taking a deep breath and giving it 24 hours. . . . Go call someone instead. You don't always have to do what that person says, but I think someone else's input is always valuable.

You may be totally smitten with the new job, so what do you need to consider?

For many, salary is the bottom line when considering an offer. Because there may not be enough wiggle room in salary negotiation, the real bargaining may have to be reserved for the other items in the deal. For example, perhaps the new employer has strict policies regarding salary: all R&D associates with your experience and background make X amount. But they want you on board and are willing to lure you with a signing bonus. This is negotiable. The first thing you must do, though, is ask for it. Be reasonable and say, "I understand that you cannot offer me more salary because [blank], but I would like a signing bonus of [blank] because I am worth [blank, blank, blank]." If the employer pushes back, remember to stay away from definitive answers, such as yes (the negotiation is over) or no (defensiveness kicks in). Say instead, "Yes, if . . ." or "I will need another day to consider . . ."

Then ask more questions. Maybe you can ask for more vacation time. Perhaps you neglected to ask when your salary will be reviewed again. Why not ask to have it reviewed in six months instead of a year? Maybe your partner has a comprehensive health care plan and you want to opt out of the new company's plan. Can the employer make up the difference somewhere else? What about stock options? Or a flexible schedule? Feel free to bargain and trade, but listen for the cue that signals enough is enough.

BCI's Horton said candidates usually get

> one shot to see if the employer is flexible. You definitely should [come back and] try one time [to boost the salary]. If that doesn't work, then you ask for a week's more vacation, a better benefits package. Or you can negotiate whom you are going to report to or what exactly your role

is going to be. When are you up for your next review? Instead of six months, ask for a three-month review.

Ultimately, how firmly you negotiate comes down to how much you want the new job.

Engelhard's Mangiarano said he knows what the candidate expects to earn at his company at the time of the offer. If the candidate absolutely seems to be the perfect fit for the job and then ups the ante, Mangiarano has to make a decision: "Is the individual so special that I'm willing to pay more than I normally would to have him or her join our company? That's my decision to make." Fit also plays a part at small companies. According to BCI's Horton, "I want the right fit. And usually $10,000 or $15,000 is not going to make or break the bank to get the right candidate." It rests on you to convince the employer that you are worth every penny that you are asking for.

IRONING OUT THE DETAILS

A lot of facts and figures have been bandied about during this process. If you didn't take notes during the interview, then sit down as soon as possible to gather your thoughts. If the offer is accepted, many companies wrap up all the details of a negotiation with an employment contract. Always read the fine print. If an employment contract is not offered to you, make sure you write down the details of all of your conversations with hiring managers as well as the individuals in human resources with whom you spoke.

Bruzzese said:

> It depends on the job you're going for. I think you should definitely get in writing your start date, your salary, the benefits you're going to be offered, your job description, whom you are reporting to, when your performance evaluations will be, because sometimes it's an honest mistake, where human resources and the people hiring you don't exactly communicate it down to the manager level, to the actual supervisor you'll be working with.

So take the initiative and put the deal in writing. If the company doesn't offer you a contract, then put the details of the negotiation in a letter that confirms your acceptance of the job. You should then mail this letter to the representative in human resources who was your primary contact. Going on record is a testament to your professionalism and ensures no miscommunication will occur.

When you accept the job, don't forget to thank every person you spoke to during the interview process for their time. In fact, even if you decline the offer, it is still a good idea to recognize these people. Remember, this is your industry—not as big and anonymous as you think—and your reputation is only as good as you make it. Build bridges, observe protocol, and then go the extra mile.

TRANSITIONING TO YOUR NEW JOB

All your hard work has paid off handsomely, and now you have a new job that will challenge you and catapult you to new heights. Congratulations! The next six months in your new job will be exciting—and challenging. You will be tempted now to sit back and heave a huge sigh of relief. By all means, take a breather … but don't relax too long. The primary emphasis of *Get the Interview Every Time* has been that you need to discover your work-self so you can make a good match with an employer. Just because you have the new job doesn't mean you can now go on cruise control. You don't want to be one of the 35 percent who leave a new job after the first six months because you failed to understand what you were getting into.

Most people feel extremely vulnerable when a new job pushes them out of their comfort zone. Think about it. Maybe you were the go-to person at your last job. You probably knew every nook and cranny of your old office, even the best time to hit the Xerox machine on the third floor. Maybe your direct reports respected your expertise and laughed at your jokes. Now you are at a new job and you know next to nothing: you even have to ask for directions to the cafeteria, not to mention that your new colleagues stare at you as though your hair is green when you make a joke. Transitioning into a new job is harrowing, and you will be uncomfortable for six months to a year. Don't take these growing pains personally. Everyone goes through it.

That's why it's important to acknowledge your own vulnerability and not jump to conclusions. Commit yourself to the new job, even if you suffer until you understand the lay of the land. In other words, give the job a chance—and hope that the employer gives you an equal shot. Everything you worked so hard to attain—by networking, doing research, creating résumés and cover letters, showing up for job interviews, negotiating salary—is on the line. That positive, can-do attitude you had during the job interview? By all means carry it over into your new job. Be yourself—the best version of yourself.

Heather McBride, a human resources manager at Fiserv, offers this advice:

> The best advice I can give to any employee when they start a new posi-
> tion is to get to know the people in your department and those outside
> your department that you will rely upon for assistance. All too often, we
> come into a company worried about getting up to speed on the processes,
> computer programs, etc. The real key to success is to cultivate your busi-
> ness network early on. Ask your boss who these key people are, then go
> introduce yourself and ask what you can do to help them in their posi-
> tion. Even better, write it down so they know you care about what they
> have to say. See if there is anything you can do to help the others in your
> department with tasks that you can pick up quickly. The only advice I
> have on what not to do is do not form impressions of people and corpo-
> rate culture based on gossip and rumors. This could lead to toxic results,
> since most often you were hired for the position because the hiring man-
> ager saw you as someone who could be a positive influence and add new
> viewpoints to a department that may not have had that in the past.[4]

McBride added:

> If you are a new manager, my best advice is to walk in the first day and
> sit down with each direct report for a few minutes to understand their
> needs—what worked well with their last boss that they would like you to
> keep doing, what didn't work well that they would like to make sure you
> don't do. And what they would like to start doing that hasn't been done in
> the past. Understanding where they are in their job satisfaction would go
> a long way with the employees that you took this on as your first assign-
> ment and didn't rely upon the documentation in a personnel file to relay
> their work history.

You are probably feeling challenged by all the recommendations that the Fortune
500 hiring professionals offered in this book. That's understandable. It's a tall order
to put your best foot forward under all circumstances and conditions. It's work!

Remember, though, you have an opportunity to be highly rewarded and regarded,
whatever work you do. The next, and final, chapter of this book will give you recommendations on how to grow in your new career. The suggestions for development
are based on the input from three executives who have risen to senior positions at
Fortune 500 companies. Their counsel should help to propel you forward in your
new job and career.

"It goes back to team-building skills, working in collaboration, acquiring new competencies, and building upon what you already have."

Charlotte K. Frank, Ph.D.
Senior Vice President, Research and Development, McGraw-Hill Education
The McGraw-Hill Companies

CHAPTER 18

Getting Ahead in Your New Job

Sometimes a job is just a job. It pays the bills, adds structure to your daylight hours, offers health insurance and retirement savings, or maybe merely provides relief from obsessive computer gaming and incessant sit-com watching. A job can be any of these things—all of them valid.

But just as often, a job is the basis of a meaningful and productive life. A new job can be a vehicle for engaging your hyperactive brain and inventive imagination. Usually you hope it will be a stepping stone in a career that offers ample compensation, stimulation, and a chance to show the world what you're made of.

Most people don't sign up for wholesale transformation when they take on a new job. Instead they hope for—and actively seek—steady promotions. And usually they accomplish this by making minor adjustments as they climb the corporate ladder.

Many books have been written about getting ahead in Corporate America. But since most people neither covet the head honcho's job nor do they feel the need to revamp their entire lives to get ahead, this chapter zeros in on making steady progress and advancing in a new job by developing certain attributes.

Three senior executives at Fortune 500 companies were interviewed about what it takes to move ahead at their companies.[1] Their input forms the basis of this chapter; they deem the following skills a means for getting ahead. Their suggestions for advancement come from the trenches of America's largest and most successful companies, so these executives have walked the walk. Their insights should help you navigate the ever-changing corporate landscape and help you advance in your career.

HAVING A PLAN AND COMMITTING TO IT

America is a mobile society. We move around a lot. Now more than ever, this typifies the workplace, too. In the past, it was not unusual to land a job and stay at a company for your entire career. Nowadays this is more the exception than the rule. Most people hold more than 12 positions in an average 30-year career. However, you cannot count on getting where you want to go if you move haphazardly from one position to the next. You need a plan.

Get the Interview Every Time has emphasized again and again how essential it is to find a position that is the right fit for who you are. And this book also stresses that a degree of self-knowledge is required if you want to find a job that works—on many levels—for you as well as the prospective employer.

Not everyone has a plan when they seek employment. Too often, people look for a new job because they no longer value their current position or employer. As Lisa Whittington, a vice president of human resources at Host Hotels & Resorts, said, "There's a saying that people join a company and leave a boss. My exit interview data confirms that." To add to Whittington's data, 35 percent of employees leave a new job after six months because "the number-one reason is that they don't feel valued and recognized." So in effect, for many people, leaving is more about getting away from an old job than moving toward a new job and a career goal.

There's nothing wrong with saying goodbye to an insecure or hostile boss, but make sure hopping to another job is not merely a desperate antidote. A solid plan should help you find a new position (even by making a lateral move) that fits you as well as provides an opportunity for growth and advancement. A plan also makes the old boss a lot more palatable because the focus moves away from the petty particulars and toward the bigger picture—your plan. Even if a boss takes all the credit for a project that you stayed until midnight four nights in a row to complete, you know that with a little patience and tolerance, you will be onto bigger and better things because you have a map and goal. A bad boss and dead-end job move out of the realm of Forever and into building your career for Tomorrow.

While you do not want to be too rigid, you should have an idea of where you want to be in 5, 10, and 15 years. Remember your job interview and the question, "Where do you see yourself in . . . ?" There's a reason why that's a favorite question. Employers know the most successful people at their companies are those who have carefully thought about their career path—and have seriously considered the steps it takes to get there.

But before taking the plan a step further, it's essential to be committed to where you are at this very minute—or at least for the duration of your current job or even job search. Work hard, maintain cordial relations, produce results, and stay in the now. Commit yourself wholeheartedly to what you are doing right this minute because success flows from that presence of mind—not from wishing you were somewhere else.

Then think long and hard about what you need to do to move forward in your career—whether it's getting another degree, enrolling in special training, signing up for assignments that are a stretch for you, working extra hours, or networking even when you don't feel like it.

All of these career challenges are going to have an impact on you—maybe even on your family. You'll have less time. You'll feel more vulnerable in unfamiliar territory. You'll go without sleep. You'll have to take some risks. But when you have a plan, the stress is a lot kinder to everyone involved. Charlotte Frank, Ph.D., senior vice president of research and development at McGraw-Hill Education, The McGraw-Hill Companies, said:

> After several years, I decided that I wasn't going to be an A.B.D. (All But Dissertation). I had to adjust my home and family time arrangements to complete my Ph.D. at NYU [New York University]. I scheduled 4:30 to 5:30 AM, almost every morning, to complete the research on the impact of ten years of "*BusinessWeek* Awards for Instructural Innovation" (which was impressive). It was always the same: I wanted to do the next thing, so I had to figure out how to get this next thing accomplished.

As Dr. Frank mentioned, a little sacrifice is called for. You can never be all things to all people, so prioritize and commit yourself to going above and beyond your day-to-day job responsibilities. For that, you'll need some self-motivation.

While it's nice to be recognized, if you rely too heavily on the pat on the back, your expectations will be dashed. Your boss has a lot to do—and it's not always possible to spend half the day cheerleading for the staff. Stop looking for constant approval and start asking yourself what you can do better to make matters run more smoothly, improve the bottom line, streamline the budget, bring in more business—or whatever you were hired to do, and then some.

Do frequent reality checks and remain proactive. It's a given: your job is going to challenge you—personally and professionally. McGraw-Hill's Dr. Frank added:

"Loyalty to the company and fulfilling your responsibilities" are essential, but "that doesn't mean that in some places I'm going to enjoy it all."

That's why it's a good idea to do an internal tune-up on your self-esteem. Reward yourself, at least until you have built up a body of work that will instead speak for you. The good news is that giving your best has a ripple effect. You produce good results for the company, for your customer, for yourself, and for your family, so acknowledge your own contribution, even if it's just, as Dr. Frank says, "I'm going to feel Wow" because of a job well done.

And don't forget to look at every job as an opportunity to build your professional reputation. Competition is stiff and Corporate America doesn't normally reward employees with plum promotions just because they have hung around for a long time. Shelley Bird, executive vice president of global communications at Cardinal Health, said, "We used to call that the 'battlefield promotion'—where people got promoted to a large degree because they were on the battlefield at the time."

While length of service and loyalty are valued at Cardinal Health, there's more emphasis on the "reciprocal relationship." In other words, moving ahead at Cardinal is a twofold process: Did the employee take every opportunity to develop professionally while growing the company's business? And did the company prepare for the employee's career advancement with succession planning? At a good company, there will be room for a lot of give-and-take, so don't hide out in your cubicle for five years. Take the company up on its offer to get special training or go to the leadership seminar being held in a less than convenient location. Bird continued, "So it's up to the individual to make choices on where [they] want to go, and then the companies need to help make that happen."

BUILDING RELATIONSHIPS

Each of the three vice presidents interviewed stressed the importance of building relationships within the department, the company, and the industry. Many job seekers think once they get the job, they can stop networking. According to the Fortune 500 senior executives, this is a big mistake. You continually need to reach beyond your comfort zone. For some, this means extending yourself to help others in the department. To others, it means a gung-ho immersion in special training outside the organization or taking on assignments with people you don't know as well, even when the thought of strange territory makes you squirm. More often than not, relationship building involves some risk.

Shelley Bird was relatively new to the company and the locale, but she didn't wait long to make a connection with another newcomer. The two women shared lunch together—and information. Bird said, "The two of us happened to join the company at about the same time, within weeks of each other. We had to relocate to this city, so she became my first friend at the company."

In lieu of playing golf, Bird and her colleague came up with the idea of getting together for dinner with a few other women in the company.

> Folks tend to get somewhat isolated in those senior levels—and you also have the pressure of the organization expecting you to have all the answers—so I think if you are self-aware it helps you reach out appropriately to complement your own skills and strengths. Reaching out to others is not a weakness. It helps you adapt to the day-to-day situations and it also helps your insight.

Bird sent out an email to locally-based senior women in various departments and got a surprising response. Twelve of the 16 locally-based women were able to meet for dinner that first time. Now the women meet informally over dinner to exchange information and build their network. Bird added:

> We do quarterly business reviews at Cardinal, so we plan a team-building evening during that week when the out-of-town members are here. One night, we cooked dinner in our cafeteria together. Not only was it fun, but it was a way to get to know the newer people—outside a strictly business sense—and I think that helps.

If the thought of organizing a work-related activity is too much of a stretch, then at least make a few friends. Exchanging information with your colleagues is one of the best ways to find out how an organization really works. If you get a new job, McGraw-Hill's Dr. Frank suggested that you ask yourself, "Is there anyone here I can ask for some advice?" She added, "If you have questions, call the person. Go to lunch with them."

At Host Resort & Hotels, Whittington said it's essential you find out "who you need to team with to get good results." Whittington's company sponsors periodic

> gatherings during business hours, so people will make those connections and meet other people from different departments. Our company has a quarterly award for teamwork, which goes to people in the company who team across different departments or outside their normal boundaries.

None of this happens overnight—it takes time to learn the basics of a new job—but to refer back to what Fiserv's Heather McBride said in Chapter 17, don't neglect building your relationships, even from the get-go. You will need allies. Coming to that realization sooner rather than later will benefit you.

And it doesn't mean merely showing up at the annual company picnic, either. McGraw-Hill's Dr. Frank said, "It's to my benefit to participate fully and enthusiastically and really give the sense that I am a real partner—that I like working with the group and people like working with me."

COLLABORATION

Work is a communal activity—even for artists and telecommuters. Nothing much is accomplished in a vacuum. A one-person operation needs customers, colleagues, suppliers, subcontractors—links to the outside world—to build a business and be commercially successful. So whether you work for a small or large company, you need the cooperation of your colleagues.

Time and again, career studies have shown that the best results are achieved when a spirit of collaboration or teamwork exists. Mavericks and iconoclasts may be adept at pulling good ideas out of thin air, but it's usually a team of players who manifest the vision. In a Coworking Institute Network newsletter, Bernie DeKoven said:

> Even when both people are friends, even when the technology for their collaboration is present and enabling, there is an art to working together—a subtle and sometimes profound art—as subtle as the art of listening. It requires that each person let the other person in.[2]

In a typical work environment, "letting others in" is about sharing the work, the tribulations, and the glory of a group effort. Certainly letting others in is not about providing the graphic details of your messy divorce, what you overheard when your boss spoke too loudly into her cell phone, or blaming others for projects running askew. A good collaborator is a worker among workers, a member of the team who is always moving forward to make sure that a shared goal has a positive outcome. That doesn't mean that you are all-business 24/7. In a collaborative environment, your coworkers will probably get a peek at who you are, at what your style is for getting things done—and maybe even whether you prefer mustard or catsup on your hot dog.

And, like everything else, collaboration is a gradual process. McGraw-Hill's Dr. Frank said:

> You have to build the process in order to accomplish something. Sometimes you can do it all by yourself, but more often it requires you extending this positive attitude in how you present [your ideas] to colleagues. . . . To get results on an ongoing basis, you have to have people comfortable and wanting to participate.

Every team—and individual—has strengths and weaknesses. If you want to improve your collaborative skills, then try to figure out how all the pieces can fit together. Dr. Frank said:

> When there's a chance to network and connect, you build on every moment. When somebody else gets a challenging task—maybe you met this person in the lunchroom or on the elevator or at the water fountain—you think maybe I should include this guy or this gal because he or she knows how to work in a group and they bring other pieces of knowledge with them that we may not have or could extend the solution that we need. It may give us a different perspective.

Try to surrender some of your territorial instincts, because in many respects, the best collaboration occurs when you are inclusive.

While consensus building is part of effective collaboration, that doesn't necessarily mean individual opinions are not welcome. At Host, Whittington said, "Our culture isn't conducive to blindly following the leader. Senior management asks for our opinions . . . and most people don't hesitate to voice their opinion. People are very vocal here." Bird of Cardinal Health added, "I don't believe in making everyone a version of myself. I try to encourage diverse styles. . . . There has to be a degree of flexibility and willingness to work together—for everyone's benefit."

Collaboration is harder for some than others. And a highly individualistic approach is not necessarily a bad thing—even in the corporate environment. Just make sure you're not too invested in a renegade sensibility. That may work at Walden Pond, but it has a way of irritating coworkers when too many deadlines are missed because you insisted on doing things your way. Instead, align your strong points so they complement the group's effort. Cardinal Health's Bird said, "You can't have an army of generals. You need roles for everyone in order for the team to be strong."

In today's work environment, making connection—or crossing the great divide to network and build a team—is even more challenging, at least on an intergenerational level. Lisa Belkin, a career columnist for the *New York Times,* said, "This is the first time in history that four generations—those who lived through World War II, Baby Boomers, Generation X and Generation Y—are together in the workplace."[3] Don't place the responsibility of building relationships on more seasoned workers. Take it upon yourself to bridge the gap by accentuating similarities—and common purpose—rather than focusing on your differences.

OPERATING UNDER ADVERSITY

While you may strive to do your best in each and every job, not all of your projects—or even jobs for that matter—will be considered a resounding success. As you advance in your career, the demands of a more senior position increase. You'll have more responsibility, more people counting on you, more pressure to produce outstanding results. Try to remember that this is what you signed up for when you made a decision to move ahead and take a promotion, so be prepared to handle adversity.

Difficult situations, according to Bird, "Shine the light on you—and how you deal with that is very important." Bird added, "My mother used to tell me that 'Adversity doesn't build character, it reveals character.' [Failing at something] provides a level of experience that you can't get any other way."

Failure is sometimes a better teacher than success. When the promotion you desperately wanted goes to another or the project that was supposed to thrust you into the limelight takes a dive into the red zone, do not retreat into a pit of despair. Host's Whittington said:

> You learn a lot from failure. I think it's made me a better HR person. I've experienced a lot of the things that people come to me for help with. I've made mistakes, and I've lived to tell about it. That gives you a lot of credibility.

Cardinal Health's Bird added, "Those lessons you learn in the valley really stay with you. They make you wise."

But McGraw-Hill's Dr. Frank didn't even like the word *failure.*

> Something that didn't work out well? I hate to accept failure. If there's something that wasn't as successful as I thought it should be, then I

always think about what it was that I missed. It should have been a better product. Whom should I speak to? If I didn't make that sale, then I want to figure out why I didn't make the sale. I don't want to fail at that again.

The key is to stay positive and make adjustments.

Your reaction to a bad turn of events will be noted. Whittington said her initial reaction to failing is

> stomach-dropping, absolute panic. But I also think covering up a mistake or tying to hide it is another mistake. Once I get over the panic, I look at what happened, and I try to come up with solutions to fix it. I will go to my peer or boss or whomever is appropriate, and I'll say, "OK, here's what happened, and here's what we can do to fix it. What do you think I should do? Can you help me?" I think you just have to put it out there.

A POSITIVE ATTITUDE

Each of the VPs thought having a positive attitude was an important competency for advancement. Dr. Frank said, "If you have a positive attitude, you also have to have a system for achieving it."

Whittington said her company does. While she personally thinks a "can-do attitude," is essential, her company goes a step further by creating a corporate culture that breeds an atmosphere of "employee engagement." Whittington added:

> Culture is very important at Host, and ours has been a work in progress for a few years. We've based the culture on a book called *Fish*. The four principles of *Fish* are: 1) Make their day, 2) Be present, 3) Choose your attitude, and 4) Have fun. And so we actually have a Fish team here who works with our CEO.[4]

Host doesn't leave a lot up to chance. Instead, it expects its employees to get on board and develop these skills if they are not already cultivated.

> One of the things we do is provide everyone who comes to work at Host training in self-leadership, which is a concept from the Ken Blanchard Company. The whole premise is that self-leadership is learning how to manage yourself and managing up to get what you want out of your job and need from your supervisor.

Host takes the idea of a positive attitude seriously by creating a framework to make sure these competencies are developed. Whittington adds:

> We work a lot, we work really hard, but we are very well rewarded for that. . . . We have a lot of Type-A overachievers here, but we really do manage to get the work hard/play hard thing balanced. We do a pretty good job of that.

Host offers an orientation for new hires that exposes them to the culture immediately, giving them a chance to see from the start what the company values and how it will help them develop these core competencies. Obviously, if you want to advance at Host, you have to have a certain temperament to align yourself with the corporate culture. Host values service, and as Mutual of Omaha's Bankey said, "It's difficult to put a square peg into a round hole." But at least Host gives its employees ample opportunity to develop and is clear about its expectations.

What if, by nature, you are serious, withdrawn, and prefer your own company? Does that mean you will never advance? Not every company casts a positive attitude in the same light. Cardinal Health's Bird said:

> I think an important part of having a positive attitude is to be open-minded and not afraid of change. Try to remain open to new ideas and don't be immobilized by change. You also want to be the type of person who is capable of bringing out a positive attitude in other people as well.

Fortunately, being positive is contagious (just as negativity has a ripple effect). Practice changing your thinking—in fact, challenge your thinking. Focus on what you have, and work toward making improvements if they're needed. Changing from negative to positive is a simple idea. Just admit that an attitude adjustment is in order, then commit to it. And surround yourself with positive thinkers in the process.

According to Wayne Tompkins of Kentucky's *The Courier Journal*:

> The negative employee is like a duck. A duck? Author and executive consultant Tom Bay explains: "Ducks are very self-centered. They start quacking when they're looking for food and that attracts more ducks. Pretty soon you have a whole bunch of ducks quacking. . . . In any company, once a duck starts quacking, he or she will attract more ducks. And

they're not producing, they're quacking. If you want to soar with the eagles, you can't hang out with ducks."[5]

COMMUNICATION SKILLS

In today's digital world, Dr. Frank said:

> In addition to speaking clearly and concisely, everyone also has to be a writer. We don't have to be a Shakespeare, but we do have to be—especially when we're in different parts of the world—able to communicate our thoughts in a way that says we are intelligent, thoughtful, and knowledgeable. Literacy skills are essential. That's why you see business communities out en masse—going to the government, going to all the political, community, and business leaders—so that we can maintain our competitiveness. We have to have a workforce that has these skills.

Dr. Frank works in the publishing industry, so it's understandable that she puts a premium on communication skills, especially reading and writing, but the other two executives (from real estate and health care industries) were equally resolute on the necessity to develop good communication skills (although with less emphasis on writing). Cardinal Health's Bird said, "I wouldn't call it writing specifically—your communication skills—although I do think there should be a degree of competency, but I think we pay particular attention to the face-to-face communication. We encourage dialogue at Cardinal Health." And Whittington added, "I think [communication skills are] very important, especially in a management position." Host addresses this need with seminars on situational leadership training from The Ken Blanchard Company, which "teaches you how to talk to people on their development level."

Communication skills run the gamut of speaking, reading, listening, and writing, and developing those skills can be challenging. In today's workplace, you have to write emails that are clear and concise. You have to use simple language to describe complex processes. You have to know when to communicate face to face or when an email, voice mail, a telephone call, or text message might be better. You need to provide thoughtful answers full of specifics, whether writing an email, speaking to your supervisor, or composing a memo directed at your business unit. Dr. Frank added, "You better know how to write. You better know how to read. You better know how to listen. It's all these communication skills. You absolutely must have them. You also have to do it quickly and succinctly."

To advance in the corporate world, you need to be credible. Trust and credibility are linchpins. That means composing reports, emails, and memos that are not riddled with errors and inaccuracies. You also need to ask for the things you want in language the employer understands. You need to be clear about your expectations and capable of persuading others if a consensus needs to be reached. And according to Dr. Frank, so much "depends on how it is presented. You have to show why this makes sense. . . . Sometimes you're selling an idea within the company, sometimes you're selling an idea to someone outside the company."

Even the blue laser scientists among us have to develop these skills because so much depends on the exchange of information, especially in today's hyperkinetic work world. Make a commitment to improving these skills. Take classes, read, use stylebooks and grammar books, become a careful writer, and practice being direct and use simple language. Every company (and industry) has its own language. Learn it and use it.

BECOMING A LEADER

Advancing in the corporate world implies that your responsibilities will increase and you likely will have more people reporting directly to you. Dr. Frank said, "Good leadership requires creating a climate where people want to continue to work together." What could be more challenging? In many workplaces, diverse personalities and divergent opinions rule the day. This one wants to do that; that one wants to do this. How do you lead a team?

Whittington said that the CEO at Host is a good example.

> He doesn't ask anyone to do anything that he wouldn't do himself. And I think that rubs off. He also thanks us and acknowledges our contribution. I think he leads us by being one of us. He works just as hard, probably harder.

Cardinal Health's Bird added:

> I think the leaders I've worked for are able to look at situations and access them quickly to bring a great deal of clarity to the change or opportunity. They are self-aware. There are the people who are confident in their own abilities, and they're not threatened by other strong performers. They thrive on it, in fact.

Not everyone is a born leader. Like all the other competencies mentioned in this chapter, there's a learning curve. The good news is that if you work for a good company, you'll have a chance to develop even your leadership skills. Gaining leadership skills is a gradual process. After all, it's fairly unlikely that you will be plucked from your role as assistant and put in the top chief's spot to run the company. If you take to managing well, you will get the opportunity to steadily increase the number of your direct reports.

Bird said:

> As we help people get the experiences that they need along the way in order to best position them for senior roles, flexibility plays a key part. Because people have to be open to the idea of moving location, moving into a different type of role where there is a gap in their experience. Or perhaps they need to make a lateral move to just broaden their capabilities.

Dr. Frank added:

> All I can tell you is that when families are productive, the parents have established the climate in that home. They don't call it leadership, but that's what it is. . . . The leader, whether at home or in the office, has to create a climate of support, growth, and friendship.

The modern workplace is a pressure cooker of tight deadlines and exceedingly high expectations, so creating an environment of "support, growth, and friendship" takes skill. Fortunately, nothing reduces stress better than a sense of humor. You can take your work seriously, but try not to take yourself too seriously. Acknowledge your humanity. Your coworkers will appreciate it. Dr. Frank thinks a sense of humor is essential:

> I always said, we need to feel comfortable, laugh, and enjoy ourselves. I like people with a good sense of humor. They make the whole discussion sensible and pleasant. It then becomes a more comfortable place to work. You can't make good decisions if people are always angry at each other. Humor levels the discussion and takes the angst out of the situation, so it improves the perspective when we have a good sense of humor.

Cardinal Health's Bird said the ability "to laugh at yourself" and develop a "healthy dose of levity" puts things in perspective for her, but she also said, "I wasn't afraid to be fired. That's not to suggest that I take unnecessary risks, because that's not my nature at all. I guess I view my career as an adventure. I want to try new things."

Define your vision of what a great job or promotion looks like and make it happen. You deserve to work in a job that engages you, a job that gives you a sense of fulfillment and productivity. While cultivating good relationships with your boss and colleagues will aid you as you advance—as much as "a healthy dose of levity" will—ultimately it is up to you to make work satisfying. Good luck!

Appendix

Sample Résumés

It can be daunting to think of revising a résumé every time you apply for a job, but don't be discouraged. Now that you know what hiring professionals expect to see in a résumé, the revision doesn't have to be extensive and is really pretty painless. Time and again, the Fortune 500 participants stressed that you need to target a particular position. An understanding of what you did at your last position and what you want to do at your next one, key words, good content and design, an emphasis on accomplishments rather than duties, and dynamic language help you to create a résumé that hits the mark.

Now that you know the importance of having a targeted résumé (an email-friendly plain-text résumé as well as an original version with more elaborate formatting), plan to experiment a little by tweaking your own résumé so that it fits an array of job descriptions.

Established rules for writing a good résumé don't exist, but there are a few constants: consistency, balance, format, and content. The following points are a good direction to follow when creating your résumé.

Consistency

Consistency is a good indicator of a logical mind. HR professionals are practiced at noticing inconsistency in the layout of your résumé, so spend a few extra minutes taking note of the following:

Spacing. Be consistent in the amount of spacing between lines, between words, and between headings.

Spelled-out Versus Abbreviated. If you spell out *September* in one line, don't use the numerical alternative in the other line. Or if you use the abbreviated version of a state name in one line, don't spell it out in the next.

Typeface. If you use boldface for your job title in one reference, make sure you use boldface for it in the next. Or if your headings are 14-point on one page, make sure they are 14-point on the next.

Indents. Tabs have a way of playing tricks on you, so make sure everything is aligned correctly.

Verb Tenses. If you use past tense in one bulleted item, use the past tense in the next bulleted item. Use present tense for your current job and the simple past tense for former positions.

Periods. End complete sentences with periods (even when the subject is implied), such as "Managed direct reports for deadline-sensitive projects."

Punctuation. Consistency is important in punctuation as well. Whether you use the serial comma (the comma before the *and* in a list) or not, make sure to exercise your choice correctly and consistently. The same is true for dashes: if you use the en-dash, make sure you are consistent. For instance, if you use an en-dash between years (1999–2000), then don't use a hyphen (2000-2004) in the next item.

Balance

"Balance" is visually pleasing. Fortune 500 professionals strongly recommend that you confine your résumé to one or two pages (there are always exceptions, several of which are included in this book), but it's a good design choice to write a full page or a full two pages. It's better to edit your two-page résumé rigorously to get it down to one page than to have two lines flop over to the second page. Also, aim for symmetry. An even distribution of lines to break up the text always works well. Finally, don't squeeze too much information on one page, as that's hard to read. Using white space to break up the page is a better alternative.

Format

Format—whether chronological, functional, or a combination of the two—will depend on how you want to display your information, but all résumés must contain key information.

Content

Content is the essence of a good résumé. Focus on the content of your résumé instead of spending hours on the layout. A simple design works well, especially because so many résumés today have to be converted into plain text; that is, email-friendly versions in which all formatting and embellishments are lost. It's more important to provide the information employers want. According to the Fortune 500 participants, employers prefer the following:

- Hard skills ("Proficiency in AutoCAD LT") rather than soft skills ("Excellent computer and people skills")
- Verifiable accomplishments ("Increased sales by 30 percent in the Northeast) rather than unsubstantiated claims ("The best salesperson in the Northeast")
- Extensive experience at profitable companies ("13 years' experience at a Fortune 500 company") rather than short-time stints at flighty businesses ("two years' experience at Hair Today, Here to Stay" [your brother-in-law's entrepreneurial venture in hair replacement therapy])
- Hard-core results ("Streamlined processes to increase turnaround by three months) rather than a listing of responsibilities ("Responsible for billing")
- Progressive promotions or responsibilities rather than clinging to the same responsibilities for the past ten years

Most people have experience that can be put into these positive terms. You may not be trained to think in this language, so make an effort to revamp your mind-set while working on your résumé.

Base your writing style on your audience. When you write a résumé, you should write in the style with which hiring professionals are familiar, even if you are a stickler for formal prose. One of the problems you will encounter when you write your résumé is space—or the lack of it. Distilling eight years of experience into four sentences can be a challenge. For that reason, don't rely solely on your ear to determine which words to choose. Style shortcuts are used—and accepted—in résumés; for example, clipped sentences and familiar abbreviations are often used. You have to get a lot of essential information into a small space, so you can't afford to be long-winded. In fact, that would be counterproductive, even if such prose sounds more correct to you. Stay away from those empty adjectives—and remember that nouns are good, but dynamic verbs are better. You want to convey yourself as a doer.

After you have looked at a few samples, you will probably begin to detect a style unique to the résumés in this book. Note the many variations of style for presenting your career accomplishments in a readable format. Because no one style is absolutely correct, you must decide what will work best for you and your industry. To review some style guidelines for the preparation of your résumé, though, I have included a checklist of style points that were used for the résumés in this book. Some style preferences are unique to writing résumés; some are standard style guidelines for all business writing.

- ❏ List town and state for all companies (not street address); two-letter postal abbreviations (rather than the standard state abbreviation) were used most often throughout this book.
- ❏ Use either hyphens (1990-1999) or en dashes (1990–1999) for dates. Newer computer operating systems automatically insert the en dash, but the older systems do not, so make a decision and then be consistent.
- ❏ Use present tense verbs to describe current jobs, past tense verbs to describe jobs held in the past.
- ❏ Use sentences with implied subjects (avoid using *I*), and put a period in a bulleted item with an implied subject; e.g., "Managed 20-person sales staff [period]."
- ❏ Dispense with periods in stand-alone sentences or lists (where white space separates one line from the next), unless the period is necessary for clarity.
- ❏ Use periods for incomplete sentences when they are followed by another sentence.
- ❏ Use full company names in the first reference but shortened forms thereafter (e.g., "Pepsi Bottling Group" the first time, but just "Pepsi" in the second or third reference).
- ❏ Use the same typeface for the punctuation after boldface, italics, and so on (e.g., "**Systems Analyst,** Microsoft Corporation" [note the bold comma after Analyst]).
- ❏ Accompany résumés lacking specific career objectives with a cover letter so the hiring professional knows what job you are applying for, where you noticed the opening, and what you have to offer the employer.

- ❏ If it's not obvious, describe the business of the companies you worked for. A word or even a brief description after the company name or in the body of your duties/accomplishments will do.
- ❏ Spell out degrees, such as *Bachelor of Science* or *Master of Arts*. If space is limited, you may use these abbreviations: BA, BS, MA, MS, MBA, PhD. If you prefer to use periods, do so consistently.
- ❏ Dispense with a comma between month and year (e.g., "January 2000," not "January, 2000").
- ❏ Use either the percent sign (%) or write percent after the numeral; do not write "fifty percent."
- ❏ Capitalize job titles (Account Executive, Media Planner, IT Director) and the names of departments (Human Resources, Accounting) within companies (notice this style was not used in the text of this book but only in the résumés).
- ❏ Only use ampersands (&) if they are part of a company's name.
- ❏ Use American spellings, unless a variant word is part of a company's or organization's name, such as "United Nations Development Programme."

Most of the samples in this book (the preceding ones as well as those that follow) are actual résumés used by actual people working in actual jobs. They are models that should generate ideas about design, language, and how to best display your information. Those who provided sample résumés are gainfully employed and not seeking employment, but some adjustments were made to reflect the input of the Fortune 500 hiring professionals. For the most part, though, only the names, addresses, and telephone numbers have changed significantly. Company names, employment histories, and tenures are virtually the same. As recommended by the Fortune 500 participants, résumés should have cover letters (especially if they do not have a focus statement), so the HR representative knows what position you are applying for and your qualifications for that position.

Tara Gutch
100 Medford Lane
New Canaan, CT 06100
Home Telephone: 203-555-1000
Work Telephone: 203-565-1000
Cell Phone: 203-554-1000
E-mail: APA100@yahoo.com

CAREER PROFILE
Fortune 500 Financial Adviser with 18 years of finance and general management experience working at IBM, Philip Morris, General Motors and as a management consultant with KPMG Peat Marwick. Bachelor's degree in Finance with expertise in:

- *Financial planning and analysis, financial modeling*
- *Cash management, strategic planning and business development*
- *Project management*

PROFESSIONAL EXPERIENCE

IBM CORPORATION. White Plains, NY   **11/99 - Present**

Principal Financial Adviser — Small and Medium Business Sector

Coordinate 2003 Global Revenue Plan for largest Sales and Distribution sector, committing $20B of revenue to IBM.
Build business cases by quickly understanding issues and translating them into business opportunities. Develop profitable strategy to capture this opportunity.

Program Manager — Integrated Product Development   **12/98 - 10/99**

Architected financial models built by deconstructing complex business issues, determining probability of occurrence and using Monte Carlo simulation tools to assign investment-level risk.
Developed Web-based Content Management Programs to leverage information across IBM organization to reduce development costs and reduce key "time to profit" metric.

C. S. BROOKS. New York, NY
(consumer products company, retails home products)   **10/97 - 11/98**

Treasurer — Corporate Officer

Maximized cash flow by monitoring and managing worldwide cash position.
Reduced cost by managing risk though interest rate and currency hedging strategies.
Drove profitability by tightening control over cash receipts and disbursements.

IBM CORPORATION. Armonk, NY   09/95 - 10/97

Senior Consultant, Internal Consulting Practice

Led multimillion-dollar business transformation consulting project in PC group as Executive Relationship Manager, Project Engagement Manager and Financial Strategy Subject Matter Expert.

AMERICAN BUREAU OF SHIPPING. New York, NY   12/92 - 09/95

Manager Cash Management and Assistant Treasurer

Reduced costs by rationalizing more than 160 bank accounts in 120 countries, establishing payments netting center and centralizing invoicing process.
Reduced cash flow variability by establishing more disciplined cash-management approach allowing for optimization of both cash flow requirements and tax considerations.
Increased the performance of $250 million pension portfolio by rigorously analyzing past performance and uncovering opportunities.

KPMG PEAT MARWICK. New York, NY   11/89 - 12/92

Manager, Corporate Finance Consulting

Developed Corporate Finance Strategy for Fortune 200 clients that included interest rate and currency hedging strategy, treasury management and optimal capital structure.

PHILIP MORRIS CORPORATION. New York, NY   09/88 - 11/89

Senior Planning Analyst

Corporate financial planning liaison between Chairman's office and Asia Pacific Tobacco organization

GENERAL MOTORS CORPORATION / E.D.S.
Canada and Brazil   09/84 - 09/88

Treasury Analyst

Managed foreign exchange exposure working in Canada and Sao Paulo, Brazil.

EDUCATION

1984   Series 7 Qualification
1984   Bachelor of Arts, Finance, University of Western Ontario, Canada

THOMAS DEPHILLIPS
100 E. 31st St., Apt. 10
New York, NY 10000
Thomas.dephillips@gs.com
Work Phone: 212-357-1000
Mobile Phone: 917-685-1000
Home Phone: 212-684-1000

PROFESSIONAL PROFILE: Fortune 500 *Equity Sales Trader* researched, designed, negotiated and leveraged highly favorable market share opportunities

---

WORK

EXPERIENCE

Goldman, Sachs & Company — Equity Sales Trading
New York, NY
July 2002 - present
• Bridge execution focus with knowledge of the research product by identifying catalyst-driven trading ideas for accounts.
• Cover accounts for both the Listed and OTC markets as a member of sales trading team.
• Understand liquidity and supply/demand in determining appropriate price levels for capital commitment transactions.
• Monitor and interpret intraday news flow for potential market impact.

Goldman, Sachs — Technology Research Sales
New York, NY
July 2000 - July 2002
• Leveraged Goldman, Sachs Technology Research franchise as a member of specialized sales team focused on technology-sector investing.
• Co-covered mid-Atlantic and New York–based accounts, including both mutual funds and hedge funds.
• Designed and marketed presentation for generalist portfolio managers, detailing tech-sector investment themes and opportunities — as well as food-chain overview.
• Developed internal database system to better identify market-share opportunities and to assist in creation of goals for all domestic tech-sales members.
• Involved with recruiting and development of post-undergraduate positions at firm; selected in the summer of 2001 as mentor for new financial analysts.

INTERNSHIP

EXPERIENCE

Goldman, Sachs — Equities Division
New York, NY
Summer 1999
• Participated in summer program consisting of presentations/classes, rotations and desk assignment.
• Shadowed employees from all areas of Equities Division, including Institutional Sales, U.S. and International Trading and Private Client Services.
• Created a "how-to" manual for Securities Lending Operations desk.
• Assigned to desk at Global Securities Lending; focused on daily management of short-sale contracts.

Lexington Management Corporation
Saddle Brook, NJ
Summer 1998
• Teamed with the domestic equities group.
• Attended analyst conferences and IPO road shows.
• Researched competitive mutual funds, developed comparison reports for Lexington Growth & Income Fund.
• Prepared research reports for senior analysts regarding stocks to be added to Growth & Income Fund.

Fowler, Rosenau & Geary, LLC
New York, NY
Summers 1996, 1997
• Worked on floor of NYSE alongside specialists.

ENTREPRENEUR

EXPERIENCE

Eagle Alliance, LLC
1997 - 2000
Co-Chairman
Eagle Alliance, LLC, was student-operated investment company licensed in Delaware.
• Goals of organization included capital appreciation for investors and education of student shareholders about financial marketplace.

EDUCATION

Chartered Financial Analyst
• Level 2 Candidate
Boston College, Carroll School of Management
Bachelor of Science — Finance. Graduated: May 2000.
GPA: 3.6 / 4.0. Major GPA: 3.7 / 4.0. **Honors:** Magna cum Laude, Dean's List, Peer Leadership Program, Golden Key National Honor Society

Doreen O'Dea
123 Bergen Avenue
Jersey City, NJ 07100

Phone: (201) 333-1000
Facsimile: (201) 333-1000
email: DDgallery@aol.com
www.ddgallery.com

GRANT WRITER

KEY FEATURES: *Recent Transaction:* $2.5 million. **Largest Transaction:** $20 million. **Project Manager** for Jersey City (a wayfinding signage program). Public/private partnership between nonprofit organizations and city of Jersey City. Wrote additional grants:

- $1.3 million grant writing. Jersey City (Bergen Avenue local lead application)
- $319,000 grant writing. Jersey City (pedestrian safety application)
- $1.5 million grant writing. Long Hill Township (ecotourism)
- $849,000 grant writing. Long Hill Township (transportation enhancement)
- $150,000 grant writing. Long Hill Township (pedestrian safety)
- $250,000 grant writing. Long Hill Township (municipal aid)
- Eligibility Research and Writing: National Register of Historic Places (for designation and subsequent tax credits for private developer)
- $342,000 grant writing. Consultant to S3x Associates (bikeway program for municipality)
- $20 million grant writing. Consultant to S3x Associates (variety of funding for private developer)
- $304,000 grant writing. Essex County Division of Cultural & Historic Affairs (NJSCA application)
- $40,000 grant writing. Essex County Division of Cultural & Historic Affairs (Staffing initiative: NJSCA)

Experience:

1982-2002 *Doreen O'Dea Gallery*

Owner. Fine art, custom framing and art appraisal business
- Marketing, sales, finance for art business
- Public relations, advertising
- Corporate and residential art collection management
- Appraisal of fine and decorative art
- Exhibition management for gallery and corporate locations (locations provided on request)
- Consultant — Artistic event planning: auctions, corporate sponsorship, arts marketing
- Consultant — Nonprofit management: fundraising, grant writing, 501(c)3 Incorporation, planning

2000-Present *City of Jersey City and Liberty Science Center*
Consultant — Project Manager — Destination: Jersey City
Wayfinding Signage Program for Jersey City
- Write grant applications.
- Facilitate and coordinate communications, meetings, committee resources.
- Act as liaison to government agencies and nonprofit organizations.
- Present materials to business community and general public meetings.
- Oversee Public Relations firm.
- Manage $2.5M budget.

1998-Present *Essex County Division of Cultural & Historic Affairs*
Consultant — Long-Range Planning
- Create, design, write agency long-range plan.
- Develop steering committee, design and lead workshops create public surveys.
- Analyze data.

Essex County Division of Cultural & Historic Affairs
Consultant — Grant Writing
- Created Essex County Block Grant Application for FY2000.
- Developed and led workshops for applicants FY2000.
- Wrote FY2000 and FY2003 NJSCA: Grant for Essex County $848,000 budget.
- Grant Panel Evaluator

Jersey City Economic Development Corporation
Consultant — Brownfields
- Developed plan for land reuse (brownfields).

Jersey City Episcopal Community Development Corporation
Consultant — Business Planning
- Created business plan and grant to federal government for non-profit agency to develop for-profit business, enabling low-income residents to gain full employment.
- Created business plan for Dress for Success license: Hudson County.

1998 *Union County Division of Cultural & Heritage Affairs*
Consultant – Grant Administration
- Essex County Block Grant Coordinator administered through Union County FY99

259

1992-1995   *Hudson County Cultural & Heritage Affairs*
Coordinator of Federal and state aid for county government agency for
promotion of arts and heritage
- Reviewed incoming grants. Wrote grant proposals.
- Administered grant budget.
- Coordinated and implemented Arts-in-Education Programs
  (60 programs).
- Designed non-profit development institute for 501c3 organizations
  (skills for administration of non-profits).
- Co-Chair American Heritage Festival Committee (Festival won the
  NJ Tourism Award: major sponsor, Bell Atlantic).
- Coordinated Arts Fair Day with local corporate businesses
  (introduction of arts to corporate community).
- Researched and wrote Hudson County Artists Directory.
- Coordinated and implemented Hudson County St. Patrick's Day
  event televised by Fox 5 WNEW.

1985-1989   *New York City Board of Education*
Teacher. High School English Teacher at Curtis HS and Townsend Harris HS.
- SAT Prep, social studies, journalism, English literature, careers
- Designed curriculum for and implemented Photography Enrichment
  program.
- Designed Writing through Word Processing Program.

Education:

1994   New York University. Art Appraisal Program
1986   Queen's College, CUNY. (M.S.Ed.)
          (Research Assistant to Dr. Phillip Anderson for Poetry Pilot in schools)
1980   Jersey City State College (now NJCU). Bachelor of Arts (Philosophy)

Professional Associations:

Commissioner, Jersey City Historical District Commission, 1994-2001
Co-Chair, Hudson County Chamber of Commerce Special Events Committee, 1999-2002
Founding Board Member - Hudson County Dress for Success
Board of Trustees, Educational Arts Team 1994-2000, President of Board 2001, 2002
Board of Trustees, Lincoln Association, 1999-2002
Media Advisory Board, Hudson County Schools of Technology, 1997-2000
March of Dimes Hudson County Chair, 1994, 1995; Jail and Bail Fundraising Committee;
    FDR Award, 1995; County Committee, 1994-1999; Promotional Chair, 1997-1999
Associate Member, American Association of Appraisers
Adjudicator: Hudson County Senior Citizen Art Show; Jersey City Board of Education Permanent
    Student Art Collection; Congressional Art Competition for HS Students

DAVID FELDMAN

100 Grand Street, #1-W, Croton-on-Hudson, New York 10100
(914) 271-0001 • E-mail: dfelsen@msn.com

QUALIFICATIONS SUMMARY

Qualified for a Business - Legal Counsel / Manager function including: corporate governance, compliance department start-up, regulatory agency liaison. Served as corporate accountant for more than 5 years. Developed training manuals / seminars. Scope of experience:

- cost and general accounting
- asset management / disposition
- accounts payable / receivable, capital budgets
- internal controls, job costing
- cost avoidance, debt financing, equity financing
- credit and collections
- financial statement analysis
- audit controls / management
- financial reporting, regulatory compliance
- profit / loss analysis

Provided more than 14 years of Human Resources support: Grievances, arbitration, policy and development. Attorney proficient in: NLRA, ERISA, FLSA, EEO, TITLE VII, ADA, FLMA, ICRA, ADR. Accomplished writer, researcher and speaker. Scope of experience:

- labor and employment relations law
- contract review / administration
- grievance and arbitration proceedings, mediation
- union negotiations and mediation
- Unemployment and Workers' Compensation hearings
- collective bargaining agreements
- litigation, discrimination claims, labor hearings
- HR policy and design

Personal Contributions: Extensive volunteerism to business and civic organizations. Served in United States Naval Reserve for six years.

PROFESSIONAL EXPERIENCE

ATTORNEY, OF COUNSEL
Law Offices of Robert J. Hilpert
Croton-on-Hudson, New York (2001-present)

Areas of practice: Commercial and Employment litigation; general labor advice
ATTORNEY, PRIVATE PRACTICE
Law Office of David Feldman
Ossining, Peekskill and Wappingers Falls, New York (1996-2001)

Areas of practice: All areas of Labor and Employment Relations Law, litigations including commercial litigation, arbitrations, mediations, labor hearings, policy manual development, contract reviews, negotiations, legal research and general labor counsel. Also served as in-house counsel to a consumer credit and collections firm.

LEGAL ASSISTANT / LAW CLERK
Parker Chapin Flattau & Klimpi, LLP
New York, New York (1988-1996)

Areas of practice: Litigation support in Labor and Employment Relations Law. Personally performed extensive legal research and writing on labor relations issues, including: NLRA, ERISA, FLSA, EEO, TITLE VII, ADA, FLMA, ICRA, ADR.

PRIOR TO 1988

- Legal Assistant: Bronx District Attorney, Bronx, New York
- Accountant: KingAlarm Distributors, Inc., Elmsford, New York
- Assistant to Controller: General Manufacturing Inc., Fort Lauderdale, Fla.

EDUCATION

- Pace University School of Law
- Bachelor of Science – Business Administration (Economics and Accounting) University of Florida

ADMISSIONS

- New York State Bar; United States District Courts for the Southern, Eastern and Northern Districts of New York, and Second Circuit Court of Appeals

| SHEILA NADIA | CELL (914) 555-1000 | E-MAIL: aK11@netzero.com |

PROFESSIONAL OBJECTIVE
To meld nine years' diverse creative and administrative expertise at top-notch companies into Marketing Manager position in entertainment industry

PROFESSIONAL EXPERIENCE

Gentlemen's Quarterly   *Sales Assistant*   2003
- Coordinate meetings and prepare sales collateral for luxury fashion and accessory clients.
- Track and process insertion orders and advertising positioning statements.
- Develop meeting calendars for fashion shows and presentations.
- Support directors, including answering phone calls, preparation of expense reports, filing, faxing, photocopying and other general administrative tasks.

Lazard-Freres & Co.   *Travel and Meeting Planner*   2002-2003
- Coordinated executive meetings; scheduled flight, lodging and limousine services.
- Recorded, processed and filed billing invoices/expenses.
- Originated calling lists and maintained department files and databases.
- Researched and compiled marketing materials for public-information booklets.

Wall Street Interactive Television   *Communications Manager*   2001-2002
- Created corporate communication materials, including company history and investment-relations content.
- Facilitated marketing outreach efforts to promote programming and public affairs segments.
- Produced online financial news, lifestyle and entertainment sound bites.
- Coordinated and launched a September 11th benefit gala and downtown revitalization PSA campaign.
- Tracked market trends to create corporate profiles and establish contacts.
- Assisted sales team in preparing sponsor/partnership proposal and collateral.
- Generated sales leads through research of financial trade publications.
- Edited and placed job placement copy; recruited, interviewed and staffed consultants and interns.

a21 Group   *Freelance Copywriter*   2001-2002
- Composed online promotional copy and press releases for photographic agency.
- Wrote and edited online corporate communications; created corporate style guide for online and print collateral.
- Recorded marketing minutes and agenda topics for distribution to board members and partners.
- Coordinated graphics layout and site architecture.

NBC Internet   *Associate Manager of Client Marketing*   1999-2000
- Conceived and implemented integrated radio, television, online and print advertising campaigns.
- Conceptualized new programs, promotions and special events for NBCi advertisers.
- Collaborated with channel producers and marketing department on optimal advertising placements, internally reporting project status.

- Created pitch material and ad copy; produced content; designed sweepstakes, contests and raffles.
- Trained sales team to pitch multimedia campaigns to prospective clients.
- Supported East Coast advertising and sales team.

NBC, Inc.   *Marketing Specialist, NBC.com*   1994-1999

- Promoted "Must See TV" contests, series premieres, cliffhangers and talent appearances on newsgroup and fan sites.
- Coordinated design and development of website marketing and affiliate programs, and "The More You Know" PSAs.
- Consulted with design and advertising teams on revisions/approvals of broadcast, online and print materials.
- Co-wrote promotional commercial for "Passions," a daytime soap opera.
- Proofread corporate communication press releases and business proposals.
- Edited and reviewed website content for MSNBC.com re-launch.
- Collaborated and produced departmental style guideline and staff handbook.
- Supervised marketing interns.

RELATED MARKETING EXPERIENCE

Carnevale di Venezia Art Exhibit   *Events Coordinator*   2003

- Compiled guest list, facilitated invitation and press announcements to arts editors and buyers of Italian-American art.
- Managed event-opening reception, with net proceeds of $4,000 on the first evening.

8minutedating   *Marketing Events Associate*   2002-2003

- Assisted marketing outreach efforts to promote singles events.
- Registered participants and facilitated social activities.

NBC 2002 Winter Olympics   *Online Content Writer*   2002

- Researched and developed sports content for Olympics website.
- Collaborated with video producers and sports experts on accuracy and style.
- Incorporated IOC and NBC style guidelines.

Ballantine Books/Random House   *Proofreader*   1995-1999

- Proofread mass-market /trade fiction and nonfiction manuscripts.

AFFILIATIONS & ASSOCIATIONS
Dining by Design Industries Foundation Fighting AIDS, Volunteer. HeartShare, Volunteer
Make-A-Wish Foundation, Volunteer. Ryze Networking Group, Member. The Joyce Theatre, Volunteer.

EDUCATION
1996   New York University, Book Publishing Certificate, Copyediting & Proofreading
1993   Marist College, Bachelor of Arts, English: Creative Writing / Minor, Photography

SKILLS
Project management, event coordination, copyediting, copywriting and proofreading
Proficiency in Macintosh and Windows platforms
Proficiency in Microsoft Office and Lotus Notes 1-2-3
Familiarity with Microsoft Publisher, Adobe Photoshop and QuarkXPress

CHARLES JONES　　　　　　　　　Telephone: 212-456-1000 (H)
100 Christopher Street　　　　　　　　Cell phone: 212-456-1010
New York, NY 10010　　　　　　　　　E-mail: hjhj@yahoo.com

Experienced Reporter capable of breaking news stories under real-time deadlines and with proven ability to translate financial terminology into plain but vibrant language.

PROFESSIONAL HIGHLIGHTS

Freelance Financial Reporter
2001-Present

- Write and cover foreign, emerging and domestic equity markets, industry sectors and mutual funds.
- Articles have appeared in *Wall Street Journal* and *New York Times.*

Worldlyinvestor.com
New York, NY

Correspondent/Mutual Funds Editor
1998-2001

- Analyzed market trends and mutual fund industry analytics in support of investing content.
- Reported on financial/investment topics, especially mutual funds, on daily basis.
- Created/developed investing-oriented content for online financial content site.
- Edited mutual fund content daily, assigned articles and managed freelancers.

Self-Employed Consultant
1995-1998

- Managed new product launch, developed newsletter/catalog for a handheld computer firm, provided financial consultation for TV production company, extensive market research in various industries.

Republic National Bank of New York
New York, NY

Forward/Spot Foreign Exchange Trader
1990-1995

- Priced swap and outright forward contracts; up to $500 million for major corporate customers.

- Traded short-dated futures contracts including: EuroUSD, EuroDM, EuroSTG.
- Analyzed yield spreads for short-term and long-term trading opportunities.
- Made markets in spot Swiss and DM/Swiss; more than 200 trades per day.

Associate Institutional Sales/Trading—International Capital Markets
1988-1990

- Marketed and traded international fixed-income products (Eurobonds, foreign bonds and foreign currency government bonds) to major international client base (central banks, mutual funds, insurance companies, bank trust departments and pension funds). Generated profits of $1,000,000 annually.
- Monitored all major international markets and worked with UST, money markets, FX, futures and options.
- Performed analysis for swaps, yield spread comparisons and hedging.

Rafidane Corporation
New York, NY

Import/Export Coordinator—Strategic Planner
1986-1988

- Coordinated activities for all aspects of merchandising; purchase and sales, import/export documentation, transportation, warehouse and storage, and futures hedging.
- Developed strategic marketing plan for major foreign product introduction in U.S.

EDUCATION

New York University. New York, NY
Graduate School of Business Administration. *1985-1987*
M.B.A. Finance/International Business

University of Vermont. Burlington, VT
B.S. Accounting. *1979-1983*
Extensive coursework in engineering

RELEVANT INTERESTS AND COMPUTER SKILLS

Proficient in Microsoft Windows and Office software
Comfortable with HTML and Internet publishing systems
Working knowledge of French and Spanish
Extensive independent international travel

Lorna Steinberg
100 East 100th Street, Apt. 1C, NY, NY
Home: (212) 410-1000 / Office: (212) 582-1000
E-mail: STB10@worldnet.att.net

SUMMARY OF QUALIFICATIONS

Multilingual Senior Executive with 15 years' experience selling high-end products worldwide. Skilled at problem-solving, financial analysis and intercultural communications. Decision-maker who can troubleshoot and has proven track record in opening and emerging markets.

EXPERIENCE

Stuart Weitzman, Inc., New York, 1989-present
Account Executive

- Develop financial and marketing strategies for customers to increase sales and gross margins (open-to-buy budgets, sell-through analysis, special promotions design, trunk shows).
- Spearhead international expansion, increasing overseas market presence to 53 countries in 2002 from 12 in 1989; new markets include China, Australia, Spain, South Africa, Mexico.
- Team with other senior executives to manage major accounts, including Saks Fifth Avenue, Browns (Canada) and Russell & Bromley (United Kingdom).
- Play key role in diversification of the Stuart Weitzman product line, introducing new products to existing clients.
- Market new brands for third parties, such as Vera Wang, growing shoe sales for this line by 80% since November 2001 launch.
- Sell product line at trade shows in Milan, Düsseldorf, New York and Las Vegas, counseling international customers on the logistics and requirements for importing.
- Train/manage sales force and customer representatives in U.S. and abroad.
- Ensure timely production and delivery, working with overseas factories.

Key Accomplishments

- Increased sales tenfold in one of the three largest accounts since 1990.
- Increased sales by an average 20% per year over the past five years.
- Improved efficiency of day-to-day operations by establishing new data management systems.

Dianne B. Corporation, New York, 1987-88
Vice President Operations/Acting Chief Executive Officer
- Managed three high-end retail stores and a wholesale operation.
- Responsible for financial planning, including sales/costs forecasting, short-term financial strategy, accounting and banking relations and product pricing
- Managed Hong Kong private label import business.
- Contributed to long-term strategic planning, including dealing with venture capitalists to finance expansion and identifying new store locations.
- Managed staff of 25 at three locations.

Chose Classique/Mishaan Innovations Inc., New York, 1985-87
Chief Operating Officer
- Planned and executed financial budget of a wholesale contemporary sportswear operation.
- Coordinated trade shows.
- Established and managed Hong Kong import division.

Sonia Rykiel, New York, 1984
Assistant Manager
- Managed and ran day-to-day business of Madison Avenue store.

Holmes Protection, Inc., New York, 1981-83
Executive Assistant to the Chairman
- Responsible for the chairman's personal finances.
- Planned, budgeted and maintained real estate holdings in the United States and abroad, including supervision of construction and contracting personnel.
- Assisted in the reorganization and automation of the company's accounting department, including training of new personnel.

De la Ronda, S.A., Bogotá, Colombia, 1978-81
Assistant Manager
- Contributed to start-up of wholesale operation for designing, manufacturing and selling swimsuit/leotard line.
- Conducted market research and analysis to launch expansion into new active wear and sportswear lines.
- Oversaw De la Ronda manufacturing operation.

EDUCATION
- **Monterey Institute for International Studies, Monterey, CA**
  Master of Arts, International Management
  Certificate in translation and interpretation (Spanish/English/French)
- **Vassar College, Poughkeepsie, NY**
  Bachelor of Arts, Anthropology

LANGUAGES
- Fluent French, Spanish, English; proficient Italian and German

William Daly
100 America Avenue
West Babylon, NY 11100

Telephone 516-558-1000(H)
Cell Phone 516-557-1000
E-mail DetMD@yahoo.com

EXPERTISE ———————————————————————

Extensive supervisory experience in criminal investigations in New York City Police
Department

OBJECTIVE ———————————————————————

To utilize more than 18 years' experience as **Commanding Officer** to provide protection
and security to targeted industries from terrorists

PROFESSIONAL HIGHLIGHTS ———————————————

- Varied background in managing and conducting criminal investigations
- Demonstrated proficiency in administration, management and training
- Proven ability to analyze, plan and reorganize
- Results-oriented — with numerous citations for excellence

EXPERIENCE HIGHLIGHTS —————————————————

46th Precinct Detective Squad • Commanding Officer
- Managed Detective Squad and addressed all administrative and operational
needs in timely, efficient and results-oriented manner.
- Supervised investigations of serious crime incidents.
- Recognized for excellence. The 46th Precinct Detective Squad amassed
highest case load as well as the Bronx's highest homicide clearance rate during tenure.
- Supervised and reviewed all case closings.

NYPD Detective Bureau Training Unit • Commanding Officer
- Administered and managed Detective Bureau Training Unit.
- Reorganized and enlarged Unit in addition to overseeing acquisition of
permanent classroom, office facilities and updated training aids for Unit.
- Analyzed training needs on continual basis for Detective Bureau.
- Managed preparation and presentation of lessons/courses for training 3,400
Detectives and Supervisors during semi-annual training cycles. Also addressed orientation
training for all supervisors and detectives transferred into Detective Bureau by administering,
preparing and presenting various courses involving specialized detective bureau issues.
- Initiated and edited monthly "Detective Bureau Training Bulletin," which was
distributed to all Detective Bureau personnel.
- Edited and wrote "Detective Squad Supervisors Handbook," NYPD Bureau
Manual, Number 764.
- Recognized for excellence. The Detective Bureau Training Unit was recipient
of NYPD Unit Citation in recognition of excellence in performance.

Bronx Robbery Squad • *Commanding Officer*
- Administered and managed operational needs of borough-wide Bronx robbery squad and oversaw managerial, administrative and investigative responsibilities of seven local precinct Robbery Investigative Units.
- Managed and supervised investigations involving serious incidents of robbery as determined by Detective Borough Commander and borough-wide and inter-borough pattern robberies.
- Provided staff and operational assistance to all Bronx precinct detective squads involved in robbery investigations.
- Expanded investigative responsibility of the Bronx Robbery Squad to include robbery incidents in which firearms were discharged by perpetrators during robbery.
- Managed administration and operational functions of the Bronx Borough Criminal Intelligence Unit.

Manhattan Sex Crimes Squad • *Commanding Officer*
- Managed Manhattan Sex Crimes Squad.
- Acted as Preliminary Operational Supervisor for all serious sex crime investigations.
- Managed and supervised all serious sex crimes to detect borough-wide patterns of sex crimes.
- Investigated incidents involving physical and sexual abuse of special-category children within Manhattan.

34th Precinct Robbery Identification Program • *Commanding Officer*
- Managed 34th Precinct Robbery Identification Program Unit.
- Managed and supervised all robbery investigations with 34th Precinct.
- Identified and investigated all patterns of robbery with precinct.

Patrol Duties
- Integrity Control Officer and Desk Officer, 50th Precinct.
- Patrol Sergeant in 25th and 26th Patrol Precincts.
- Detective Anti-Crime, 30th Precinct, Police Officer, 30th and 32nd Precincts.

EDUCATION / RANKS / MILITARY

- Currently enrolled in John Jay College of Criminal Justice, NY. Coursework in International Terrorism and Crime. Projected graduation: 2008
- Associate of Applied Science, Criminal Justice, Rockland Community College, NY: Graduated cum laude
- U.S. Marine Corps, Honorable Discharge
- Progressive promotions from Police Officer to Detective (Grade 3) to Sergeant to Lieutenant to Lieutenant Commander (Detective Squad)
- Proficient in Microsoft Word, PowerPoint, knowledge of Macintosh.

Terrence DePhillips
10 Oak Street
Dayton, Ohio 46100

(937) 444-1000
(937) 445-1000, ext. 1000
DeP1990@yahoo.com

CHIEF TECHNICAL OFFICER

CAREER PROFILE:
- Senior information technology professional with extensive experience managing large-scale development projects and organizations. Personal strengths focus on understanding business objectives, organizing teams and delivering solutions.
- Highly developed skills in organizational leadership, specifically in areas of staff and project management, organizational planning, budgeting, and staff development and the development of "best practice" policies.
- Development efforts focused on highly integrated applications that included revenue/yield management (pricing and discounts based on trends), sales and marketing (CRM-type focus on tracking customer activities), financials (General Ledger, Accounts Payable, ATMs).

Development technologies have included:
- Web – Java, XML, Sybase
- Client/server – PowerBuilder, C++, SAS, Sybase
- Mainframe – COBOL II, Assembler, IMS, DB2

PROFESSIONAL EXPERIENCE

NCR Corporation, San Jose, CA
Managing Director, Applications Development   *2002 - Present*
Director, Applications Development   *2001 - 2002*

NCR provides global IT infrastructure. Led organization that developed and supported applications for multiple business lines as member of senior management team. Direct management responsibilities including development staff that supported project activities across IT services and a management staff that supported department planning, budgeting and staff support.

- Managed development staff that supported ATM deployers that now easily transition to a complete application platform. This business unit sells technology/ATM services to various industries. The development team:
  - Developed, rolled out and supported products that provided customers with Internet Distribution Systems (IDS) and Global Distribution Systems (GDS) connectivity.
  - Developed a Web-enabled product (Easy Access) that allows customers to update information in multiple GDS databases through a single transaction.

- Managed development staff that supported customer information and billing systems.

- Managed a team of dedicated project managers assigned to manage selected efforts across business lines. These managers used MS Project and PowerPoint on project efforts for:
  - Managed Web-hosting, data center and network project activities associated with implementation of several Internet-based applications.
  - Implemented the Help Desk product in Phoenix.
  - Managed the data analysis associated with a major system conversion project.

- Managed a team responsible for department planning and financials. Corporate Finance required that all department expenses be quantified on an hourly basis. Actions taken:
  - ➤ Created new team composed of manager and analysts.
  - ➤ Developed budgeting processes that gathered plans from all business units.
  - ➤ This team and processes created resulted in year-end recoveries within 1% (positive) of total expenses.

- Managed team responsible for department people issues. Development staff grew significantly. Serious attention was paid to recruitment, retention and training.
  - ➤ Created a new team with technical experience and strong interpersonal skills.

- Selected by NCR Corporation management to participate in cross-organizational management teams that addressed IT best practices.
  - ➤ The Project Management team developed a "best practices" handbook.
  - ➤ The Human Resource team developed new policies and procedures.

EDAaptive Computing
Director, Applications Development	*1999 - 2001*
Manager	*1998 - 1999*
Project Leader	*1997 - 1998*

EDAptive Computing is an award-winning company that deals with complex electronics systems in aircraft and space vehicles. Expanding leadership responsibilities included supporting global systems. Direct responsibilities included management of projects and systems that included business relationships, systems analyses and designs.

Led teams that developed highly integrated systems supporting full business cycle. They included:
- Yield Management
- Sales
- Marketing
- Operations
- Financials

Recognized by management as leader and team player by selection to participate in key organizational teams:

- Selected by management as one of 40 people from corporation to drive and manage corporate re-engineering efforts.
- Selected by IT management as one of the lead people to work with consultants to identify department issues and to implement change.
- Selected by IT management to create a Project Review committee that evaluated larger scale development efforts and provided guidance and assistance to project teams.

EDUCATION
Ohio State University (Bachelor of Science, Psychology)

MARY WARD
171 Belmont, Jersey City, NJ 07100 (201) 432-1000 (201) 333-1000 Mar@hotmail.com

OBJECTIVE

Marketing Director at large daily newspaper in metropolitan area where management, creative and leadership skills will have positive impact on community and create revenue-building programs for company

CAREER HISTORY

NEWHOUSE PUBLICATION - EVENING JOURNAL ASSOCIATION: 1996 - Present

Marketing Director

- Develop highly successful publicity campaigns for daily newspaper:

  The Jersey Journal

  Plus five weeklies:
  Go Out!
  Coming Up.
  El Nuevo Hudson
  This Week in Bayonne,
  This Week in Jersey City

- Create revenue-building programs for newspaper.
- Supervise internal resources and outside agencies in the management of marketing projects; provide writing, editorial and creative concepts.
- Supervise and train circulation customer-service representatives.
- Plan and coordinate all trade shows/special events and conduct related research.
- Direct creative staff of eight responsible for artistic and creative input.

MARCH OF DIMES   1994 - 1996

Community Director

- Coordinated two major *"WalkAmerica"* sites, company's largest fundraising event.
- Responsible for marketing, fundraising, special projects and events for nonprofit organization
- Spokesperson for national nonprofit agency

FREELANCE JOURNALIST 1992 - 1994

- Hosted on-air fundraising for WNJT, New Jersey Network.
- Researched and interviewed published authors; worked as media consultant for dental practice.
- Conducted interviews, assisted assignment editor with future stories for daily news programs.
- Designed script for restaurant voice-over tape.

FOX TELEVISION, "A CURRENT AFFAIR" 1992 - 1993

Production Assistant

- Assisted reporters in all aspects of production, including topic research, screening story ideas for future productions.
- Facilitated and coordinated on-site taping and interviewing.

FLORIDA STATE LOTTERY 1987 - 1991

Promotional Director

- Became member of original start-up team.
- Developed, organized and implemented Florida State Lottery procedures.
- Managed promotional events, such as lottery-sponsored 1991 Super Bowl.

ORGANIZATIONS/AFFILIATIONS

- Chairman–Hudson County Chamber of Commerce Small Business Committee   1999 - present
- Member–National Federation for Female Executives   1998 - present
- Committee Member–St. Joseph's School for the Blind, Phil Rizzuto Golf Classic   1996 - present
- Board Member–Hudson Cradle, Home for Infants   1995 - present
- Committee Member–Valerie Fund, Children with Cancer   1995 - present

EDUCATION

Rutgers College of Arts & Sciences, Bachelor of Arts, Journalism

CONFIDENTIAL

CHARLES AHERN
10 America Avenue
Babylon, NY 11000
(718) 652-1000
cax2130@aol.com

QUALIFICATIONS: TECHNICAL STAFF MEMBER
More than 10 years' systems and programming experience in **Brokerage** and **Financial** applications.
Wide background in IBM hardware, software and programming languages. Experienced with **full project life cycle** and **project control methodologies.** Extensive experience with **COBOL, COBOL II, VSAM, CICS,** and **DB2. Extensive user contact.**

Hardware:	IBM 3094, 3090, 3083, 3033, 4381
Software:	IBM MVS/ESA, DOS/VSE, TSO/ISPF, VM/CMS, Arthur Andersen Foundation and IEF (CASE), **CICS, DB2,** SPUFI, ISQL, QMF, IMS, IDMS, **VSAM, I**NTERTEST, EDF, XPEDITER, PRO-EDIT, File-AID, Data Expert, SDF, UTILITIES; IDCAMS, SYNCSORT, COMPAREX, Panvalet, Librarian; Windows, WordPerfect
Languages:	**IBM COBOL II,** SQL, BAL, OS/JCL, DOS/JCL, PC-DOS, EASYTRIEVE

EXPERIENCE

Port Authority of New York and New Jersey   **11/97 - Present**
Senior Manager — Programmer/Analyst
Code and modify programs that combine the BARAMIS and AVPS systems. Daily system analysis and program development utilizing ADABAS, **COBOL II, CICS,** SDF, **VSAM,** QSAM, OS/JCL. Key member of the BARAMIS System Y2K conversion team. Changed **COBOL II batch and online programs,** record layouts and SDF maps; converting **VSAM** and QSAM files, and OS/JCL date parms. **CICS** programs were tested using INTERTEST and Xpediter used for batch programs.
Environment: MVS/ESA, TSO/ISPF, VM/CMS, ADABAS, Xpediter, Panvalet: Windows, WordPerfect

Credit Suisse, New York   **6/93 - 9/97**
Senior Manager — Programmer/Analyst
Worked on pilot project to convert part of Warehousing System from Texas Instruments IEF (Information Engineering Facility) to standard **COBOL, CICS, DB2.** System processes and displays global customer information utilizing both batch and online programs. Analyzed the IEF high-level program code and converting the programs to native **COBOL, CICS, DB2** source code. Also tested and documented each program. Promoted from Manager to Senior Manager in 1995. Platinum, QMF and SPUFI used for accessing **DB2** tables and creating test data. File-AID and IDCAMS for creating and changing **VSAM** files. **Environment:** MVS/ESA, TSO/ISPF

Lehman Brothers, New York   **10/92 - 5/93**
Senior Programmer/Analyst
Worked on Maintain Securities Information (MSI) process of Multi-Currency Accounting and Reporting System (MARS). This large global security system processed corporate actions and pricing information received from financial organizations. Analyzed, designed and coded programs that performed validation of the vendor input data and creation of output transaction tables used to update the MARS database. Programs were written in **COBOL II** and **CICS** with embedded **DB2.** Platinum, QMF and SPUFI were used for testing **DB2** queries, ad hoc reports and creating test tables. **Environment:** MVS/ESA, TSO/ISPF

EDUCATION: Bachelor of Science, Queens College

David J. Rosen

100 Glenwood Avenue, Leonia, NJ 07100
Home: (201) 461-1000 Cell: (646) 431-1000 E-mail: djr100@nyu.edu

STATEMENT OF PURPOSE

Recent college graduate responsive to deadlines and with multifaceted intern experience seeks entry-level administrative and editorial support position at publishing house that requires the ability to multitask; has strong writing, proofreading and editing skills.

EDUCATION

- B.A., 2003, New York University, Gallatin School of Individualized Studies Concentration in English and Communications: 3.3 GPA

SKILLS

- Proficient in Microsoft Word, Works and Excel
- Familiar with Macintosh

EMPLOYMENT

Intern, Show Business Weekly, February 2003 – June 2003

- Proofread articles
- Wrote casting notices
- Proposed cover concepts
- Phone duties
- Data entry
- Wrote photo captions

Human Resources Intern, Time Warner Cable, Palisades Park, NJ, summer 2000

- Improved organization of office materials to upgrade efficiency.
- Assisted reporters at press conferences.

Clerical Assistant, NYU Undergraduate Admissions Office, October 1999 – May 2001

- Advised prospective students of upcoming events and off-campus functions.
- Filed important and confidential documents.

Customer Relations, Corporate Investor Communications, summer 1999

- Entered data and performed telephone duties.

STUDENT ACTIVITIES: Co-Junior Class Representative, Gallatin School Student Council: Helped initiate student council and implement new programs. Staff Member, *Minetta Review,* NYU Literary Magazine, 3 years: candidate for Editorial Position. Treasurer, Gallatin First Friday Organization: Helped organize monthly arts festival.

Terrence Martz
WIRE ROPE ENGINEER
100 Breuhaus Lane
Seaville, NJ 08230
(609) 624-1000 (Cell)
Tmar@hotmail.com

Objective: Managerial position in Wire Rope Industry where engineering expertise in suspension bridges can further advance the application of new wire rope technologies

➤ More than 10 years' experience as engineer in Wire Rope business
➤ Specialized in contract negotiation and specifications for pre-stressed products in bridges and cable-supported structures

---

J.A. Good Consultants, Cape May Courthouse, NJ   **1992-Present**

Manager/Field Engineer   **1997-Present**
Prepared and **tested** socketed strand assemblies to develop an approved methodology for subsequent field application.
Developed marketing strategies to increase customer base and increase usage of structural strand and wire rope products within construction sector.
Managed contracts for Warrior River RR Lift Bridge, Burlington Northern RR Life Bridge, Camas Prairie RR Lift Bridge, Texaco Pipeline Suspension Bridge, Capitol Center Sports Arena, Denver Sports Arena.
Provided estimates and then managed contracts for McKenzie River Bridge, Point Pleasant Canal Lift Bridge, Ben Franklin Bridge.
Recent field work includes:
➤ Replaced suspenders and handropes on Golden Gate Bridge.
➤ Made corrective repairs to suspender assemblies and handropes on Golden Gate.
➤ Inspected wire ropes on Harlem River 125th Street Lift Bridge.

Assistant Manager   **1994-1997**
Coordinated three warehouses and inventory management. Conducted transportation cost-analysis studies. Negotiated freight rates and developed national transportation policies that improved time-to-market and reduced costs by 20%. Wrote specifications for pre-stressed products in bridges. Proficient in Microsoft Office.

Senior Wire Rope Product Engineer   **1992-1994**
Provided engineering services to original equipment manufacturers and strip mining companies while acting as National Customer Technical Service Representative. Highly skilled in field investigation, negotiation, settlement of claims.

EDUCATION: Stevens Institute of Technology, Hoboken, NJ   **1990-1992**

Myles Byrne
WEBMASTER
1 Northland Avenue
Appleton, WI 54100
(920) 444-1000 (Home)
(920) 445-1000 (Cell)
Mylie111@msn.com
www.mylie.com

OBJECTIVE: To combine expertise as **editor** and **writer** with computer skills as highly proficient **Assistant Webmaster** for **Webmaster** position at large corporation in Wisconsin

---

Assistant Webmaster, SYS-CON Media, Montvale, NJ. 2001-2004

SYS-CON Media, listed in *Inc. 500* three years in a row as the fastest-growing, privately held publishing company in America, is leading publisher serving the i-technology markets.

As **Assistant Webmaster,** maintained and enhanced various publications' Web sites, including *Wireless Business & Technology, Java Developer's Journal, XML-Journal, Web Services Journal and ColdFusion Developer's Journal,* where it was necessary to type, scan, import and edit text. Additionally, wrote, edited, researched and solicited as well as acquired additional information for Web sites.

Skills and **qualifications** necessary to successfully fulfill requirements were knowledge of Macintosh, WYSIWYG and graphics software, HTML, QuarkXPress.

Expertise in Internet technologies, such as CGI and JavaScript, Adobe GoLive. Proficient in Word, WordPerfect, MS Works, PowerPoint.

Sports Editor/Copy Editor, *North Jersey Herald & News,* Passaic, NJ. 2000-2001

Worked as **Assistant Editor** and **Copy Editor** at metropolitan newspaper covering Paterson and surrounding area. Competently met daily deadlines in high pressure atmosphere. Wrote sports news briefs and copyedited daily section.

Skills required for position: thorough knowledge of AP style; thorough knowledge of sports (even minutiae); acquired skills in Macintosh, Quark, PhotoShop. Honed skills as writer and editor, with emphasis on accuracy and clarity.

Unrelated experience:

South Coast Deli, Santa Barbara, CA 1995-1998.

Prepared sandwiches and worked cash register 20 hours per week during school semesters. Developed **skills**
- interacting with public
- working long hours
- taking direction from four supervisors simultaneously

EDUCATION: University of California, Santa Barbara, Bachelor of Arts, **English.** Minor in **Computer Science.** 1998. GPA: 3.2.
- Involved in many intramural sports (volleyball, basketball).

- See www.mylie.com for sample work.

Sharon M. Smith
559 Holly Court
Mahwah, NJ 07100
(201) 760-1000
Suz559@aol.com

OFFICE MANAGER *with definitive strengths in managing day-to-day administrative and financial operations*

Traphagen & Traphagen, CPAs, Oradell, NJ
October 1981 to Present

Office Manager/Administrative Assistant/Administrative Partner
- Supervise front office staff.
- Supervise entire staff for firm policy compliance.
- Manage time accounting and billing system.
- Accounts Receivable
- Accounts Payable
- Liaison between partners and clients
- Prepare firm financial reports.
- Facilities maintenance (250-year-old historic structure)
- Equipment maintenance
- Property management for rental properties
- Prepare promotional material.

SUMMARY OF ACCOMPLISHMENTS

- Led computer conversion for firm's billing and accounts receivable system.
- Assisted in restoration of historic structure.
- Assisted state-funded program for victims of September 11th in receiving nonprofit organizational status — worked directly with governor's office.
- Volunteer for March of Dimes

SKILLS

MS Windows, Word, Excel, PowerPoint, Peachtree, Quickbooks, Unilink TB Plus, Lacerte and Steno

EDUCATION

Berkeley Secretarial School, Executive Secretarial Program
Graduate of Dale Carnegie Effective Communications Course

JAMES HENRY
100 Walnut St. • Brookline, MA • 02100 • (617) 277-1000
henry.cat@verizon.net

Education

Tufts University, Medford, MA   *1988-1990*
University of Massachusetts, Amherst, MA   *1990-1992*
- Bachelor of Arts, Psychology, December 1992
- Cum laude graduate

Experience

May 2000 - present   *Program Analyst*
Vaxgen, Inc., Brisbane, CA

- Provide SAS programming support for Phase III clinical trial involving experimental AIDS vaccine.
- Perform validation and creation of summary tables supporting Phase I/II reports submitted to FDA.
- Create semiannual summary tables for submission to Data Safety Monitoring Board.
- Act as sole support for contract laboratory data.
- Create and maintain Contract Payment System responsible for quarterly payments made to 61 participating clinical sites for Phase III clinical trial.
- Maintain company intranet with respect to summary tables and subject listings for Clinical and Data Management departments and remote staff.

November 1998 -
May 2000   *Consultant*
Statistical Programming Consultant for Trilogy Consulting and
Atlantic Search Group
Programmer/Data Manager, Warner-Lambert Company,
Morris Plains, NJ *(Trilogy)*
Analyst, Pharmacyclics, Inc., Sunnyvale, CA *(ASG)*

- Provided consulting services/SAS programming support for clinical study applications and NDA submissions of Phase I/II clinical trials.
- Inspected existing systems, SAS code and report generation for accuracy.
- Created data warehouse through the construction of SAS data sets and analysis files from source data (e.g., SAS, ASCII, spreadsheets, transport, text, etc.).
- Executed database queries on protocol specifications and

follow-up for resolution with clinical/data management groups.
- Generated complex data reports.
- Assisted in the development of department-wide SOPs and the standardization of SAS code generation.
- Created finalized status reports for related programming and data management activities.
- Trained/developed new staff for all data management aspects and auditing data listings.

April 1998 -
November 1998

Programmer Analyst
Abt Associates, Inc., Cambridge, MA

- Represented Law and Public Policy area in all company-wide programming issues.
- Wrote reports of study results for funding agencies.
- Cleaned and analyzed data for Senior Scientists in Law and Public Policy Area and investigators at federal offices.
- Wrote and debugged SAS code for several projects.
- Served as internal resource adviser and mentor in statistical programming for junior staff.
- Interviewed and evaluated prospective Abt employees in programming and statistical skills.

July 1995 -
April 1998

Senior Research Associate (1997-1998)
Research Associate (1996)
Senior Research Assistant (1995)
New England Research Institutes, Watertown, MA

- Conducted site visits to study centers in New York, DC, Chicago, San Francisco and Los Angeles to monitor adherence to study laboratory protocols.
- Tracked central specimen repository containing 400,000 specimens.
- Used SAS to select specimens to be retrieved from specimen repository for individual substudies.
- Acted as primary contact with central repository staff.
- Served on protocol development team for substudy involving NIDA.
- Worked directly with NIAID Program Officer during study renewal.
- Performed exploratory statistical analysis and analysis for eventual manuscripts in SAS for a multicenter study of women and HIV disease progression.
- Served as primary contact to multiple working groups, including Epidemiology-Statistics, Retention, Shipping, Laboratory and all lab-related subgroups.

- Collaborated directly with principal investigators and site project directors on data management and analysis issues.
- Produced monthly reports on protocol compliance, accrual and retention of study participants.

June 1994 -
July 1995

Research Assistant
Medical Research International, Burlington, MA

- Programmed in SAS on multiple studies involving pharmaceutical companies.
- Provided database management support for multiple studies.
- Acted as primary contact with overseas office regarding international study status.
- Assisted in coordination and implementation of database construction using SAS.
- Assisted in development and implementation of internal quality assurance procedures.
- Collaborated with systems development staff on design of study-specific data-management systems.

December 1991 -
January 1993

Senior Team Leader
Laboratory for Behavior Assessment, University of Massachusetts

- Recruited subjects for laboratory behavior studies.
- Distributed and monitored tasks performed by research assistants.
- Oversaw all activities performed in laboratory.

Professional Organizations

Golden Key National Honor Society
Psi Chi (The National Honor Society in Psychology)

Computer Skills

SAS through 8.01; basic methods (sort, merge, retain, formats, freq, etc.), macros, report generation (data null, tabulate, report, graphics, etc.), statistics (proc means, tabulate, univariate, etc), arrays (implicit, explicit), SAS SCL programming, AF Frame creation, SAS/Graph, time series graphing, Shell scripting, SPSS, S-Plus, FoxPro, Paradox, WordPerfect, Microsoft (Word, Access, Excel, PowerPoint, Outlook), Quattro Pro, Netscape, Internet Explorer, Eudora Pro, FTP, Windows NT and UNIX environments

BARRY MITCHELL

100 Baxter Avenue
New Hyde Park, NY 11010

Home: 516-437-1000
E-Mail: mitch@msn.com

PROFESSIONAL EXPERIENCE

THE DEPOSITORY TRUST & CLEARING CORPORATION (DTCC)
1998-2003
Manager, Corporate Communications

Conceive and write/edit annual reports, policy papers, talking points, internal/external newsletter articles, speeches and press releases while also creating marketing collateral material for trade shows, industry conferences and direct-mail pieces. Respond to media inquiries and pitch stories to trade publications. Converted complex topics into readable copy for all business units.

ANTON COMMUNITY NEWSPAPERS OF LONG ISLAND
2001-Present
Syndicated Columnist, "Eye on the Island"

Write weekly public affairs column for 18 Nassau County, Long Island, newspapers. The Anton papers have a subscription base of more than 75,000 households. The current piece is online at www.antonnews.com/feature.

THE NEW YORK STATE BANKING DEPARTMENT
1996-1998
Public Information Officer

Primary media relations contact for agency that regulates much of New York's financial services industry. Wrote speeches, press releases, talking points and other key correspondence for governor and superintendent of banks. Managed staff that processed hundreds of Freedom of Information Act (FOIA) requests each year.

CORPORATE COVERAGE
1992-1996
President

Operated a public and governmental relations firm that included among its clients Jamaica Water Supply (a subsidiary of Emcor, a publicly traded corporation), the Oyster Bay-East Norwich, New York, public schools and Jay Leno's Big Dog Productions.

TOWN OF NORTH HEMPSTEAD
1989-1991
Public Information Officer

> Primary media relations contact for municipality of 210,000 in northern Nassau County, Long Island. Wrote press releases, speeches, issue backgrounders, legislative memoranda and constituent correspondence for town's elected officials.

MANHASSET PRESS
1984-1988
Editor

> Edited and wrote hard news and features for Nassau County weekly newspaper with a circulation of more than 3,500 households. Supervised freelance writers. Broke numerous stories before daily news media.

ELECTIVE OFFICE
Village of Manorhaven
1991-1993
Trustee

> Elected to two-year term with more than 60 percent of vote in village that is home to almost 7,000 in Port Washington, New York. Voted in favor of garbage contract that increased recycling and against largest property tax hike in Manorhaven's history. Moved out of village and did not seek re-election in 1993.

EDUCATION

> *Fordham University*
> Bachelor of Arts (Communications)
> Earned Dean's List honors and was catcher on varsity baseball team.

SELECTED ACHIEVEMENTS

Public & Media Relations

- Created DTCC's first-ever Recruitment Brochure, Code of Ethics manual, and employee guide to Customer Support Center.

- Developed marketing collateral materials that boosted sales for DTCC products, such as Security Position Reports and its Data Delivery Service.

- Served as key media relations contact for DTCC's Board of Directors and frequent speechwriter for DTCC's Chairman/CEO.

- Generated story ideas and was major editorial contributor to @*dtcc*, the company's external newsletter — and *The View*, its internal publication.

- Business units requested reprints of numerous @*dtcc* articles for sales-generation purposes and to keep current customers up-to-date.

- Coordinated Harvard's Henry Louis Gates's DTCC appearance (press release, Chairman's speech, company-wide publicity) as part of company's African-American history month celebration.

- Served as primary point of contact for DTCC Managing Directors seeking assistance with correspondence and presentations. Edited for content, style and readability.

- Supervised all of New York State's regulatory media relations activities pertaining to the Chase Manhattan-Chemical merger and the one between Union Bank of Switzerland (UBS) and Swiss Bank Corporation (SBC).

Governmental Affairs

- Developed remarks and position papers for Governor Pataki and New York's Superintendent of banks regarding their financial regulatory policies.

- Interacted with the New York Bankers Association (NYBA), trade groups, and key legislators on the "wild card" law, the ATM Safety Act, and the creation of the state's Holocaust Claims Processing Office.

- Monitored Freedom of Information Act (FOIA) requests closely, recognizing that some would generate subsequent media inquiries.

- Edited the *Weekly Bulletin*, a document that summarized branch bank closings/openings as well as Mortgage Broker and Banker activity statewide.

Journalism

- Write/research weekly column that covers politics, government, sports, and entertainment— and profiles Long Island personalities.

- Appeared as frequent guest on WLIW-TV's "The Editor's Desk," a current events program aired on Long Island's public television station.

- Acted as guest lecturer, St. Joseph's College, Patchogue, New York.

- Have a wide array of editorial contacts at various news outlets, including the *Wall Street Journal* and the Associated Press.

LiAnn Chu
100 Cinder Road
Edison, NJ 08100
Telephone: (H) (732) 744-1000

Email: LiAn@hotmail.com

Work History
September 2002 - Current
Senior Consultant
Technovision Inc., Clark, NJ

Project: Post-Trade Transaction Processing System for SIAC
- Familiar with new Post-Trade Transaction Processing. Analyze and test performance of newly developed programs using MQ Series and JCL.
- Design and develop new batch programs to identify and process Gaps during the Post-Trade Processing.
- Test performance of new programs.

Oct. 1998 - June 2002
Senior Programmer Analyst
Company: **(i) Structure, Inc.,** Parsippany, NJ

Project: Customer Information Database for Pershing, Credit Suisse First Boston
- Analyzed and specified Cash Management, IRA and COD account business editing rules.
- Designed and developed Cash Management editing, creating, viewing and bridgeback programs to interface with PONA (CICS,VSAM System), and other Web-based Front-end using CICS, COBOL II, DB2 and MQ Series.
- Analyzed, designed and developed Cash Management Batch Conversion and Bridgeback Processing to convert the existing Cash Management information from PONA to CID tables and to bridgeback information from CID tables back to temperate files for verification.
- Tested and supported all developed programs in DEV, SIT and UAT by using Message Manager Tester, XMLLink MsgExplorer and InterTest.

March 1999 - December 1999

Project: Paradigm (Integration System for Online Brokerage) for Pershing, DLJ
- Developed new Inquiry, Add and Update programs for Investment Objectives to Interface with the GUI Front-end (MQ Series) in Paradigm system.
- Analyzed, designed, developed new programs and modified old programs of PONA (Online Name and Address) system to interface with the GUI Front-end (Planetwork) for New Accounts Approval Processing in Paradigm.
- Supported the GUI Front-end team with PONA Knowledge.

Environment and Resources: IBM mainframe, CICS, COBOL II, DB2, INTERTEST, MQ Series and ENDEVOR.

October 1998 - March 1999
Company: **ETS**

Project: DANTES, GMAT Y2K Renovation Projects for Educational Testing Service.
- Coordinated the Renovation Team, Testing Team and the Customers for Y2K Renovation of DANTES and GMAT testing systems.

Main tasks were:
✓ Managed the progress of renovation and testing.
✓ Documented and solved issues raised by renovation, testing team and customers.
✓ Liaison between renovation, testing team and customers

Environment and Resources: CICS, COBOL II, VSAM, IDMS (ADSO)

April 1997 - September 1998
Programmer Analyst
Company: **Andersen Contracting,** Melbourne, Australia

Project: FLEXCAB (Flexible Charging and Billing System) for Telstra, Australia
As *Migration Coordinator and Data Representative*
Main tasks were:
✓ Maintained and controlled the versions of programs and data elements.
✓ Reconciled updated programs and data elements with production versions.
✓ Defined new programs and data elements in Design/1 and Endevor.

As *Lead Programmer Analyst*
Main tasks were:
✓ Analyzed the Change Requests.
✓ Designed detail solutions for Change Requests for each quarterly release.
✓ Coded and unit tested the programs for Change Requests
✓ Documented all new changes in the Design/1.

Environment and Resources: MVS JCL, CICS, COBOL II, DB2, SAS, SPUFI, ProEdit, Access for DB2, SCLM, SmartEdit, SmartTest and DESIGN/1, ENDEVOR

November 1995 - July 1996
Software Consultant
Company: **TaskForce Computer Service,** Melbourne, Australia

Project: GRCS for State Revenue Office (Ferntree Computer Corporation) VIC Australia (GRCS is a Generic Revenue Collecting system developed under MVS, COBOL II, DB2, CICS and GUI interface.)
Main tasks were:
✓ Maintained Land Tax and Payroll Tax collection programs.
✓ Solved User Requests and Production problems.
✓ Designed and developed new reports within existing programs.

Environment and Resources: MVS, COBOL II, DELTA (Cobol Generator), DB2, CICS and SPUFI, File-Aid for DB2, ENDEVOR.

May 1994 - Oct. 1995
Programmer Analyst
Company: **Andersen Contracting,** Melbourne Australia

Project: FLEXCAB (Flexible Charging and Billing System), Telstra Australia.
Environment & Resources: MVS JCL, COBOL II, DB2, SPUFI, File-Aid, SAS and Design/1, ENDEVOR, MS Project, CTM

January 1989 - April 1994
Programmer Analyst
Company: **NEXUS Business Software Pty. Ltd.,** Melbourne, Australia

Project: NEXUS (Integrated Accounting System)
Environment & Resources: IBM-PC, C++, DATAFLEX

IT SKILLS SUMMARY

IBM mainframe DB2 SQL	Excellent	8 years
IBM mainframe MVS JCL, COBOL II	Excellent	8 years
IBM mainframe CICS COBOL	Excellent	5 years
IBM mainframe IMS(DL/1)	Familiar	1 year
UNIX COBOL	Good	2.5 years
PASCAL, GW-BASIC	Familiar	
MS-DOS DATAFLEX	Good	5 years
SAS, C++	Familiar	1 year
Software Utilities (Package)		
ENDEVOR	Very Good	8 years
DESIGN/1	Very Good	2 years
File-AID	Good	7 years
SPUFI, PROEDIT	Good	7 years
File-AID for DB2, Access/DB2	Good	6 years
SmartEdit SmartTest	Good	1 year
SCLM	Familiar	1 year
MQ Series	Familiar	1 year
MS Project	Familiar	0.5 year
Microsoft Word, Excel	Excellent	6 years

Education:
* Master of Science: Software Engineering **ZhongShan University,** China 1985
* Bachelor of Science: Computer Science & Software **ZhongShan University,** China 1982

JOHN SMITH
100A EXETER STREET
BOSTON, MA 02100
(617) 266-1000

JS100@worldnet.att.net

EDUCATION	Babson College, Master of Business Administration (1981) Villanova University, Master of Science Math (1969) Villanova University, Bachelor of Science Electrical Engineering (1965)

EXPERIENCE

1997-PRESENT   SKYCADY
BOSTON

Principal
Involved in variety of consulting assignments both for venture capital groups and with small and medium-size companies. A member of the BOD of Savior Technology, Campbell, CA.; Finale Inc, Boston, MA; Asic Alliance, Woburn, MA; and Site Technology, Sunnyvale, CA. Completed several acting CEO assignments.

Boston University, Boston; Dean College, Franklin, MA; and University of Phoenix, Braintree, MA

Part-Time Instructor
Taught undergraduate/graduate level in Computer Science Department.

1989-1998   DATA GENERAL CORPORATION
WESTBORO, MA

Vice President Worldwide Channels
Responsible for all activities associated with DG's distribution channels. This includes P&L, credit, technical support, account management, training, advertising and promotion. Budgets in excess of $1 billion. Member of operations committee, which approves product directions, sets marketing strategies, determines corporate expense plans and partner investment.

Vice President of Americas Sales and Service
Managed all sales, support, field marketing, customer service and national account activities in North and South America. Built a $600M open system business from scratch in five years while simultaneously

289

increasing sales productivity by 50% and generating more than 70% of this business from accounts new to Data General. Completely restructured field function to integrate VARs, OEMs, ISVs, telesales, teleservice, agents, subcontractors, integration channel partners, major accounts and end users. Responsibilities included revenue budgets in excess of $700M, associated profit budgets and professional staff of more than 2,000 people.

1985-1989   **APOLLO COMPUTER CORPORATION**
CHELMSFORD, MA

Vice President of North American Sales Operations
Managed all sales, support, field marketing and national account activities. Sales, revenue and profit responsibilities for all markets through all channels. Took over sales when 85% of sales were to OEMs and expanded sales into major accounts, new accounts and VARs. Grew major accounts 40% and doubled new accounts each year. Member of operations committee, which approves product directions, sets marketing strategies, determines corporate expense plans and partner investment.

1983-1985   **DIGITAL EQUIPMENT CORPORATION**
MAYNARD, MA

Northeast Regional Sales Manager
Managed all the field and sales marketing activities in the Northeast. Sales and revenue responsibilities for all markets through all channels. Fastest-growing and #1-performing region in the company in 1984.

1981-1983   *United States Distribution Manager*
Managed the operations activity for all distribution channels. Group consisted of approximately 60 people involved in operations, technical support, account management, training, advertising and promotion.

1969-1983   *Sales and Sales Management*
Various sales and sales management positions in Manhattan and Boston. Overachieved goals in every year of eligibility. Managed Digital's top district for three consecutive years.

1976-1977   **NEW YORK INSTITUTE OF TECHNOLOGY**
WESTBURY, NY

Adjunct Faculty
Instructor for undergraduate statistics course

1965-1969   **TECHNITROL INC., & U. S. ARMY (Civilian Employee)**

Electrical Engineer
Various electrical engineering assignments in test equipment design

CATHERINE SMITH
1 Madison Street #1C
Hoboken, NJ 07010
Telephone: 201-792-1000
E-mail: csss10@hotmail.com

Professional Experience

2000 - Present   **TD SECURITIES (USA), Inc.**   New York, NY
Associate, Media & Communications Group

- Active member of several four-person deal teams that structured, originated and executed six new/amended and restated senior leveraged credit facility transactions within the cable, programming and publishing sectors for which TD Securities acted as Agent Bank and earned more than $7.5 million in fee income. Responsibilities included performance of due diligence, preparation of credit and valuation analyses, construction of transaction terms, negotiation of loan documentation and frequent interaction with prospective investors during syndication phase to support due diligence initiatives.

- Acted as primary Transaction Manager for 13 accounts totaling $600 million within Media & Communications Portfolio, which involves active monitoring of financial and operational performance, reassessment of credit risk and enterprise valuation as well as preparation of formal analyses used to regularly update senior credit committee members.

- Serve as bank's primary representative in workout phase and Chapter 11 filing of an Internet broadband company. Responsibilities included the development and update of credit analysis and recovery scenarios, calculation and recommendation of loan loss provisions and frequent direct communication with key credit committee members, including the Chief Credit Officer.

- Negotiated with domestic and international counsel and with client management to remedy loan defaults of two Argentine cable companies caused by extreme local economic and political conditions, which resulted in partial receipt of interest payments and loan principal.

Summer 1999   **ARGUS RESEARCH CORPORATION**   New York, NY
Summer Associate, Sell Side Equity Research

- Constructed quantitative models used to project earnings and equity valuations for several telecom service companies.

- Researched and prepared written analyses of a telecom equipment company and a telecom service company to initiate research coverage of its equities.

291

- Composed daily and monthly client reports that summarized current events in telecom services/equipment and cable/media industries and projected their potential impact on equity prices.

1996 - 1998	**BANKERS TRUST COMPANY**	New York, NY

Assistant Vice President, Internal Audit Department

- Evaluated accuracy of market and credit risk statistics used by derivatives trading desks.

- Composed audit reports directed to senior management, including Chief Information Officer and Senior Managing Director of Sales and Trading.

1992 - 1996	**DELOITTE & TOUCHE LLP**	Parsippany, NJ

Senior Accountant, Accounting and Auditing Services

- Analyzed quarterly and yearly financial statement balances related to investment activity and researched material differences.

- Identified and substantiated variances in client portfolio performance vs. market trends.

Education: **NEW YORK UNIVERSITY**   New York, NY
Leonard N. Stern School of Business
Master of Business Administration, May 2000
Emphasis in Finance/Economics

- GPA: 3.77/4.0: Graduated *with Distinction*

LEHIGH UNIVERSITY   Bethlehem, PA
Bachelor of Science, Accounting, June 1992
- GPA: 3.5/4.0: Graduated *cum laude*
Minor in American Literature

Certification: Certified Public Accountant since 1993, Series 7/Series 63

Language: Fluent Spanish

Nicholas Murray   **1 Mount Walley Road**
Nicmc@yahoo.com   Waltham, MA 02100
(781) 899-1000

EDUCATION
Harvard University
Bachelor of Arts, with honors (cum laude) in 2003
GPA: 3.25 (3.30 in major)
Relevant Coursework: Introduction to Investments, Political Economy of Japan, Calculus

RELATED WORK EXPERIENCE
Morgan Stanley (Boston)   6/02 - 9/02
Financial Services Intern
• Identified potential market strategies by contacting outside fund companies. Presented these strategies to upper management.
• Researched current market conditions and fixed-income industry segments.
• Analyzed portfolios, using Bloomberg and Nasdaq information services. Made suggestions to identify strengths and weaknesses.
• Attended research meetings over live video feed from New York.
• Prepared client reports using Microsoft Excel.

Fidelity Investments (Boston)   6/01 - 9/01
Trade Analyst
• Acted as liaison between 40 Investment Managers and custodian bank to research and answer client inquiries. Provided quick resolution to problems. Answered inquiries in efficient and timely manner.
• Compiled and analyzed variety of securities, failed trades and trade metrics for company's database to streamline operations.
• Forecasted potential overdrafts by monitoring global cash balances.

Sullivan and Cogliano Companies (Staffing Solutions, Waltham, MA)   6/00 - 9/00
Research Analyst
• Located and contacted potential candidates for recruiting firm.
• Researched client company profiles for sales division. Familiarity with Macintosh. Proficient in Microsoft Windows and Internet research.

OTHER WORK EXPERIENCE
Harvard University Athletic Operation   09/01 - 09/03
Facilities Staff: Monitored facilities after hours and assembled facility equipment prior to athletic competitions. Committed 15 hours per week to defray cost of education and maintained high GPA.

Harvard College Fund   9/00 - 12/00
Student Fundraiser: Raised more than $20,000 each semester by contacting alumni by telephone for various branches at Harvard. Honed telephone and customer service skills. Learned value of following up with customers.

ACTIVITIES
Member of Harvard Varsity Baseball Team, 09/99 - 2003. Member A.D. Club, Harvard Finals Club, 09/01 - 2003, Harvard Student Thank-a-Thon Committee Member, 09/00 - 09/02

Marissa Capelli
Cape3@bc.edu

Current Address
1000 Commonwealth Avenue
Apartment 100
Brighton, MA 02100
(617) 787-1000

Permanent Address
1 Monroe Court
Harrington Park, NJ 07000

(201) 767-1000

EDUCATION

Boston College
College of Arts and Sciences
Bachelor of Arts, projected graduation: May 2007
Major: Communications
Cumulative GPA: 3.6/4.0
Honors: Dean's List (5 semesters); Golden Key International Honor Society

---

WORK EXPERIENCE

The Brunswick Group
London, England
Research and Information Intern
June 2006

✓ Assembled specific information regarding clients using programs such as Bloomberg, Lexis Nexis, Multex, Hemscott and Reuters.

✓ Created a media overview and press analysis of particular company, tracking national and regional coverage, and third-party comments on company funding.

✓ Researched quarterly reporting dates and figures for many Brunswick clients and their competitors.

✓ Summarized controversial AGMs (annual general meetings) and compiled a casebook to serve as a reference guide for Brunswick's future client situations.

Boston College Career Center
Chestnut Hill, MA
Peer Adviser
Academic year 2005

✓ Training in communication skills, résumés, cover letters and interview skills.

Boston College Career Center (continued)

✓ Conducted résumé, cover letter and interview workshops for undergraduate students and provided individual assistance to teach basic skills.

✓ Directed recruitment project by creating advertisements for Boston College newspaper, mass e-mails and fliers to recruit peer advisers for next academic year.

The Lily Pad Academy
Hackensack, NJ
Day Care Assistant
Summer 2003

✓ Planned and ran activities for children ranging from 1 to 5 years of age.

✓ Assisted in personal development of each child through activities and individual nourishment.

The Limited & Co.
Paramus, NJ
Salesperson
Winter 2003

✓ Assisted in the visual display of merchandise, exceeded daily sales goals, managed client relationships.

ACTIVITIES
BC-GESS Mentoring Program, Thomas Gardner School
Allston, MA
Mentor
Fall 2004

✓ Promoted academic achievement and instilled values in children at academic and social risk.

✓ Received training on mentor tasks and roles, communication skills, child abuse prevention and cultural diversity.

SKILLS

Computer: Proficient in Microsoft Office, Knowledgeable in Multex, Bloomberg and Reuters
Language: Conversational in Spanish

Roseanna Pollack
1 Main Street
Newton, NJ 07100

Telephone: (973) 300 1000
Fax (973) 300 9100
E-mail: R10@aol.com

EDUCATION
Graduate of Montclair State University, January 1994
Received Bachelor of Arts (Language)
Graduated in 3½ years with 4.0 GPA

PROFESSIONAL HIGHLIGHTS

Customer Follow-Up Coordinator
April 1999 - Present

> *McGuire Chevrolet:* July 2001 - Present
> *Franklin Sussex Auto Mall:* April 1999 - Present
> *Condit Ford World:* April 2001 - April 2003
> *Prestige Volvo:* February 2001 - October 2001

Sales • Marketing • Service Skills
Contact customers who have visited each dealership via telephone and **document** respective Sales/Service experiences. **Answer** customers' questions regarding dealers' policies and procedures. **Chart** results of telephone calls, as well as dates and times of attempted calls, making sure three attempts are made to contact customer — all within three business days. **Write** Customer Feedback Reports whenever there is a concern. **Verify** that each report is immediately forwarded to appropriate manager and it is promptly **resolved, documented** and **reviewed** with personnel involved. **Draw up** Trend Analysis Reports for each dealer based on information **collected** from customers, **evaluating** where each dealer is strong and where each requires improvement. **Design** reports that correspond to reflect each vehicle manufacturer's specification (e.g., Chrysler's Five Star Program, Ford's Blue Oval Certification, etc.). **Acting as liaison** so that these reports are available for inspection by each vehicle manufacturer. **Remind** customers to fill out and return manufacturers' surveys. **Improve** each dealership's CSI score each quarter.

__Jump Lumber Company, Inc.__ Newton, NJ
June 1997 - Present

Bookkeeper • General Office
Balance books at end of business day. **Adjust** computer inventory to match physical inventory, entering customer payments and purchase orders. **Match** purchase orders with receivings and bills to ensure all figures are correct. **Print** checks, making sure bills and taxes are paid on time. **Run** customer statements at end of each month. **Mail** out in timely manner, **filing** customer receipts, **backing up** the computer after closing, **updating** the computer system at end of each month, quarter and fiscal year. **Input** weekly payroll each week and verify that hours have been added up correctly.

__United Parcel Service, Inc.__ Parsippany, NJ
May 1993 - February 1997

Customer Service Account Executive
Youngest woman **promoted** to Management in North Jersey District; directly responsible for 11,000 shippers in Morristown area. **Set up** new accounts. **Sold** UPS services. **Persuaded** customers from using competition. **Inspected** damages, **settling** claims, **responding** to customer concerns, **maintaining** solid relationships with customers, as well as **establishing** new contacts. **Taught** customers to utilize new technology. **Wrote** and **submitted** logistic study analysis to **improve** customers' shipping procedures. **Initiated** and **approved** incentive pricing. Coordinated donations to United Way. **Oversaw** customer counter that is open to the public during Christmas holiday.

UPS Customer Service Intern
Discovered good locations for UPS overnight letter boxes. **Set up** contracts with property owners and **coordinated** placement of letter centers. **Canvassed** areas and **created** new overnight/international shipping accounts. **Worked** on various advertising projects for UPS letter centers. **Qualified** driver leads and assisted Account Executives in customer follow-up.

ALICE A. THOMAS
15 East 10th Street, Apt.10, New York, NY 10100 (212)533-1000
E-mail: Alito@aol.com

PROFESSIONAL OBJECTIVE
College-educated and bilingual Administrative Assistant with 14 years' experience seeks to support management at architectural firm with excellent accounting, communication and computer skills.

- Proficient in MS Word, Excel, PowerPoint, and Lotus and Internet
- Fluent in Spanish

EXPERIENCE
Ambassador Construction, New York, NY   1995-2004

Administrative Assistant
- Promoted to Administrative Assistant in Insurance Department.
- Streamlined accounting procedures.
- Created highly workable file structures.
- Assigned special projects.

Executive Secretary
- Composed and prepared routine correspondence.
- Liaisoned between immediate managers and high-level executives.
- Organized official company documents for prospective clients.
- Edited and proofread reports.
- Maintained accounting procedures.

Dow Jones & Co., Inc., New York, NY   1993—1994
Executive Secretary at NBEW's Advertising Department
- Composed and prepared routine correspondence. Adept at bookkeeping, filing, typing, heavy phones and customer service.
- Coordinated and created promotional materials.
- Maintained personnel attendance log.
- Arranged reservations and travel.

Globus/Cosmos Tourama, Rego Park, Queens, NY   1989—1993
Word Processor/Travel Documentation Assistant
- Initiated procedure to coordinate travel documentation with issuance of airline tickets to clients; **process was instituted nationally by the company's Documents Department.**
- Prepared travel itineraries and hotel lists worldwide.

EDUCATION Hunter College. Projected graduation: 2007

Raymond Thomas *Public Relations*
1 Licoya Bay, Nashville, TN 37215 ● (615) 677-1000
FAX: (615) 677-1001 ● RT100@worldnet.att.net

ATTRIBUTES
- Excellent communication and interpersonal skills
- Capable of meeting tight deadlines
- Works independently to complete assignments with limited supervision
- Pays close attention to details
- Positive attitude and outlook

HIGHLIGHTS OF EXPERIENCE
- Promotions given in each position
- Reduced printing costs with quality control measures
- Brought new clients aboard with creative marketing strategies
- Member of team that made ergonomically correct adjustments to office space
- Consistently selected to attend Web page development seminars and courses

RELEVANT EXPERIENCE
R.D. Murray Communications, Nashville, TN
Marketing Manager
January 1999 to Present
Wrote all marketing materials. Part of a team that created ad campaigns that increased revenue by 22 percent. Supervised six people. Promoted from marketing coordinator in 2002. Created new business opportunities, some with Fortune 500 companies.

CloudNine Graphics, Columbia, SC
Marketing Coordinator
September 1995 to November 1999
Developed Web site and wrote marketing materials, both online and hard copy. Reduced mailing and printing costs by 5 percent. Worked on tight deadlines and was responsible for proofing all marketing materials while supervising freelance writers and editors. Promoted from marketing assistant in 1997.

EDUCATION
University of Tennessee, Bachelor of Arts (Communications) 1995
Computer Skills: Microsoft Word, Access, WordPerfect, HTML. Web Page Development Certification from Waldon Community College (2000)

Scott Peterson
1000 Canon Avenue
Oakland, CA 94602
Sco1000@yahoo.com
h. 510-336-1000 c. 510-335-1000

CAREER OBJECTIVE: Energetic and committed media planner (and gamer) blends multimedia production and marketing experience at company in interactive entertainment industry

Education
Tufts University, Medford, MA
1990-1994
Bachelor of Arts: English, Film

RELATED WORK EXPERIENCE

Media Planner
Foote, Cone & Belding
San Francisco, CA
2000-Present

· Design and implement media marketing initiatives for national brands, including Compaq, Blue Shield of California, LucasArts and MoMA (SF).
· Work in all mediums (TV, print, radio, out of home, guerilla marketing) with an emphasis on interactive, online and new technologies.
· Entrepreneurial endeavor within agency was conception, design and creation of a new media lab: part education center, part brainstorming space, part hands-on technology produced with the intention of introducing the agency and our clients to new media (interactive television, wireless, instant messaging, broadband, gaming)

Director/Producer
"Land Without Blood"
Boulder, CO
1999-2000

· Wrote and submitted grant to Boulder Arts Commission.
· Made digital video documentary about Tony Perniciaro, an 85-year-old illiterate Sicilian ghetto bricklayer from Williamsburg, Brooklyn, who, at age 55, altered his life's course to become a poet/primitive artist. Produced,

directed, wrote and edited the film. Piece premiered at Puffin Room (SoHo, NYC) for one month as supplement to exhibit showcasing Tony's artwork.

Grant Writer/Office Manager
New York, NY
1996-1997

· Researched and wrote grants for nonprofit organizations, including P.E.N.C.I.L. (Public Education Needs Civic Involvement In Learning) and P.O.V. (PBS's documentary showcase).
· Managed office for grant writer, independent film producer and theater set designer.
· Post-production office coordinator credits on two films: D.A. Pennebaker's documentary "Moon Over Broadway" and Tim Blake Nelson's first feature "Eye of God." Duties included: accounting, day-to-day office management, interaction with diverse groups of people.

Other Work Experience

Sous Chef
15 Degrees
Boulder, CO
1998-1999

· Butcher, baker, and chef (pastry, pantry and line) for gourmet restaurant. Duties included: cooking, designing specials, inventory, customer satisfaction.

Prep Cook
Daily Bread Café
Boulder, CO
1997-1998

· Worked as sandwich maker at independently owned bakery/café. The alternative to Starbucks and other chains, Daily Bread's cornerstone was high-end, gourmet customer service. Duties included: inventory, preparation of food, menu, specials creation and customer service.

World Traveler
Lived/worked in Thailand, Ireland, Nepal, Prague. Traveled extensively within U.S.

MARIE ELENA RAMOS
100 VARICK STREET•JERSEY CITY•NJ 07100
PHONE (201)432–1000 • FAX(201)432–1000
EMAIL: mariram@comcast.net

OBJECTIVE: Development Associate

Strategic writer with eight years' experience fundraising more than $2 million and developing —
from start to finish — successful, long-term nonprofit, government and corporate projects

WORK HISTORY:

1999-Present
    Consultant/Freelance Writer
• Create, assist and implement strategies for clients in nonprofit organizations with special events, fundraising publications for cultivation and solicitation of foundation and corporate prospects and membership base.

1997-1999   Jersey City Episcopal Community Development Corporation, Inc.,
Jersey City, NJ
    Social Services Coordinator
• Collaborated with development team to procure more than $2.1M grants for start-up and administration of social service programs in Jersey City.
• Created and spearheaded innovative cultural and recreational center for seniors.
• Obtained grants and designed enrichment program for two after-school programs and program start-up of third after-school program.
• Collaborated with other nonprofits to provide social service educational conferences, town hall meetings and seminars. Advocacy to address urban issues affecting women and children.
• Commended by the executive director and board of directors for expertise, hard work and dedication "as critical components in helping us grow from a small start-up organization to a multipurpose social service and housing agency."
• Identified and implemented solutions impacting 160 units of low-income housing by organizing two active tenant councils. Skilled advocate effective in stressful environment requiring personal diplomacy mediation.
• Wrote newsletter with other staff members and publication's contributor.

1995-1997   Learning Community Charter School, Jersey City, NJ
    Founding Family
• Developed, with core group of community activists, the first progressive Bank Street model public elementary school in Hudson County.
• Grant writing committee yielded $335K in Community Development Block Grants and foundation grants. Grass roots fundraising yielded $60K.

1995-1997   Garden Preschool Cooperative, Inc., Jersey City, NJ
    Founder and Director
• Launched first progressive nonprofit cooperative preschool in Jersey City. Procured $55K in municipal, state and foundation grants.
• Developed award-winning community garden plan, curriculum and philosophy.

- Instituted active scholarship fund.
- Hired consultants, staff and directed 80+ volunteers.

1988-1994   *The Village Voice,* **New York, NY**
   Assistant Production Manager
- Supervised pre-press operations for weekly national newspaper. Managed fast-paced, tight deadline office, with concurrent projects.
- Acted as liaison to multiple departments for final sign-off.
- Promoted from typesetting department to production staff. Knowledge of design, typography, Atex ad composition, type processing.

EDUCATON:
   University of South Carolina: Bachelor of Arts, English, 1993. Dean's List: 1991, 1992, 1993
   Recipient of Quarto Prize for Outstanding Literary Achievement

FELLOWSHIPS AND TRAINING:
2001 - Present   **Jersey City Museum**
   Currently being trained on **Raiser's Edge fundraising software** to provide assistance to the Manager of Marketing, Membership and Special Events.

1997-1998   **Pew Charitable Trust**
Charlottesville, VA
   Fellow. Pew Civic Entrepreneur Initiative. Selected for national/local leadership training program.

1997   **Center for Non-Profit Corporations**
   Participated in grant-writing workshops.

1997   **La Leche League International**
   Accredited as *Breastfeeding Peer Counselor Program Administrator,* a program designed to decrease infant mortality and morbidity by increasing the rate and duration of breastfeeding.
1993   Accredited by La Leche League International as a *Leader* serving Hudson County.

ADMINISTRATIVE AND COMPUTER SKILLS:
   Proficient in Internet research skills; skilled at Microsoft Word; familiarity with MS Office and Atex software. Currently in training for **Raiser's Edge** fundraising software program. Portfolio and writing samples available on request.

VOLUNTEER:
2003   Currently serve on boards of two nonprofit organizations; volunteer on newsletter staff of community development corporation.

Sean Kowalski
100 Thompson Street, Apartment 1, New York, NY 10010
Home Phone 212.473.1000   Cell Phone 917.687.1000   E-mail lkow@optonline.net

Objective
Become an integral part of a sales team while providing quality outside sales by generating revenue and achieving set goals for an Internet media or media company

Experience
Sales Manager, Salon Media Group (6/00-3/08)
Recruited based on sales background, adaptability and strong communication skills. Identified and cultivated new clients in undeveloped sales territory. Exceeded expectations and grew territories while congruently building relationships with top national and New York advertising agencies and brands. Adept at listening to clients' needs and developing mutually beneficial relationships.

- Sold 31% of entire company sales team's revenue in first quarter of 2008.
- Generated 21% of all sales in 2001.
- Awarded raise as reward for strong performance.
- Ranked Number One East Coast Salesman last fiscal year.
- Promoted for continual success and highest sales-growth rate in company.
- Awarded raise based on accomplished goals.
- Designed and sold customized marketing opportunity that did not previously exist.
- Achieved sales goals 83% of time since being hired.
- Won Top Performer Award, 4th Quarter (2006).
- Won two of the four company-wide sales contests in 2005.
- Won lead generation contest both months eligible.

Sales Representative, GV Publications (6/99-9/99)
- Provided print advertising opportunities for clients while achieving set sales goals.
- Conducted outside sales with local businesses in community.

President, GLG Promotions (12/97-12/98)
- Promoted local bars and clubs and recruited 500 to 1,200 people nightly.
- Built company from ground up and developed existing venues.

Manager/Waiter, El Charro Café (3/98-5/00)
- Operated as headwaiter and promoted to manager after increasing food/beverage sales.
- Provided basic facilitator and server duties.

President, Sigma Phi Epsilon Fraternity (10/96-10/97)
- Operated as liaison between local chapter, national headquarters, and University Dean of Students.
- Maintained daily operations for 120 men while organizing weekly chapter meetings and events.

Education
The University of Arizona, Tucson, Arizona (1994-1999)
Degree: Bachelor of Fine Arts
Major: Media Arts
Minor: Communications and Sociology

Communication Skills
Language: Speak, read, and write Spanish
Computer: Operate Microsoft Word, Works, PowerPoint, Outlook, ACT, Excel, Salesforce, Palm

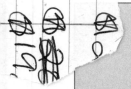

TRISH MURPHY
10-00 Dogwood Lane
Greenbrier, TN 37073
615/643-1000
MBB10@aol.com

Career Objective:
College-educated Office Systems Assistant with more than ten years' experience at Fortune 500 company seeks Administrative Assistant position at large Engineering firm where technical and communication skills as well as computer savvy can be used for preparation of reports and specs.

Work History
> *Travelers Insurance*, Nashville, TN. 1993-present
> *Littlejohn Engineering Associates*, Nashville, TN. 1993
> *Brentwood Professional Center*, Brentwood, TN. 1992-1993
> *ProCuts Inc.*, Antioch, TN. 1991-1992

Summary of Qualifications
- Develop specialized safety reports used to aid in prevention of employee illness and injuries.
- Proof and edit project contracts and proposals.
- Complete highly protected risk reports that require high degree of accuracy and technical knowledge.
- Complete real estate contracts and proposals.
- Develop billing reports.
- Resolved issues with engineers regarding completion and content of reports.
- Schedule and maintain appointment calendars.
- Address customer complaints and resolve quickly.
- Maintain high volume switchboard.

Computer Skills
- Proficient with Word 97, Word 98 and Word 2000
- Proficient with Windows 3.1, Windows 95 and Windows 98
- Knowledge of Flow Chart 3.2
- Knowledge of Excel 5.0, Excel 97 and Excel 2000
- Knowledge of WordPerfect 5.1
- Knowledge of Lotus 1, 2, 3
- Proficient with Internet research

Education
Murray State University, 1990
Bachelor of Science: Agriculture
Minor in Office Systems Administration

Mary Frances McKiernan

100 Waldwick Avenue • Waldwick, NJ 07100
(201) 444-1000 (H) • (212) 555-1000 (W)

mfk100@optonline.net

EXECUTIVE SUMMARY

Senior Developer/Manager excels in financial business applications. Possesses analytical, design and programming experience — combined with excellent communication skills — with more than 13 years' experience. Technical expertise includes, but is not limited to, DB2/CICS and MQ Series.

CAREER OBJECTIVE

Senior Manager in systems analysis and development at financial services organization

TECHNICAL SUMMARY

Software: MQ Series, COBOL II, CICS, DB2 (SPUFI, QMF, BMC, FD), VSAM, OS/JCL, IBM MQ Utilities, File-AID, OS/MVS/XA, SDF-2, INTERTEST. **System:** XPEDITER, SHADOW SERVER DEBUGGING FACILITY, STROBE, CATS, ENDEVOR, MS Office, TSO/ISPF

SKILLS, EXPERIENCE AND CONTRIBUTION

10/93 - Present • METROPOLITAN LIFE INSURANCE • New York
Manager - Programmer/Analyst

• Promoted to manager after one year. Each year responsibility increased. Currently managing 12 people in department.
• Designed, developed and implemented Excess Claims (ECS) and Environmental and Toxic Tort (ETT) Systems.
• Adept at ECS, which provides Excess Claim Department personnel with the ability to view policy and claim information as well as automate the processes of creating, abstracting and segmenting claims, financial activities, claim and policy indexing.
• Redesigned the Loss Management System (LMS), which was replaced by ECS and ETT systems, preparing system flow charts for the user review. Reduced costs significantly.
• Monitored performance of all newly created modules using STROBE prior to its implementation, which circumvented performance problems in production environment.
• Supervised group that created VB screens.
• Conduct production turnovers in ENDEVOR environment.
• Monitored bases ETT Replication on daily basis and resolved all issues concerning the process, which required user interface (QMF, SQL Server, Shadow Server).

2/92 - 10/93 • DEAN WITTER • New York
Programmer/Analyst

• Member of team that developed the Unit Trust Automated Redemption System (ARS) and Equity Information System (EIS)
• Expedited the redemption process by providing UIT personnel with complete information concerning redemption based on risk factors.
• Created, designed and analyzed flow charts on tight deadline.
• Wrote detailed program specifications and designed online screens, which required user interface.
• Handled daily transactions and production support for newly created and existing systems.
• Created VSAM files.

1/89 - 12/91 • CHASE MANHATTAN BANK • New York
Programmer

• Designed and maintained business applications, including payroll, human resources and transaction control information systems.
• Wrote program specifications.
• Participated in software development, starting with system design and finishing with detailed program specifications, coding, testing, implementation and production coverage.
• Prepared and designed economic tasks for financial applications.

EDUCATION

1982-1987 • Bachelor of Science • Pace University

ADDITIONAL TECHNICAL TRAINING

Advanced software analysis • Tel Tech Education (New York) 1991
Certificate of completion of CICS Command Level Programming

Caryn Andrea
100 10th Street
New York, NY 10003
(212) 674-1000
cary@aol.com

Film Production Experience

Muse Film and Television, Co-ordinating Producer of *Civilization by Subway*, proposed pilot for professional development video series involving New York City cultural institutions and serving New York City public school teachers

Present

Magic Box Productions, Associate Producer of documentary on the School Arts Rescue Initiative, commissioned by the 9/11 Fund and the New York Times Foundation

Intern, Researcher, WCBS-TV News

1982

Development, Marketing, and Management Experience

Management Consultant, Advisory Committee Member, Dancenow/NYC. Work with directors to create marketing and funding strategies to facilitate the organization's expansion. Assist with all aspects of producing two-week dance festival.

Present

Work for various cultural organizations, including:

1998 - 2003

Educational Outreach at the 92nd Street Y. Developed and implemented strategy; researched potential clients to increase number of schools participating in "Musical Introduction Series." Assisted with administration of arts education programs reaching thousands of New York City public school students.

New York City Museum School. Created "white paper" to explain its alternative model to educational community.

The Pearl Theatre Company, Co-Chairperson, Development Committee, Trustee. Developed and implemented fundraising strategies with development staff and fellow board members. Researched potential high-net-worth individuals, corporate, and foundation funders.

Barnard Business and Professional Women, President. Oversaw
general operations of alumnae membership organization and planning
for conferences and events.

Shearman & Sterling, Marketing Specialist. Worked with partners
to win new business. Researched potential clients and competitors.
Wrote/edited letters, brochures, and other marketing material. Created
models for development of practice group brochures and proposals
and developed systems to manage and disseminate information.

1995 -1998

Altman Foundation, Program Officer. Evaluated prospective
grantees through site visits, interviews, and analysis of written
materials. Researched best practices in the four fields of interest to
foundation – arts, education, health, and social welfare. Prepared
written and oral reports regarding potential grantees.

1989 -1993

Victoria Marks Performance Company, Manager. Managed all
aspects of the dance company's fiscal and general management.
Developed and implemented fundraising, marketing, and touring
strategies. Created a not-for-profit entity with a board of directors to
oversee the company.

1988 -1989

Shearman & Sterling, Corporate Legal Assistant Coordinator.
Managed team of legal assistants. Researched and reported on
current and potential clients.

1987-1988

Assemblywoman Louise Slaughter, Senior Legislative Aide,
Louise Slaughter for Congress, Fundraising Coordinator.
Managed Assemblywoman Slaughter's Albany office. Researched
and developed legislative proposals. Served as liaison between the
Assemblywoman and constituent groups and lobbyists. Managed all
fundraising for Assemblywoman Slaughter's successful congressional race.

1985 -1986

Jacob's Pillow Dance Festival, Associate Director of
Development. Developed and implemented corporate, foundation,
and government solicitation strategies. Analyzed potential funding
sources for specific projects.

1983 -1985

Education

1983   Bachelor of Arts, English. Barnard College, Columbia University

Computer Skills
Microsoft Word, Access, Excel, PowerPoint, Netscape and Internet
Explorer, Windows NT

100 DARTMOUTH STREET, BOSTON, MA 02100
TELEPHONE (617) 901-1000 CELL PHONE (617) 901-1010 E-MAIL HC2@HOTMAIL.COM

HEATHER CASH

EDUCATION

Boston College
Arts & Science
Majored in communication. Honors
GPA: 3.8. Projected graduation: 2004

Fordham University
Liberal Arts
Cumulative GPA: 3.3
1999-2000

WORK EXPERIENCE

WCVB-TV Channel 5   Newton, MA
Intern   5/02 - 8/02
- Conducted daily station tours, interacting with public and exhibited excellent communication and people skills.
- Wrote press releases and viewer response letters, meeting all deadlines.
- Assisted with public service effort, *Keeping Kids on Track.*
- Worked with Director of Programming, using computer skills, such as Microsoft Word, Excel, Access.

Reagan Communications Group   Boston, MA
Intern   6/01 - 8/01
- Wrote calendar listings, press releases, feature stories. Honed proofreading and editing skills.
- Worked at special events, exhibited communication and people skills.
- Updated contact information, using computer skills.
- Scheduled photo opportunities, bringing together an assortment of people on a timely basis.

Dirtpile.com   South Boston, MA
Public Relations and Sales   5/00 - 8/00
- Acquired new customer base; maintained customer relations and satisfaction.
- Maintained continual customer contact through telephone, computer and mail correspondence.
- Research, update and input in Web pages; familiarity with HTML.

Sterling Equipment   East Boston, MA
Salesperson   6/99 - 8/99
- Sold construction equipment.
- Advised customers on purchases.
- Managed flow of new merchandise.
- Maintained basic accounting (cash register, sales slips, book balancing), utilizing computer skills.

IZABELA KIESLOWSKI

100 Avenue E, Apt. 1   (201) 432-1000
Edgewater, NJ 07100   IzzyK@yahoo.com

OBJECTIVE: *Multi-lingual college graduate melds strong communication and interpersonal skills with leadership and computer savvy to management-training position in human resources*

- Hard-working and well organized; able to work with little supervision
- Detail-oriented and analytical; able to see whole picture
- Highly adaptable in solving problems and working in multitask environment
- Demonstrated leadership in training/supervision
- Creative but able to meet deadlines
- Ability to master new skills, concepts and ideas quickly
- Computer proficiency in Windows 95/98, Microsoft (Word, Works, Excel, Access, PowerPoint), Internet Explorer, Claris Works, WordPerfect and Netscape Navigator

EXPERIENCE:

2007	Liberty State Park, Jersey City, NJ
Office	Greeted visitors at front desk. Answered customers' queries relating to park activities.
Assistant	Received Employee of the Month award.
	Handled bank transactions; issued boat launch permits; collected appropriate fees.
	Performed office-related duties such as data entry, answering telephones, filing, and faxing in timely, positive and efficient manner.
2001-2006	Hudson County Occupational Center, Jersey City, NJ
Job Coach	Educated students in occupational setting on work ethics.
	Trained students to perform basic job functions.
	Developed lesson plans and scheduled events related to job placement, such as résumé writing and interviewing-skills workshops.
	Assisted in research projects, utilizing Internet skills.
2000-2001	Jersey City Housing Authority, Jersey City, NJ
Student	Assisted supervisor in various office-related activities, such as data entry, proofreading,
Intern	organizing monthly statistical data, filing, copies and faxing.
	Gathered information to update various spreadsheets for upper management's use.
	Accurately and responsively coordinated flow of work.
	Reduced costs and updated inventory of supplies.
1999-2000	Academic Affairs, New Jersey City University, Jersey City, NJ
Office	Maintained administrative and personnel records.
Assistant	Entered and verified data in appropriate formats.
	Responded to students' inquiries and requests.
	Managed incoming and outgoing correspondence.

LANGUAGES: *Multilingual — Fluent in English, Polish, Ukrainian, and some Russian*

EDUCATION: *Bachelor of Science, Management, May 2001*

New Jersey City University	Deans List, Fall 1996 and Spring 1997
Senior Class Vice President	Pre-Law Society member

Notes

PART I

Introduction

1. Leonhardt, David. "Losers All: 'Egalitarian Recession' Keeps Anger at Bay." *New York Times,* 15 June 2003.
2. Peters, Jeremy W. "Jobs Report Finds Growth Still Moderate." *New York Times,* 7 July 2007.

Chapter 1

1. Easton, Nina. "Losing the American Dream." CNNMoney.com, 19 July 2007.
2. Onrec.com. "Run-of-the-mill recruitment sites = best practices?" Onrec.com, 9 January 2001, *www.onrec.com/content2/news.asp?ID=592.*
3. See *www.blr.com/landingPR/index.aspx?landingPRID=1* at *HR.BLR.com.*
4. Lublin, Joann S. "College Students Make Job Hunting Tougher with Weak Résumés." *Wall Street Journal,* 29 April 2003.
5. A telephone interview with Meghan Gonyo, an account manager at The Creative Group, a division of Robert Half International, was conducted in May 2007.

Chapter 2

1. Maher, Kris. "Online Job Hunting Is Tough. Just Ask Vinnie." *Wall Street Journal,* 24 June 2003.
2. "Monster.com waited five days to disclose data theft." Reuters, 24 August 2007.
3. Adelson, Andrea. "Big Job Sites Try to Think Small." *New York Times,* 29 October 2002.
4. For company research, an excellent site is *www.hoovers.com.*
5. Collins, Jim. *Good to Great.* New York: HarperBusiness, 2001.
6. For P&G's mission, see *www.pg.com/company/who_we_are/ppv.jhtml.*
7. For a look at career advice at P&G, see *www.pg.com/jobs/cac/overview.jhtml.*
8. For a comprehensive overview on occupations, visit *www.bls.gov/oco/home.htm* from the Department of Labor.

Chapter 3

1. Bombardieri, Marcella and Tracy Jan. "MIT dean quits over fabricated credentials." *The Boston Globe,* 4 April 2007.
2. Whitcomb, Susan Britton. *Résumé Magic.* Indianapolis: JIST Publications, 1999.
3. The job description was taken from *www.barnesandnobleinc.com/jobs/jobs.html,* the career site for Barnes & Noble.
4. Wastler, Allen. "Objection to Objectives." CNNMoney.com, 22 September 2004.

5. Mushkat, Norma. See *www.multiculturaladvantage.com/job/recruiters-top-10-resume-pet-peeves.asp.*

Chapter 4

1. Lublin, Joann S. "College Students Make Job Hunting Tougher with Weak Resumes." *Wall Street Journal,* 29 April 2003.
2. See *www.ohio.edu/careers/students/resources.cfm* for additional information.
3. See *http://members.microsoft.com/careers/newsletter/newsletters.htm* for additional information.
4. "IBD's 10 Secrets to Success." *Investor's Business Daily,* 10 January 2003.
5. Lancaster, Hal. Promoting Yourself: *52 Lessons for Getting to the Top and Staying There.* New York: Simon & Schuster: 2002.

Chapter 6

1. Kleinschmidt, Cory. See *www.traffick.com/article.asp?aID=63* for additional information.
2. The description of the overview of the hiring process at Alltel was taken from the company's career site. See *www.alltel.com/corporate/careers/careers.html* for more information.
3. These recommendations for keywords were taken from the Southern Edison career site. See *www.edison.com/careers/applying.asp.*
4. Kiviat, Barbara. "The New Rules of Web Hiring." *Time,* 24 November 2003.
5. See *www.edison.com/careers/applying.asp.*

Chapter 7

1. Greenhouse, Steven. "Job Training That Works, and It's Free." *New York Times,* 10 August 2003.
2. Tejada, Carlos. "Applicant Flood Makes It Tough to Hire Wisely." *Wall Street Journal,* 24 December 2002.
3. For more information, see "Beyond the Basics: Career Strategies That Work" at *www.chicagojobs.org/comm/network1.html.*
4. Keller, Emily. "Acing the Informational Interview." *BusinessWeek,* 25 June 2007.
5. Kotter, John P. *A Force for Change: How Leadership Differs from Management.* New York: The Free Press, 1990.
6. Kiviat, Barbara. "The New Rules of Web Hiring." Time, 24 November 2003.
7. "IBD's 10 Secrets to Success." *Investor's Business Daily,* 10 January 2003.
8. See *www.time.com/time/2005/100books/the_complete_list.html* for a list of the 100 books.

Chapter 8

1. Permission was granted by Dan Bankey for Figures 8.1 and 8.2. They are from the career site of Mutual of Omaha.
2. A telephone interview about Wynn Casino was conducted with Kevin Marasco, marketing director of Recruitmax, in April 2005.
3. Telephone interviews with Philip Thune, president of HireMeNow.com, and Nick Murphy, operations manager of WorkBlast.com, were conducted in July 2007.
4. Cullen, Lisa Takeuchi. "It's a Wrap. You're Hired." *Time,* 4 October 2007.
5. Jennings, Angel. "Diddy Rants on YouTube to Recruit New Assistant." *New York Times,* 30 July 2007.

PART II

Chapter 11

1. Bolles, Richard. *What Color Is Your Parachute? A Practical Manual for Job-Hunters and Career-Changers.* Berkeley: Ten Speed Press, 2004.

2. Kelly, Matthew. *The Rhythm of Life: Living Every Day with Passion and Purpose.* New York: Fireside Publishers, 2004.

3. An interview with Chrystal McArthur, associate director of career services at Rutgers University, was conducted in January 2005. For more information about the career center at Rutgers University, see *www.careerservices.rutgers.edu/career.*

4. For more information regarding alumni connections at University of Nebraska, see *www.unl.edu/careers/hhl/.*

5. For more information on Jessica Turos class at Bowling Green State University, see *www.bgsu.edu/colleges/edhd/hesa/hied/curstudents.html.*

6. For more information on career services at the University of New Mexico, see *www.career.unm.edu/.*

7. Fisher, Ann. "Uncle Sam's hiring spree." CNNMoney.com, 26 July 2007.

8. For more information on Massachusetts Division of Career Services, see *www.detma.org.*

9. Bruzzese, Anita. "Keep Track of Your Value to the Company." *The Ithaca Journal,* 7 July 2005.

10. Bill Vlcek mentions 67 career competencies from Lominger, the Leadership Architects. Lominger Career Architect®, *www.lominger.com/67_336.htm.*

11. The job posting, February 7 2005, comes from the Morgan Stanley Career Page. For more information see *www.morganstanley.com/about/careers/.*

12. For more information on the job interview at CarMax, visit this site: *www.carmax.com/dyn/companyinfo/careers/interview.aspx*

13. See *www.alltel.com/corporate/careers/* for more information.

14. Corcodilos, Nick. "Ten Stupid Hiring Mistakes." 10 November 2004, *www.asktheheadhunter.com/hatenmistakes1.htm.*

15. See *www.cco.purdue.edu/About/AsktheDirector.shtml* for more information.

Chapter 12

1. See *www.bls.gov/news.release/nlsoy.nr0.htm* for more information.

Chapter 13

1. Peters, Jeremy W. "Company's Smoking Ban Means Off-Hours Too." *New York Times,* 8 February 2005: Section C, 5.

2. For more information on reference checking at PSEG, see its site at *http://skillsurvey.com/HCM_main.php.*

3. Koeppel, David. "What to Do When the Ideal Job Proves Not to Be as Advertised." *New York Times,* 27 March 2005: Section 10, 1.

Chapter 14

1. A telephone interview with Barry Martin, a director of staffing and development at Timken, about hiring practices at his company was conducted in March 2005.

2. Zinsser, William. *On Writing Well.* New York: Harper Perennial, 1998.
3. Fisher, Ann. "Starting a New Job, Don't Blow It." *Fortune,* March 7 2005: 48.
4. *Insurance Journal.* "Happy with Your Boss? New Survey Reports Contempt for Managers Across the Board." 21 January 2005.

Chapter 15

1. Go to *www.copydesk.org* for the "Editing Booklet."
2. A telephone interview with Peter Thonis, executive vice president of communications at Verizon, was conducted in January 2005.
3. A telephone interview with Neil Bussell, a group manager with the PepsiCo Business Solutions Group, was conducted in December 2004.

Chapter 16

1. Collins, Jim. *Good to Great.* New York: HarperBusiness, 2001.
2. Wojnarowski, Adrian. *The Miracle of St. Anthony.* New York: Penguin, 2006.

Chapter 17

1. Interviews were conducted with Ted Horton of BCI Partners and Anita Bruzzese, a Gannett career columnist and author of *Take This Job and Thrive,* in March 2005. Ruth Shlossman's negotiating seminar for Watershed Associates forms the basis of the negotiating skills section of this chapter. Additional questions were answered by Shlossman via e-mail in April 2005.
2. Corcodilos, Nick. Ask the Headhunter. "Divulging salary history." *www.asktheheadhunter. com/faqsalary1.htm.*
3. Sahadi, Jeanne. "Feeling Underpaid? Try This." 18 July 2003. *http://money.cnn. com/2003/07/17/commentary/everyday/sahadi.*
4. McBride, Heather, human resources manager at Fiserv, was interviewed July 2007 about starting a new job. Her response ends Chapter 17.

Chapter 18

1. Interviews were conducted in June 2007 with Lisa Whittington, a vice president of human resources at Host Hotels & Resorts, Charlotte Frank, Ph.D., senior vice president of research and development at McGraw-Hill Education, The McGraw-Hill Companies, and Shelley Bird, executive vice president of global communications at Cardinal Health, on what it takes to get ahead at a new job.
2. DeKoven, Bernie. Coworking Institute Network Newsletter. For more information, see *http://coworking.com/?pg=workinprogressitem&id=19.*
3. Belkin, Lisa. "When Whippersnappers and Geezers Collide." *New York Times,* 26 July 2007.
4. Lundlin, Stephen C. Ken Blanchard, John Christensen, and Harry Paul. *Fish! A Remarkable Way to Boost Morale and Improve Results.* New York: Hyperion, 2000.
5. Tompkins, Wayne. Originally appeared in *Courier Journal.* Can be found at *USA Today* at *www.usatoday.com/careers/news/usa051.htm.*

Bibliography

Ace Your Interview: The WetFeet Insider Guide to Interviewing. San Francisco: WetFeet, 2004.

Bermont, Todd. *10 Insider Secrets to Job Hunting Success!* Chicago: 10 Step Publications, 2002.

Bolles, Richard. *What Color Is Your Parachute?* Berkeley: Ten Speed Press, 2004.

Bruzzese, Anita. *Take This Job and Thrive.* Manassas Park, Virginia: Impact Publications, 2000.

Collins, Jim. *Good to Great.* New York: HarperBusiness, 2001.

Cunningham, Helen, and Brenda Greene. *The Business Style Handbook: An A-to-Z Guide for Writing on the Job with Tips from Communications Experts at the Fortune 500.* New York: McGraw-Hill, 2002.

DeLuca, Matthew. *Best Answers to the 201 Most Frequently Asked Interview Questions.* New York: McGraw-Hill, 1997.

Farr, Michael. *The Quick Résumé & Cover Letter,* 2nd ed. Indianapolis: JIST Publishing, 2003.

Fox, Jeffrey. *How to Become a Great Boss.* New York: Hyperion, 2002.

Kador, John. *201 Best Questions to Ask on Your Interview.* New York: McGraw-Hill, 2002.

Kelly, Matthew. *The Rhythm of Life: Living Every Day with Passion and Purpose.* New York: Fireside Publishers, 2004.

Kotter, John P. *A Force for Change: How Leadership Differs from Management.* New York: The Free Press, 1990.

Lancaster, Hal. *Promoting Yourself: 52 Lessons for Getting to the Top and Staying There.* New York: Simon & Schuster, 2002.

Lundlin, Stephen C. Ken Blanchard, John Christensen, Harry Paul. *Fish! A Remarkable Way to Boost Morale and Improve Results.* New York: Hyperion, 2000.

Nadler, Burton Jay. *The Everything Résumé Book,* 2nd ed. Avon, MA: Adams Corporation, 2003.

Richardson, Bradley G. *Jobsmarts for Twentysomethings.* New York: Vintage Books, 1995.

Rosenberg, Arthur D., and David Hizer. *The Résumé Handbook.* Avon, MA: Adams Media, 1996.

Smith, Rebecca. *Electronic Résumés & Online Networking.* Franklin Lakes, NJ: Career Press, 2000.

Waldroop, James, and Timothy Butler. *Maximum Success: Changing the 12 Behavior Patterns that Keep You from Getting Ahead.* New York: Currency/Doubleday, 2000.

Whitcomb, Susan Britton. *Résumé Magic.* Indianapolis: JIST Publications, 1999.

Whitcomb, Susan Britton, and Pat Kendall. *eRésumés.* New York: McGraw-Hill, 2002.

Wojnarowski, Adrian. *The Miracle of St. Anthony.* New York: Penguin, 2006.

Zinsser, William. *On Writing Well.* New York: Harper Perennial, 1998.

Index

About the Author

Brenda Greene is coauthor of *The Business Style Handbook: An A-to-Z Guide for Writing on the Job with Tips from Communications Experts at the Fortune 500*. In addition, she is the author of *Get the Interview Every Time* and *You've Got the Interview ... Now What?* She was previously an editor at *Working Women* and Whitney Communications, as well as marketing manager at a business-to-business venture. She is currently working on a biography about Gertrude Ederle.